CHIEF THUNDERWATER

Chief Thunderwater, ca. 1910.
Image courtesy of Mona Lee Secoy.

CHIEF
THUNDERWATER

An Unexpected Indian
in Unexpected Places

GERALD F. REID

UNIVERSITY OF OKLAHOMA PRESS : NORMAN

This book is published with the generous assistance of the Kerr Foundation, Inc.

Library of Congress Cataloging-in-Publication Data

Names: Reid, Gerald F., 1953– author.
Title: Chief Thunderwater : an unexpected Indian in unexpected places / Gerald F. Reid.
Description: Norman : University of Oklahoma Press, [2021] | Includes bibliographical references and index. | Summary: "Biography of Oghema Niagara, a Sauk-Seneca activist from Cleveland, Ohio, who played an important, but unrecognized, role in the rise of Haudenosaunee nationalism in Canada in the early twentieth century" —Provided by publisher.
Identifiers: LCCN 2020021373 | ISBN 978-0-8061-6731-2 (hardcover) ISBN 978-0-8061-9118-8 (paper)
Subjects: LCSH: Thunderwater, Chief, 1865–1950. | Seneca Indians—Kings and rulers—Biography. | Sauk Indians—Kings and rulers—Biography. | Supreme Council of the Tribes. | Six Nations—Politics and government. | Iroquois Indians—Politics and government. | Indians of North America—Canada—Politics and government. | Indians of North America—Ohio—Cleveland—Biography. | Businesspeople—Ohio—Cleveland—Biography. | Cleveland (Ohio) —Biography.
Classification: LCC E99.S3 R45 2021 | DDC 974.7004/9755460092 [B]—dc23
LC record available at https://lccn.loc.gov/2020021373

The paper in this book meets the guidelines for permanence and durability of the Committee on Production Guidelines for Book Longevity of the Council on Library Resources, Inc. ∞

CONTENTS

ACKNOWLEDGMENTS

I must begin by acknowledging Larry Hauptman, whose encouragement of my work on Thunderwater goes back many years. After setting aside the project for a time, it was a conversation with him that led me to return to the research that resulted in this book. Airy Dixon, Larry's colleague and friend, played a similar role, and I thank them both for their support. In a similar vein, I thank Taiaiake Alfred, who first put me onto the Thunderwater story and encouraged me to look at it in a new light. I also express my gratitude to the anonymous reviewers of the various drafts of my manuscript. Their comments, questions, and recommendations were invaluable to me in organizing, fleshing out, and presenting Thunderwater's story. I extend a special note of thanks, as well, to Gary Dunham, who encouraged me in this project and who opened the door for me to the University of Oklahoma Press.

Mona Lee Secoy and Dalene Kelly, both great-great-granddaughters of Chief Thunderwater, were vital to this project as sources of inspiration and support and by providing me with important documentary evidence about their "Grandpa Chief." Ms. Secoy, in particular, was generous with her time and patient in answering my many, many questions. I am especially grateful to her, her mother, Beverly Joy Palmer, her husband, Mike, and her sister, Marion, for their hospitality and good company when I visited them in March 2019.

Kanatakta Wendell Beauvais of Kahnawake has expressed an interest in this project for many years, and our conversations about Thunderwater and the history of his community in the early twentieth century have been a regular source of insight and clear thinking with regard to this project. I am deeply grateful for his input. I am especially thankful to Teiowí:sonte Thomas Deer, Cultural Liaison at the Kanien'kehá:ka Onkwawén:na Raotitióhkwa Language and Cultural Center in Kahnawake. In addition to pointing me to key archival sources, his probing questions and ideas about the Thunderwater movement were very helpful in my own thinking and writing about the life and times of Oghema Niagara. I also want to thank Rosie Beauvais, her daughter Roseanne, and their family for their kindness and generosity during my visits to Kahnawake. From Akwesasne, I would like to thank Darren Bonaparte and Ellison King for their assistance at various stages of this project. From Tyendinaga I would like to thank Lisa Maracle, director of community services for the Mohawks of the Bay of Quinte, for her assistance during early stages of this project. More recently for their assistance, I would like to thank Jennifer Walker, Deborah Greene, and Clarence Green. A very special note of gratitude goes to Trish Rae, historical researcher for the Mohawks of the Bay of Quinte, for her regular support and invaluable assistance throughout this project.

I thank Ann Sindelar, Danielle Peck, and Heather Robinson-Mooney of the Western Reserve Historical Society (WRHS) in Cleveland, Ohio, for their assistance in consulting the museum and library collections of the WRHS. Ms. Peck, senior registrar at the Cleveland History Center, facilitated my access to a number of Thunderwater items in the WRHS collection, giving me important insights into Thunderwater that helped me to bring his story to life. I owe a special debt of gratitude to Ms. Sindelar, reference supervisor for the Cleveland History Center, for her assistance and patience in facilitating my work with the Oghema Niagara manuscript collection and for arranging digital reproductions of some key documents and images. I also want to acknowledge the assistance and support of the Kanhiote Library in Tyendinaga Mohawk Territory, the Kanien'kehá:ka Onkwawén:na Raotitióhkwa Language and Cultural Center in Kahnawake, Library and Archives Canada, and the National Anthropological Archives of the Smithsonian Institution. For their assistance in obtaining illustrative material, I thank Patrick Osborne, rights and licensing specialist at Library and Archives Canada, and Daisy Njoku, media resources specialist at the National Anthropological Archives. I also thank Erin Greb for her work in preparing the maps used to illustrate the text. At the University of Oklahoma Press, I acknowledge Alessandra Jacobi Tamulevich, senior acquisitions editor, and Stephanie Attia Evans, senior manuscript editor, for their valuable guidance and support. I am especially grateful for the work of copyeditor Kerin Tate. A note of gratitude also goes to the late Roy Wright; our many conversations about the Thunderwater story were a regular source of insight and encouragement for this project.

My wife, Mary, and my children, John and Emily, have been a strong and constant source of support during my work on this project, and especially so since the work of writing began in the summer of 2017. Thank you so much!

INTRODUCTION

*Chief Thunderwater was not an Indian, but a Negro from Cleveland
and the cultural content which formed the basis of his organization was not
traditional Iroquois . . . but rather a fake concoction of pseudo-Indian features.
It is obvious that Chief Thunderwater's motives were far from honest. Around
1920 . . . he disappeared with amounts claimed to be as large as $50,000
collected from his "warriors" in Caughnawaga and elsewhere.*
—Susan Koessler Postal, writing about Chief Thunderwater and the
Thunderwater movement in "Hoax Nativism at Caughnawaga,"
Ethnology (1965)

In the autumn of 1916 Chief Thunderwater, a charismatic but shadowy figure
who in reality was a black man from Cleveland, Ohio, galvanized the Mohawk
community of Kahnawake in Southern Quebec into an outburst of nativism
and cultural revival. With pretended Indian symbolism and rituals, promises
of fighting for Native rights, and a major rally in the community in September
of that year, Thunderwater inspired the heavily assimilated people of Kahnawake, sparking their remote sense of Haudenosaunee identity and interest in
reestablishing long-forgotten political and cultural traditions. Kahnawake's
very distance from that identity and those traditions left them vulnerable to
Thunderwater's manipulations. "Thunderwaterism" had swept through the
reserve, and more than half of its 1,800 residents had become dues-paying members of the "Council of the Tribes," an organization formed by Thunderwater
that purported to advocate for Indian welfare and interests. In fact, the organization, of which Thunderwater was the "Oghema Niagara," or supreme leader,
was a cleverly disguised effort to fleece the innocent people of Kahnawake out
of their hard-earned money. In early 1920 one of Thunderwater's opponents in
Kahnawake confronted the charlatan at a public meeting in the town hall and
exposed him as an impostor, setting off a near riot by his supporters. The local
constable had to be called to restore order, and in the confusion, Thunderwater
escaped, absconding back to the United States with tens of thousands of dollars

of ill-gotten funds. Discouraged by the sudden turn of events and embarrassed by their own gullibility, Thunderwater's followers abandoned their leader, and the Thunderwater movement collapsed.

Derived mainly from an article written by Susan Koessler Postal titled "Hoax Nativism at Caughnawaga" and published in *Ethnology* in 1965, this story of Chief Thunderwater became an amusing but minor footnote in the anthropological and historical literature on the Haudenosaunees. It was reprised in the *Biennial Review of Anthropology* in 1967 and was given somewhat wider circulation in *Current Anthropology* in 1971, when one scholar in an essay on crisis cults drew on the 1965 account of the "hoax" Thunderwater movement and derided Thunderwater as "a Cleveland Negro who in 1920 swindled the Caughnawaga Iroquois of some $50,000 through a preposterous farrago of pseudo-Indianisms he had thought up himself." Fifteen years later, in a major study of Duncan Campbell Scott and the administration of Indian Affairs in Canada in the early twentieth century, E. Brian Titley reiterated Postal's account and suggested that Thunderwater's "hoax nativism" had actually spread to a number of other Haudenosaunee communities in Canada. He also suggested that the Indian Department, concerned about the cultural frenzy Thunderwater had stirred and having confirmed his true identity as an African American named "Palmer," had justifiably taken a direct hand in exposing Thunderwater as a con artist and an impostor posing as an Indian. In addition, Titley suggested that the Indian Department had learned that Thunderwater had abused a twelve-year-old Mohawk boy from Akwesasne and used that information, as well, to discredit him and undermine the cultural movement he was leading. Circulating the damaging information to its agents in the field and opponents like the one in Kahnawake, the Indian Department exposed Thunderwater, his supporters abandoned him, and his Council of the Tribes collapsed.[1]

According to Titley, the "comic-opera" of Chief Thunderwater's life had not actually ended with his public outing in Kahnawake in 1920. With "one scene left to be played," he noted, Thunderwater resurfaced several years later in Louisville, Kentucky, where he was involved in a business scheme in which he attempted again to pass himself off as "Indian." With assistance and detailed information provided by Canada's Indian Department, city newspapers ran a full-page exposé on Thunderwater, revealing him once more to be a fake and an immoral cheat. Humiliated, Thunderwater attempted to salvage his reputation by suing the newspapers for libel. After a long and protracted effort, he failed and returned to Cleveland, finally bringing the "curious saga" of Chief Thunderwater to a close. Reinforcing the notion that Thunderwater was a fraud and that his "hoax nativism" was of little cultural or political consequence, Titley concluded that the end of Thunderwaterism in the early 1920s coincided with the development of a *"genuine* Indian movement which aimed to unite all the native people of Canada . . . the League of Indians of Canada."[2]

That is the story of Chief Thunderwater and the short-lived Thunderwater movement.

Or is it?

I first became aware of the story of Chief Thunderwater and the Thunderwater movement several years ago while conducting research on political and cultural revitalization in Kahnawake during the late nineteenth and early twentieth centuries. Established in part by Haudenosaunee and Huron converts to Christianity in the late seventeenth century, Kahnawake had received little attention from scholars because it was a *Catholic* Mohawk community. Iroquoianists, who were primarily interested in studying historic and contemporary Haudenosaunee communities in an effort to better understand Haudenosaunee society and culture prior to European contact, had shown little interest in Kahnawake. This was especially true with regard to the community in the late nineteenth and early twentieth centuries, by which time they considered it to be well on its way to assimilation into the larger Euro-Canadian society and therefore not worthy of their attention. What information I could find about the community during this period came mostly from the files of Canada's Department of Indian Affairs and the stories and recollections of friends and colleagues in Kahnawake. To my surprise, these archival and oral history materials were rich and suggested that between 1870 and 1925 Kahnawake experienced a period of intense political resistance, social upheaval, and cultural revitalization and that these processes were linked closely to similar developments in other Haudenosaunee communities in Canada. It was a picture decidedly at odds with the view presented by Postal and others that Kahnawake was a heavily assimilated Mohawk community.[3]

For some time I accepted Postal's and Titley's version of the Thunderwater story and drew on their work to inform my own analysis of political and cultural revitalization in Kahnawake. "Rarihokwats" offered the only alternative view on the Thunderwater story, which he published under the title *How Democracy Came to St. Regis* in 1971. He lampooned anthropology and Canada's Department of Indian Affairs and drew on an extensive file the Indian Department maintained on Thunderwater to point attention to the underhanded tactics used by Indian Department officials to discredit Thunderwater and undermine similar Native political efforts to improve economic and social conditions on Indian reserves. In addition, Rarihokwats's work was useful in helping me to understand the Thunderwater movement as a much broader Haudenosaunee political phenomenon, a point that became very clear once I delved into the Indian Department's Thunderwater file for myself. The file contains hundreds of pages and includes more than just the reports of Indian agents and correspondence and memoranda between department officials about Thunderwater's activities on Haudenosaunee reserves. It also includes petitions and protests from Thunderwater's supporters and opponents in Akwesasne, Tyendinaga, Kahnawake, and Grand River, newspaper accounts of Thunderwater's activities, and extensive correspondence from Thunderwater himself. For me, the Thunderwater story that emerged from the contents of the file was not the story of "hoax nativism" told by Postal and Titley. It seemed that there was much, much more to the story of Thunderwater and the Thunderwater movement.[4]

There were many questions: Who *was* Chief Thunderwater? Was he, in fact, an impostor and a con man? What was his connection to Cleveland? What drew so many people from Kahnawake and other Haudenosaunee communities to Thunderwater? How did Thunderwater and the Thunderwater movement fit into the larger picture of modern Haudenosaunee political development? What was it about Chief Thunderwater and the Thunderwater movement that compelled Indian Department officials to make such a concerted effort to expose him as an impostor and a fraud? What brought the movement to such a swift end? What happened to Thunderwater after he disappeared back to the United States?

These questions about Chief Thunderwater and the political movement he triggered in Haudenosaunee communities led me on a search that resulted in extensive research in genealogical and census records, newspaper archives, correspondence, and conversations with Thunderwater descendants in Ohio and Arizona and, most important, to a small file of Thunderwater's personal papers archived at the Western Reserve Historical Society in Cleveland, Ohio. The Chief Thunderwater who surfaced from this search is a person very different from the one scandalized by Postal and Titley. The story of his life and the political movement he energized is much deeper, more complex, and more important than I could have ever imagined.

The story of Chief Thunderwater's rich and complicated life widens our frame of Indigenous life in the United States in the early modern era and helps move us beyond the popular image of Indians as reservation-bound and broken, and as vanishing people slowly and inevitably assimilated into the dominant Euro-American society. As a Sauk and a Seneca, as a child of the Indigenous diaspora of the mid-nineteenth century, as an entertainer and itinerant salesman, as an urban entrepreneur and humanitarian, as a formally uneducated but highly literate and charismatic speaker, as a pan-Indian activist who promoted Indigenous autonomy and self-determination, as a political leader whose advocacy of Native sovereignty contrasted with the assimilationist goals of Progressive-era American Indian intellectuals, and as a marginalized Indian forced to defend his ancestry, character, and identity, Thunderwater's life story brings into better view the diversity and complexity of Indian life in the United States at the turn of the twentieth century. In addition, with his longtime connection to Cleveland, Ohio, and as an active and central figure in its Native community for most of his adult life, Thunderwater's story also sheds light on the history of that city and, more generally, on urban Indian experience during this period.

The story of Thunderwater's life and political work also provides insight into the transnational nature of Haudenosaunee life in the United States and Canada during the late nineteenth and early twentieth centuries. His personal experience and connections to others in Six Nations communities in the United States and Canada sharpened his awareness of and concern with the economic and political importance of border crossing for the Haudenosaunees and anticipated the more formal and organized efforts to establish and defend their border-crossing rights in the mid-1920s. In addition, the story of Thunderwater's work on this and other matters adds to our limited understanding of social and political life in Seneca and Mohawk communities in New York, Quebec, and Ontario during this period.

Perhaps most important, Thunderwater's story contributes in significant ways to our understanding of Six Nations cultural and political revitalization in Canada during the late nineteenth and early twentieth centuries, and at Akwesasne, Kahnawake, Kanehsatake, Tyendinaga, and Grand River in particular. Serving as a bridge between political currents that formed in these communities during the final decades of the nineteenth century in response to the assimilationist pressures of the Indian Act system and the Six Nations sovereignty movement in Canada in the 1920s and beyond, the political movement led and facilitated by Thunderwater stands as an important moment in the rise of modern Haudenosaunee nationalism. More broadly, the organization he established and the movement he led was one of the first steps toward the development of modern

First Nations political organizations in Canada. His story offers insight into the tactics used by Canada's Department of Indian Affairs to neutralize Indigenous activists and to contain organized Indigenous movements that sought autonomy and self-determination for First Nations people.

Philip Deloria has written insightfully about "Indians in unexpected places," Native people at the turn of the twentieth century who confronted modernity as entrepreneurs, actors, musicians, artists, ministers, doctors, lawyers, academics, and activists.[5] They challenged stereotypes, crossed borders, and transcended expectations. Thunderwater should be counted among them. Like them, he was motivated by a range of desires—escape, adventure, liberty, survival, survivance, notoriety, influence, and political interest. Above all else, being "Indian" and fighting for Indigenous interests, both small and large, was at the center of his life. Against the backdrop of early twentieth-century stereotypes of Indians as primitive, defeated, dependent, illiterate, reservation-bound, and doomed to cultural extinction, Thunderwater's life was a lived example of the incongruity and diversity of Indian experience at the beginning of the twentieth century. He defied expectations of what an "Indian" should look like and how an "Indian" should behave. He was worldly, forward-looking, entrepreneurial, savvy, opportunistic, self-interested, and flawed. He was articulate, urban-oriented, and at ease in the economic and social circles of Euro-American society, seeking both individual gain and the advancement of Native, and especially Haudenosaunee, causes and interests. As with other "anomalous" Indians of the early modern period, in his personal, professional, and public life, Thunderwater sought to respond to the economic, social, political, and cultural challenges of being Indian in the late nineteenth and early twentieth centuries. Like them, he was constrained by, but also exploited, disrupted, and consciously subverted the dominant expectations and stereotypes of Indians. In some ways, as well, Thunderwater also challenged the model and hopes and expectations of Native intellectuals who saw themselves as the vanguard of Indian advancement. Formally uneducated, but highly literate, he was an entertainer and showman who promoted himself and his causes in Plains Indian regalia rather than a suit and a tie. He was more often confrontational than cooperative with government officials, and his aim was to advance Native—and in particular Haudenosaunee—welfare, self-determination, and self-government. Chief Thunderwater was a most unexpected Indian in the most unexpected places.

CHAPTER 1

WHO *WAS* THUNDERWATER?

Oghema Niagara, Chief Thunderwater. Born 1865, 10th day of September,
Tuscarora Indian Village, Lewistown, New York. Hut of Two Kettles. Osaukee
mother Au-Paw-Chee-Qua-Paw-Qua. Seneca father Jee-Wan-Ga.
Osaukee grandfather Keokuk. Dances by Seneca Tribe and Tuscaroras on
Canada side under [Niagara] Falls to name baby September 15, 1865.
—From a handwritten and illustrated record of Chief Thunderwater's birth
and family history given to him by his uncle, Moses Keokuk, on his
twentieth birthday in Cleveland, Ohio, 1885

On the wall of Beverly Joy Palmer's bedroom in her daughter's home in Paines-
ville, Ohio, hangs a framed, yellowing document. Dating to 1885 and handed
down to her by her "Aunt Mona," the document will in time be handed down
to her daughter, Mona Secoy, and from her to her children. Hand printed and
illustrated, it measures eleven by seventeen inches and details the birth and family
background of Mrs. Palmer's great-grandfather, "Oghema Niagara." "Oghema
Niagara" is the birth name of Chief Thunderwater. A sweetgrass headband
once worn by her "Grandpa Chief" decorates the treasured family document
(see figure 1).[1]

The Chief Thunderwater birth and family history document is signed and,
presumably, authored by Thunderwater's maternal uncle, Moses Keokuk, and
was presented to Thunderwater to mark the occasion of his twentieth birthday.
A personal note and signature written in cursive at the end of the document
reads, "I give this birthday September 10 day 1885. Oregon Street Cleveland in
Ohio—Moses Keokuk." Moses Keokuk was the son of Chief Keokuk, a political
leader of the Sauk (and later Sauk and Fox) people in the early decades of the
nineteenth century and whom he succeeded as the principal chief of the Sac
and Fox Tribe in 1848. The note and signature appear to be authentic, as the
handwriting and signature are identical to that on the flyleaf of a book given
by Moses to Thunderwater a few years earlier. That book was an 1838 edition

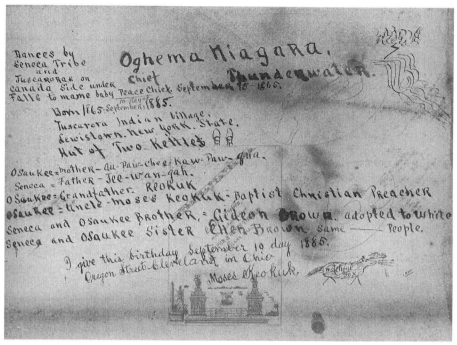

FIGURE 1. Oghema Niagara (Chief Thunderwater) genealogy. This handwritten and
illustrated document was prepared for Thunderwater by his uncle, Moses Keokuk,
and presented to him in Cleveland, Ohio, in 1885 on his twentieth birthday.
Image courtesy of Mona Lee Secoy.

of Benjamin Drake's *The Life and Adventures of Black Hawk with Sketches of
Keokuk, the Sac and Fox Indians, and the Late Black Hawk War.* The inscription and signature read, "To Oghema form [*sic*] Moses Keokuk to keep much
time—1878." The Thunderwater family history is written and sketched on the
reverse side of a photograph of Niagara Falls that dates to the same time period
and is the work of C. H. Nielson, an American photographer and printmaker.
Nielson was active in his work between 1880 and 1900 and is best known for his
images of Niagara Falls. The black and white photograph presents a view from
Terrapin Point on Goat Island in the United States, looking across Horseshoe
Falls toward Niagara Falls, Ontario, in Canada.[2]

   According to the family history document, Thunderwater was born on
September 10, 1865, in the "Hut of Two Kettles" at "Tuscarora Indian Village" in
"Lewistown [*sic*], New York State." "Tuscarora Indian Village" is undoubtedly

a reference to the Tuscarora reservation, a nine square mile tract of land within the town of Lewiston, about ten miles northeast of Niagara Falls and the international border between the United States and Canada. Located on land acquired from the Senecas and the Holland Land Company, the reservation was granted to the Tuscaroras by the U.S. government in 1803, about seventy years after they had been forcibly displaced from their traditional homeland in the Carolinas, resettled on Oneida land in central New York, and adopted into the Haudenosaunee Confederacy. "Two Kettles," at whose "hut" Thunderwater purportedly was born, is represented in the document by the hand-drawn image of two large, long-handled, three-legged cooking pots. The "hut" referred to was probably a small, single-room, wood frame cabin, a common type of dwelling on the Tuscarora reservation in the mid-nineteenth century.

The family history document also indicates that five days after his birth, Thunderwater was formally named "Oghema Niagara" at a ceremony "under Falls," that is, under Niagara Falls, on the Canadian side of the international border. "Oghema" ("ogimaa" in Ojibwe and "okimawa" in Sauk), may reflect his mother's Native ancestry and translates as "boss" or "chief." "Niagara," or "onguiaahra," a term of possible Neutral, Seneca, or Mohawk origin and perhaps drawing on his father's ancestry, translates as "thundering waters" or "resounding with great noise." "Oghema Niagara," thus, renders as "Chief Thunderwater." The name is illustrated in the document with a hand-drawn image of roiling clouds and a single bolt of lightning striking above a turbulent waterfall. According to the document, Oghema also was named a "peace chief" at the falls, and the event was marked with "dances by Seneca Tribe and Tuscaroras."[3]

The document also provides detailed information about Thunderwater's parents and other family members. It identifies his mother as "Au-Paw-Chee-Kaw-Paw-Qua" and her tribal affiliation as "Osaukee" (Sauk) and his father as "Jee-Wan-Ga" and "Seneca." The document also identifies Thunderwater's "Osaukee" grandfather as "Keokuk" (Chief Keokuk) and his "Osaukee" uncle as "Moses Keokuk, Baptist Christian Preacher." Also named in the document are two "Seneca and Osaukee" siblings, a brother, Gideon Brown, and a sister, Ellen Brown, who, according to the document, had been adopted by "White People." As noted above, the document includes the personal note and signature of "Moses Keokuk." Adjacent to the signature are the hand-drawn images of an eye and a four-legged, bushy-tailed animal, with its intent forward gaze emphasized by a fanned spread of outwardly directed lines. Written on the body of the animal are the words "Watchful Fox." The image and words are a reference to Chief Keokuk, or "Kiyo'kaga" ("one who moves about alert" or "watchful fox"). Moses Keokuk, born in 1823 and named "Wunagisa" ("he who leaps quickly from his lair"), was the son of Chief Keokuk. He adopted his Christian name in 1877 when he converted to Christianity and became a Baptist minister. The "Oregon Street" address in Cleveland to which the family history document refers and where it was presented to Thunderwater, is very likely the location of the home of longtime Indian friends or associates of one or both of Thunderwater's parents.[4]

Thunderwater's familial connection to Chief Keokuk is one of the more intriguing details in the document. The son of a Sauk father and a mixed-lineage mother, Keokuk was born about 1780 at Saukenuk, the principal village of the Sauk people on the Rock River in present-day western Illinois (figure 2). He rose to prominence among his people during the War of 1812 and was recognized as a "war chief," but more for his political and oratorical skills than his actions as a warrior or military leader. As a member of the Fox clan, Keokuk was eligible for such recognition, but not so for the inherited role of a "peace" or "civil" chief. He was a complicated and controversial political leader among his people and, later, among the Meskwaki (Fox) people, as well, after the two nations became more formally linked in the 1820s. Recognizing what he viewed as the superiority of American power and the inevitability of American expansionism, Keokuk developed a reputation as a political realist and effective negotiator with the U.S. government, a standing that drew many supporters among the Sauks and Meskwakis, but also some critics. His main detractor and political rival was Black Hawk, who favored armed resistance against the United States. In 1830, led by Keokuk, the Sauks and Meskwakis signed a treaty with the United States in which they surrendered their claim to twenty-six million acres of land east of the Mississippi River in exchange for territory in present-day Iowa. Black Hawk and his followers opposed the treaty and sought to keep their lands and principal village in Illinois, a position that eventually led to the short-lived and failed Black Hawk War of 1832. Keokuk worked successfully to discourage support for Black Hawk and in 1831 led a relocation of the Sauks and Meskwakis out of Illinois to the Iowa lands.[5]

Following Black Hawk's defeat, which resulted in the cession of six million acres of Sauk and Meskwaki lands in Iowa, the U.S. government rewarded Keokuk

FIGURE 2. Chief Keokuk (Kiyo'kaga, "Watchful Fox"), ca. 1780–1848.
Chief Keokuk, a political leader among the Sauk and Meskwaki people during
the first half of the nineteenth century, was the maternal grandfather
of Oghema Niagara (Chief Thunderwater).
Image courtesy of National Anthropological Archives.

for his cooperation by officially recognizing him as the principal "peace" or "civil" chief of the Sauk and Meskwaki people. However, because his position and actions during the war had been controversial and because he did not belong to the traditional ruling clan of the Sauks, many of those people, the Meskwakis in particular, did not support him in his new position. Suspicions about corruption in his use of tribal resources further eroded his support. Despite his cooperative relationship with the U.S. government, Keokuk was a steadfast opponent to the introduction of teachers and missionaries among his people. Nevertheless, acceding to American land pressures, he led negotiations for the sale of the Sauk and Meskwaki lands in Iowa in 1836, 1837, and 1842 and the relocation of his people to Kansas in 1845. There they found poor economic and living conditions, and as their circumstances worsened, dissatisfaction with Keokuk's leadership intensified and continued until his death from dysentery in 1848.

As noted, according to the Oghema Niagara family history document, Thunderwater's mother, "Au-Paw-Chee-Kaw-Paw-Qua," was the daughter of Chief Keokuk. This connection is difficult to corroborate. Keokuk is known to have had at least three wives. These included an unnamed first wife, who was born in Illinois about 1785 and whom he married in 1806. A second wife, "Har-quo-quar," was born at Saukenuk in 1803 and joined him about 1818. A third wife was "No-Kaw-Quale-Quale," who was born about 1800 and whom Keokuk married at Rock River in 1823. Genealogical records for Keokuk identify five children born to these three wives. Au-Paw-Chee-Kaw-Paw-Qua is not among them. However, Keokuk reportedly had more than these three wives, perhaps as many as seven, and it is quite possible that he had one or more children by the additional wives.[6]

To try to puzzle out the possible connection between Thunderwater and Chief Keokuk, we can begin by assuming that Thunderwater's mother was approximately twenty to thirty years of age when she gave birth to him in 1865 and, thus, that she was born sometime between 1835 and 1845. In addition, there is some evidence in Thunderwater's personal papers that Au-Paw-Chee-Kaw-Paw-Qua's maternal ancestry was Ojibwe. Considering these details, it is unlikely that Keokuk's first wife could have been Au-Paw-Chee-Kaw-Paw-Qua's mother, as she would have been approximately fifty years old or more at the time of the birth. It is also unlikely that Har-quo-quar, Keokuk's second wife, was her mother. She would have been about thirty-five years of age at the presumed time of Au-Paw-Chee-Kaw-Paw-Qua's birth, but she appears to be of Sauk, not Ojibwe, ancestry. It is possible that Keokuk's third wife, No-Kaw-Quale-Quale, was the mother of Au-Paw-Chee-Kaw-Paw-Qua, but she may have been about forty years of age or more at the time of the birth. The most likely possibility is that Au-Paw-Chee-Kaw-Paw-Qua was born to one of Keokuk's younger, and later, unidentified wives, a fact that Thunderwater acknowledged toward the end of his life.[7]

FIGURE 3. Moses Keokuk (Wunagisa, "He Who Leaps Quickly from His Lair"),
ca. 1821–1903. Moses Keokuk, son of Chief Keokuk and the principal chief
of the Sac and Fox Tribe from 1848 to 1884, was the maternal uncle of
Oghema Niagara (Chief Thunderwater).
Image courtesy of National Anthropological Archives.

Moses Keokuk was born to Keokuk's second wife, Har-quo-quar, at Saukenuk about 1821, making him Au-Paw-Chee-Kaw-Paw-Qua's older half brother
(figure 3). Moses assisted his father in the 1842 negotiations that resulted in the
sale of the Sauk and Meskwaki lands in Iowa and in 1848 succeeded him in his
position as the principal chief of the Sac and Fox tribe. Moses continued his
father's cooperative relationship with the U.S. government, signing a treaty in

1859 that resulted in the allotment of the Kansas reservation, another treaty in 1867 that resulted in removal of the Sauks and Meskwakis to a new reservation in Indian Territory, and a third treaty in 1891 that resulted in the allotment of the Indian Territory land. After he converted to Christianity in 1877 and became a Baptist minister, he encouraged his people to attend Christian religious services and assimilate to the Euro-American way of life. Moses Keokuk died in 1903.[8]

"Jee-Wan-Ga," Thunderwater's purported Seneca father, appears to have been born about 1840. Genealogical information about him, too, is limited, but there is some independent corroboration of his identity, age, and ancestry. In the late 1920s Thunderwater became embroiled in a legal battle in Louisville, Kentucky, in which two of the city's newspapers raised doubts about his character and Indian identity. As part of a libel case he brought against the papers, Thunderwater collected a number of legal depositions from longtime associates who testified to his identity and family history. One of those depositions was from Chief Isaac Hill, "Skyendockyeh," an elderly pine tree chief at the Six Nations of the Grand River reserve near Brantford, Ontario. Identifying himself in the deposition as eighty-four years of age, Hill would have been born about 1846, making him a contemporary of Thunderwater's father. Hill stated that he had known Thunderwater since his boyhood and had been associated with him for many years. He went so far as to note that he knew of a slight physical disfigurement by which Thunderwater could be identified, stating, "[He] has a left-right scar under his left knee, which was caused by a hatchet . . . cut to the bone at the time he was near Buffalo. This scar will identify Chief Thunderwater at any time." Chief Hill also addressed the matter of Thunderwater's parentage and ancestry, stating "that he was well acquainted with the father and mother of Oghema Niagara, Chief Thunderwater, and that the name of the father was Jee-Wan-Ga and of the mother Au-paw-ghee-paw-qua . . . that the father of the said Oghema Niagara, Chief Thunderwater, was a full blood Iroquois Indian of the Seneca Tribe, and that the mother of the said Oghema Niagara was the daughter of a prominent western Chief of the Sauk and Algonquin Nation, and that she, also, was an Indian . . . that he often played La Cross with the said Jee-Wan-Ga at and about Buffalo, New York."[9]

Jee-Wan-Ga's familial and social connections to the Seneca communities in New York—Cattaraugus, Oil Spring, Allegany, and Tonawanda—if any, are unknown. Cattaraugus, Allegany, and Tonawanda connections are at least possibilities, as Thunderwater would have some political involvement with members of those communities later in his adult life. A connection to Tuscarora is also a possibility since Thunderwater was purportedly born in or near that community. In addition, he had some political involvement with the Tuscarora community later in his life, as well. Another possibility is that Jee-Wan-Ga's roots lay in the Buffalo Creek Seneca community, which was located near the city of Buffalo and dispersed with the dissolution of their reservation in 1842. Thunderwater's connection to Buffalo appears to have been a strong one, as events later in his life suggest. Still another, though more remote possibility, is that Jee-Wan-Ga's Seneca tie was to the Senecas of the Sandusky and that his family was part of the diaspora of that group after their removal from northern Ohio to Indian Territory in 1831. One final point worth noting may provide some understanding of the relationship between Thunderwater's parents. In the mid-eighteenth century, after being displaced south from their homeland in the western Great Lakes region and migrating east from present-day Illinois, some Meskwakis settled along the Genesee River in New York at the border of Seneca territory. While the Meskwakis in Illinois eventually aligned themselves with the Sauks, over time those who had relocated east developed close social and political ties with the Senecas in the Genesee Valley region and eventually assimilated along with them into the Tonawanda, Cattaraugus, Buffalo Creek, and Allegany communities.[10]

Additional testimony in Thunderwater's legal case in Louisville in the late 1920s included an affidavit from one of Thunderwater's longtime connections, Minnie Peck of Cleveland, Ohio. Peck's affidavit, taken in June 1927, is also helpful in unraveling the mystery of Thunderwater's identity and family history. In addition, it provides some insight into the Indian community of Cleveland, to which Thunderwater was closely connected throughout much of his adult life. Peck, seventy-two years of age at the time of her deposition, stated that she had known "Oghema Niagara" for more than sixty years and that she had been well acquainted with his father and mother, whom she described as "full blooded Indians." Recalling the circumstances of Thunderwater's naming soon after his birth, Peck stated that she was present at the home of Peter Bennett, on Oregon Street in Cleveland, when Niagara, "a babe in arms," had been brought there after a recent visit to Niagara Falls with a party that included a "Mr. and Mrs. Palmer." She identified "Mrs. Palmer" as Niagara's "God Mother" and described her, her husband, and Bennett also as "full blooded Indians" who "wore long hair." Bennett's home on Oregon Street may have been the location where, twenty years later, the handwritten and illustrated record of his birth and family history prepared and signed by his uncle Moses was presented to Thunderwater. Though her account is somewhat confusing on this point, she stated that Thunderwater was named "Oghema Niagara" during a thunderstorm, either at Niagara Falls or at Bennett's home, and that several months later, in the spring of 1866, he, his mother, and "several other Indians" left Cleveland and returned to Niagara Falls. "The baby had been taken to the base of the falls or under the same," she stated, "and there given the name of Niagara." "Festivities" were held at that time, she added, perhaps referring to the "dances" by the Senecas and Tuscaroras noted in the Thunderwater family history document. In her deposition Peck also indicated that Thunderwater's mother was known throughout the Oregon Street neighborhood as "the daughter of one of the Chiefs of the Black Hawk war" and that his father was a "hunter and trapper [who] dealt in skins or hides and also sold herbs for medicine." She continued, "Many people around Oregon Street bought herbs from [Thunderwater's father]." Providing additional insight into the Native community of Cleveland to which Thunderwater and his parents were connected, she stated that "the home of Peter Bennett was frequently filled with travelling Indians" and that Bennett, Thunderwater's parents, the Palmers, and others "were very friendly to whites." She added, "Niagara and the rest of the Indians went and came frequently, sometimes being absent for a long time."[11]

Moses Keokuk's reference in the 1885 family history document to the naming of Oghema Niagara as a "peace chief" at the time of his birth is an important element of Thunderwater's biography and one that he would refer to frequently in the creation of his public persona later in life. Peck also refers to this point in her 1927 deposition, identifying him as a "Chief by inheritance or Peace Chief." Though not stated explicitly in the family history document, this may refer to the connection through his mother to Chief Keokuk and to a position within the Sauk Tribe. Throughout his adult life Thunderwater would emphasize his Sauk ancestry and assert that he was a chief within the Sauk Tribe by inheritance, doing so to promote both himself and the political causes with which he became engaged. It would be a claim repeated by his many friends and associates, presumably based on that assertion. On the one hand, Thunderwater's claim to an inherited position of political leadership would appear to be without foundation. Among the Sauks a "peace chief," sometimes referred to as a "civil chief," was a status controlled by a clan within the tribe and to which an adult male member of that clan was appointed. Typically, individuals were not assigned, nor did they inherit chieftainships at birth. In addition, any claim that Thunderwater could make to the position of "chief" within the Sauk Tribe would have to have been based on the connection through his mother to Chief Keokuk. However, Keokuk's position as chief in the early nineteenth century was that of a "war chief," recognized by some within the Sauk Tribe as a leader due to his political and oratorical skills; his was not an inherited status. Also, as a member of the Fox clan within the Sauk Tribe, Keokuk did not belong to the patrilineal line within the Sauk Tribe through which inherited tribal leadership descended. Keokuk solidified his position as a chief in the 1830s when the U.S. government recognized him as the principal "peace" chief of the Sac and Fox Tribe. Though it was an appointed position, Keokuk treated it as an inherited one, and when he died in 1848, the title passed to his son, Wunagisa (Moses), Thunderwater's uncle. Moses Keokuk remained the principal chief of the Sauk and Fox Nation until about 1884 or 1885, then served as an assistant principal chief until his death in 1903. According to Sauk tradition, Thunderwater could not have inherited political leadership status from Chief Keokuk.[12]

On the other hand, it is noteworthy that Moses Keokuk, who at the time was the U.S. government-appointed chief of the Sac and Fox Tribe, himself identified "Oghema Niagara" as a "peace chief." One possibility is that the statement means only that Thunderwater was in the familial line of political leadership within the Sauk Tribe, not that he inherited the position at birth. Another possibility is that during the mid-nineteenth century, Sauk rules of access to political leadership, along with other cultural and political norms, were breaking down or changing as the people sought to cope with the stress and upheaval associated with the warfare, social division, loss of land, and relocation they had experienced. Yet another possibility is that in identifying or naming Thunderwater a "peace chief," Moses Keokuk intentionally disregarded Sauk customs, as his father before him seems to have done, and sought to pass the line of political leadership to one of Chief Keokuk's descendants. In any event, throughout his adult life Thunderwater *did* make claims to inherited political leadership, but that claim is problematic and raises questions about his motivations in doing so.

Little is known about Thunderwater or his family between 1865 and 1875. According to the family history document, a white family by the name of "Brown" had adopted his two siblings, "Gideon" and "Ellen." A biographical note in Thunderwater's personal papers indicates the family, or perhaps just he and his mother, traveled periodically between "Saukee Town" in central Iowa and Montreal, Quebec, near which, according to the note, "resided many Musquakees after the Black Hawk War." Along this route they often stayed with Native friends and hosts in Cleveland, perhaps at the Oregon Street home of Peter Bennett, and other towns and villages along the way. It seems likely that "Saukee Town," and perhaps the Montreal area, as well, represented important social connections for Thunderwater's mother. "Saukee Town" is most likely a reference to "Indian Town," which was located between Tama and Marshalltown, Iowa, and established in 1857 by Meskwakis who had not relocated to Kansas with the other members of the Sac and Fox Tribe in the 1840s. Today "Indian Town" is known as "Meskwaki Settlement" and is the home of the Sac and Fox Tribe of the Mississippi in Iowa. The St. Lawrence River region in southern Quebec and southern Ontario was the traditional homeland of the Sauk and Meskwaki peoples, but they were driven from the area by colonial pressures in the seventeenth century. From there they migrated to northern Michigan, then to Wisconsin near Green Bay, and eventually to northern Illinois in the 1730s. Black Hawk's great-grandfather, Nanamakee, was born near Montreal and led the Sauk migration to northern Michigan about 1629. Some Meskwakis may have returned to and resettled in the Montreal area after the Black Hawk War of 1832 and might have been the source of Au-Paw-Chee-Kaw-Paw-Qua's tie to the Montreal area. Perhaps it was an important connection for Thunderwater as well. The migrant life of Thunderwater's family during this early period of his life may help to explain his apparent lack of formal schooling during his childhood or adolescence, a noteworthy point because in his adult life he would prove to be a very competent writer and correspondent. He may have spent some of his time between 1865 and 1875, and perhaps beyond, in Cleveland with his godmother, Mrs. Palmer, as some familiar with him from that time period knew him by that surname. The transiency and time spent in Cleveland during this formative period of Thunderwater's life might also explain his apparent lack of fluency in a Native language (see map 1).[13]

In 1875 Thunderwater's parents were recruited to work in the Centennial International Exposition in Philadelphia, the first official World's Fair. Held from May to September 1876 to celebrate the one hundredth anniversary of the signing of the Declaration of Independence, the exposition included more than two hundred buildings constructed on a 265-acre fairgrounds, featured agricultural, horticultural, mechanical, and artistic exhibits, and attracted nearly ten million visitors. One of the highlights of the exposition was an "Indian Encampment," which included over three hundred Indians from fifty-three different tribes, with Thunderwater's parents, and perhaps Thunderwater himself, apparently among them. According to an official history of the exposition, the Indian Encampment featured "redskins [who were] in many instances famous chiefs and their families. . . . They were selected for their perfection of form and physical development, or for their distinguished deeds; so that they constitute

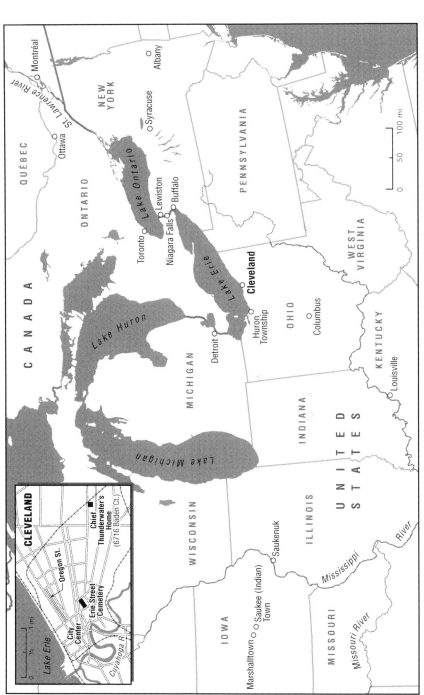

MAP 1. Important places and locations in Chief Thunderwater's life.

Map by Erin Greb.

the very aristocracy of the Indian nation. . . . The object of the encampment is
to show, in as perfect a degree as is now possible, the original inhabitants of
this country and their modes of life." The exposition was a great success, but
according to one source, there was at least one somber moment when news of
Custer's defeat at the Little Big Horn River by the Lakota, Northern Cheyenne,
and Arapaho arrived several weeks after its opening and "cast a dark shade over
the festivities."[14]

Following the Centennial Exposition, Thunderwater's family continued to
engage in Indian entertainment and exhibitions for the next ten years, work
he then continued on his own for another fifteen years or more. At some point
during this period Thunderwater even performed in Buffalo Bill Cody's Wild
West Show. Cody, as is well known, made his name in the late 1860s as a famed
buffalo hunter, began entertainment work in Chicago in the early 1870s, and
founded *Buffalo Bill's Wild West* in 1883. The circus-like show and exhibition
toured annually for two decades and traveled throughout the United States and
to Great Britain and Europe. Over time, Cody employed hundreds of Native
people in his shows, including Pawnees, Arapahos, Kiowas, Cheyennes, and,
almost exclusively by the early 1890s, Oglala Lakotas from Pine Ridge and other
reservations in South Dakota. The importance of Thunderwater's connection
to Buffalo Bill is suggested by correspondence between the two later in his life
when Cody wrote to him as follows: "How, Thunderwater, My Chief: I am glad
to know there is one Indian who is trying to better the conditions of his Red
brothers, the first Americans, a proud, romantic race. Keep the good work going,
and whenever I can help you, call on me." Like other Indian entertainers and
performers of this era, it is likely that Thunderwater's parents and then Thunderwater himself engaged in exhibition and Wild West work out of economic
necessity. Like the others as well, they also may have sought escape, adventure,
and personal freedom.[15]

Thunderwater's entertainment work brought him into close contact with other
Indian performers, Oglala Lakotas in particular. A newspaper photograph from
1901 titled "Big Pow-Wow of Indian Chiefs" shows Thunderwater as part of a large
group of mostly Oglala Lakota performers who were participating in the "Indian
Congress and Village" at the Pan-American Exposition, held during the fall of
that year in Buffalo, New York (see figure 4). In the photograph Thunderwater
and three others are seated on the ground before a large, standing group, many
of whom are dressed in traditional Native regalia. Thunderwater himself wears
a feathered headdress, beaded shirt, leggings, and moccasins. Like many other

FIGURE 4. Chief Thunderwater and Lakota entertainers at the Pan-American
Exposition in Buffalo, New York, in 1901. Thunderwater and the Lakota performers
participated in the "Indian Congress and Village" at the exposition. Thunderwater is
seated near the center in the front row, alongside Chief Iron Tail of the Oglala Lakota.
Image courtesy of the Western Reserve Historical Society, Cleveland, Ohio.

Native entertainers who catered to the expectations of non-Native audiences, his
regalia is in the Plains Indian–style, a habit of dress for public appearances that
he would maintain throughout his life. Seated to his immediate right, dressed
more plainly, is Chief Iron Tail, the Oglala Lakota political leader from Pine
Ridge who had become a star performer in Cody's Wild West Show.[16]

The Lakota connection Thunderwater developed through his entertainment
work appears to have been deep and sustained. In his Louisville libel case in 1928
Thunderwater obtained a number of character witness statements from Lakota
friends and associates who testified to not only his Native identity and ancestry,
but also to his close ties with and service to individuals from the Rosebud and
Pine Ridge Agencies. One of these associates was sixty-six-year-old "Makes
Mad," who identified himself as "the son of Ben Charging Hawk of Tribe Oglala
Sioux and Lacota Nation situated on the Indian Reservation at Rosebud South

Dakota." He gave sworn testimony that Oghema Niagara had been known to the Lakota since 1876, the year of the Centennial Exposition in Philadelphia, and that he personally knew Thunderwater to be "a full-blooded Indian." Henry Eagle Head, self-described as a "full blood Sioux residing at Pine Ridge Indian Reservation, Manderson South Dakota," gave similar sworn testimony. Eagle Head also stated that he had known Thunderwater since the late 1800s and that he "has been . . . trusted, admired by, and has the full confidence of hundreds of Sioux Indians." He went on to state that Thunderwater had assisted him in various business matters and that he had done so "honestly, faithfully and without charge of any amount of money or reward." In their depositions both Makes Mad and Eagle Head referred to Thunderwater as "Minniwakyon." "Minni," or "mni," in Lakota translates as "water" and "minniwakyon," or "mni wakan," translates as "holy water," "water is sacred," and "sacred water." Later in life Thunderwater sometimes boarded Lakota and other Indians in his home in Cleveland. One of those was Sherman Charging Hawk, a "showman" who was from the Rosebud Agency and a lodger in Thunderwater's home in 1910.[17]

In the late 1880s Thunderwater spent some time in Detroit, Michigan, where he had a relationship with a white woman by the name of Euphemia Waters. Born in that city in 1872, Euphemia was the second of the five children of John and Effie Waters, both working-class Irish immigrants. As an adolescent, she was employed in domestic work, and at about age seventeen or eighteen she married Joseph Antoine Blanchard of Windsor, Ontario. In 1889, about the time of her marriage to Blanchard, she gave birth to a son fathered by Thunderwater. The son was named "Louis Keokuk." Euphemia, still married to Joseph Antoine and the mother of several other children, died in Detroit in 1899 at just twenty-seven years of age. Her death certificate lists the cause of death as tuberculosis and "exhaustion."[18]

Following Euphemia's death, Thunderwater and young Louis relocated to Ohio and eventually to Cleveland. There, in the city that was so well known to him and his family, Thunderwater would make a home and name for himself as a businessman, concerned citizen, Indian-rights activist, and lifelong resident. By 1915 he would establish the Council of the Tribes and help spark political resistance and revival among Haudenosaunees across southern Quebec and Ontario.

CHAPTER 2

THUNDERWATER AND CLEVELAND'S INDIANS

One of the most interesting ceremonies held yesterday in connection
with the decoration of graves in the various cemeteries [in Cleveland]
was at the old East St. cemetery, when the Indian chief, Thunderwater,
and members of his family and tribe held an impressive service at the grave
of their famous old warrior, Joc-O-Sot. In full Indian costume, with war paint
and feathers, Chief Thunderwater, on a prancing steed, accompanied by
members of the tribe of the Sac and Fox, gathered around the grave,
which had already been decked with flags and flowers, and held the
consecration service peculiar to the Indian faith.
—From the *Cleveland Plain Dealer* (May 1908)

Sometime in the early 1900s Thunderwater and his son, Louis Keokuk, relocated from Detroit to Huron Township, Ohio, on the southwestern shore of Lake Erie near the city of Sandusky, about fifty miles west of Cleveland. The reason for their move is unclear, though one possibility is that it was related to the death of Louis's mother in 1899. Little is known about Thunderwater's activities in Huron Township, though he began business ventures there that he would continue after relocating to Cleveland a few years later. In 1907 and 1908 Thunderwater visited Cleveland on several occasions out of concern for the remains of Joc-O-Sot, a Sauk chief who had died in Cleveland in 1844. Joc-O-Sot, or "The Walking Bear," was born about 1810 and had fought in the Black Hawk War of 1832. Soon after the war he settled in Cleveland, worked as a hunting and fishing guide, and eventually found employment with a theatrical troupe that toured American cities performing plays about Indian life. In 1843 Joc-O-Sot joined an American company touring England with an early version of a Wild West show and even made an appearance in artist George Catlin's "Real Indian" exhibition in London. In June 1844, while still on tour, he became gravely ill with tuberculosis and returned to the United States and Cleveland. Joc-O-Sot died just a few months later and was buried in Cleveland's Erie Street Cemetery.[1]

Thunderwater regarded Joc-O-Sot as a personal hero, perhaps because of their common tribal background, shared experience in entertainment work, and connection to the city of Cleveland. In 1907 the city was considering commercial development of the Erie Street Cemetery, and Thunderwater initiated a campaign to raise funds to have the remains of the Sauk chief transferred elsewhere and for the new grave to be marked with a suitable memorial. His visits to Cleveland for this purpose received the attention of one of the city's main newspapers, the *Plain Dealer*, which in its reporting referred to him as a "peace chief," a member of the "Sac and Fox nation," and the maternal grandson of Chief Keokuk. "He has not the tall, lithe form usually connected with the American aborigine," the *Plain Dealer* noted. "His eyes, however, stamp him a thoroughbred. They are black, ceaselessly active and inscrutable as the grave. His conversation is that of an educated man, but he has not learned in books." Ultimately, in part through the attention brought by Thunderwater's campaign, the Erie Street Cemetery was preserved, and Joc-O-Sot's grave remained undisturbed. On Memorial Day in May 1908 Thunderwater led a commemoration service at his grave site, an event the *Plain Dealer* reported on under the headline "Memorial Day Observed— Chief Thunderwater Near Grave of Old Warrior." Accompanying the article was a picture of Thunderwater, the first of many of him that would appear in Cleveland papers over the coming years. Heavyset and broad-faced, dressed in Native regalia that includes a full-feathered headdress and beaded buckskin shirt and leggings, he sits astride a large horse, seated in a leather saddle and holding a set of leather reins. With another Indian rider to his right, Thunderwater is pictured shaking hands with a mounted representative of the Grand Army of the Republic, a national association of Union Civil War veterans. According to one report of the event, family members and "members of the Sac and Fox" assisted Thunderwater at the service.[2]

Thunderwater and his son, Louis, moved to Cleveland around this time and took up residence on the city's near-east side, which then was home to many working-class European immigrants. With an economic core of steel and oil production, Cleveland in the early twentieth century was a prosperous, burgeoning city that saw its population rise from about 380,000 in 1900 to over half a million by 1910. Thunderwater's eventual home, at 6716 Baden Court, was a rambling seventeen-room house located about two miles from the Oregon Street neighborhood that his family frequented in the 1860s and 1870s. The 1910 U.S. Census lists him at the Baden Court address and identifies him as "Oghema

Niagara Chief Thunderwater," "Indian," forty-five years of age and a widower. As noted, Thunderwater had a relationship with a white woman from Detroit who bore his son and died in 1899. However, there is no record that he married her or any other woman prior to this date. In subsequent censuses he would identify himself as single, and he remained unmarried throughout the rest of his life. The 1910 census lists Thunderwater's birthplace as New York and that of both of his parents as Illinois. The members of his household included his son, Louis, and Louis's wife, Blanche, age twenty-two. Louis and Blanche (Beckwith) married in 1908, and the 1910 census identifies both as "Indian." Thunderwater, his son, and his daughter-in-law are also listed in the Indian Population Schedule of the 1910 U.S. Census for Cleveland. The schedule identifies Thunderwater as "Oghema Thunderwater" and a member of the "Osaukee" tribe. His mother and, erroneously, his father are identified with this same tribal affiliation. In addition, the Indian Population Schedule records Thunderwater as being of "full" Indian blood, with no "White" or "Negro" blood. Louis, also identified as "Osaukee," is recorded as being "full" Indian blood as well, though this is incorrect since his mother was white and of Irish ancestry. Blanche Keokuk, with no tribal affiliation listed, is recorded as "9/16" Indian and "7/16" white. She is also identified as a "graduate" of the "Ohio Soldiers and Sailors Orphan Home," a community near Xenia, Ohio, established in 1869 for the care of the widows and orphans of civil war veterans.[3]

Thunderwater's principal source of income during these early years in Cleveland and throughout much of his later life included making and selling herbal medicines, a trade that he likely learned from his father. The U.S. censuses of 1910 and 1920 list his occupation as "manufacturer" and record Louis as an employee. Among the medicines that they produced and sold were "Thunderwater's Mohawk Oil," and "Jee-Wan-Ga," an herbal tea named after his father. Thunderwater also produced and sold a tonic for asthma, the recipe for which consisted of a quarter ounce of belladonna leaves added to a pint of water; for treatment, the mixture was boiled and the steam inhaled. Another prescription was for "spasmodic asthma" and consisted of an "infusion" of catalpa beans and a "dose of tincture," an alcoholic extract. For a time in the early 1900s Thunderwater also owned and operated "Camp Niagara," a campground near Huron Township managed by Louis and which they rented out for "picnics" and "forest fetes." "Camp Niagara" letterhead listed Thunderwater as the proprietor under the name "Oghema Niagara" and featured a likeness that may have been Thunderwater himself, but also bears a resemblance to popular images of Sitting Bull, the Hunkpapa Lakota warrior and spiritual leader. He belonged to the Cleveland businessmen's "Taft Club," which in 1908 invited him to participate in festivities related to a visit by presidential candidate William H. Taft.[4]

Thunderwater soon developed a reputation in Cleveland for his civic and charitable work. In 1908, for example, he organized and served as treasurer for an amateur baseball team, the "Thunderwaters." Originally known as the "Camp Niagaras," the team consisted of Thunderwater's son, Louis, who played first base and served as team manager, at least one other Native player, and a number of non-Native players. Team meetings were held at Thunderwater's Baden Court home. According to the *Cleveland Plain Dealer* sports pages, in May 1910 the "Thunderwaters" routed the rival "Acorns" thirteen to five and bested them again two weeks later by a score of six to three in a three-hit, fourteen-strikeout performance by "Deering," their star pitcher. In 1910, under court appointment and supervision, Thunderwater volunteered to rehabilitate a malnourished young man whose mother was arrested for child neglect. After two months' care he brought the nineteen-year-old back to good health and, as reported by the *Plain Dealer*, "built him into a husky young man." When the judge in the case offered Thunderwater his congratulations, "the chief smiled with delight."[5]

In January 1911 Blanche Keokuk gave birth to a daughter, who was named "Mahoniall Au-Paw-Chee-Kaw-Paw-Qua," in acknowledgment of Louis's grandmother and Thunderwater's mother. Eleven months later, in a ceremony reminiscent of Thunderwater's own naming as "Oghema Niagara" forty-five years earlier, Mahoniall was "baptized" at Niagara Falls. The event attracted considerable public and press attention, and the news reports were indicative of the complexities of the Thunderwater story. According to the *Plain Dealer*, the baptismal party included Thunderwater, Louis, who was described as a "half-breed Indian," Blanche, described as a "white woman," eleven-month-old Mahoniall, and the infant's godmother, "Away-Ehsee," and godfather, "Cah-New-Dey-Day." After dining at noon at a hotel on the American side of the Falls, the party, followed by a number of tourists, walked "in true Indian fashion" a half mile to Horseshoe Falls on the Canadian side of the Niagara River and descended some two hundred feet to the Cave of the Winds. There, "with the mist from the immense waterfall beating upon the group, the aged chief baptized and formally endowed the little princess with her title."[6]

There may have been some dispute between Thunderwater and his daughter-in-law over the ceremony that was to take place beneath the falls. In its reporting, the *Plain Dealer* noted that Blanche Keokuk refused to allow the baptism without an ordained clergyman present. Purportedly, Thunderwater objected, declaring that he was baptized "without help from the palefaces" and that he preferred his granddaughter be named in the same way. "I was named under the Horseshoe Fall in 1866," he stated. "There was no white man there and none who does not understand our customs should be called now." The *New York Tribune* told a somewhat different story. According to its reporter, a minister from St. Paul's church in Buffalo performed the baptism and "anointed the infant of eleven months with spray from the cataract." Following the ceremony, Thunderwater, "with a handful of people about him," made an address for the "pagan faith." "The Christian says that the pagan is a fool," he reportedly stated. "I was raised a pagan. I have lived a pagan and I shall die a pagan. . . . This child is christened because she lives under a Christian nation and will have to obey Christian laws. But she shall later be named a pagan and when she is old enough to decide for herself, she shall choose between Christ and Manitou." Over the next several days the *Tribune* account was picked up and reprised by a number of newspapers around the country under such headlines as "Defends His Faith" in the *Topeka* (Kansas) *Daily State Journal*, "Indian Chief Raises Protest to Baptism" in the *Omaha* (Nebraska) *Daily Bee*, "A Sturdy Old Savage" in the *Ocala* (Florida) *Evening Star*, and "An Indian Chief's Protest" in the Keokuk, Iowa, *Daily Gate City.*[7]

According to the *Plain Dealer* account, Mahoniall's "baptism" by Thunderwater "formally endowed" her with the title of "princess." The newspaper also reported that through the ceremony she was "proclaimed a princess with all the pomp and splendor which marks an Indian coronation." Mahoniall's status as an "Indian princess" is well established in Thunderwater family lore, and newspaper articles reporting on her activities later in life frequently referred to her as a "princess." Nevertheless, the grounds for claiming such status are problematic. The notion of royalty implied by the term "Indian princess" did not exist in Sauk, Ojibwe, Seneca, or other American Indian cultures. It was, in fact, a concept that had deep roots in Euro-American stereotypes of Indian women that served to cast them as legitimate mates (and ancestors) for whites and which rationalized European conquest and colonization. Historically, whites sometimes used the term to refer to the daughters of legitimate Native tribal leaders. However, it is certain that Mahoniall's father, Louis, was not a recognized tribal leader of any sort. In addition, Thunderwater's status as a chief by inheritance is problematic, and there appears to be no basis for a claim of authority to confer a title of this sort on his granddaughter. It is possible that the interpretation and reporting of the events proclaiming Mahoniall an "Indian princess" was partly the product of the newspaper reporters drawing on popular cultural tropes regarding Indians in order to attract readers. Another possibility is that Thunderwater was using the "Indian princess" claim for his granddaughter in a self-serving way to validate his own status as a "chief." Perhaps it was a combination of both of these factors.[8]

Thunderwater did not limit his activism and engagement with Cleveland's Native community during these years to his efforts to protect the grave of his hero Joc-O-Sot. In 1907, while still living in Huron Township, he spoke out publicly in the city against a campaign led by the Women's National Indian Association (WNIA) against Native traditional dances. Founded in 1879, the WNIA advocated for enforcement of Indian treaties and protested white encroachment on Indian lands, but also promoted the Christianization and assimilation of Native people in the United States. In 1907 the organization, which was based in New York City and made up mostly of white female social activists, took an official position that Native dances were immoral, primitive, and incompatible with the demands of a modern, Euro-American way of life. They succeeded in introducing a bill in Congress that would ban such dances nationwide. "The National Indian association is composed of a lot of meddlesome old women," Thunderwater complained at one of his Cleveland meetings. "Blood will surely flow if the government listens to the National Indian association and attempts to abolish the time honored Indian dances in different parts of the country."

"The big Indian scornfully denounces the National Indian association," the *Cleveland Plain Dealer* reported, "declaring that it is composed of wolves in sheep's clothing, false friends. Denying the charge of immorality leveled against the Indian dance, he counters by asserting that the waltz and two step of the white man . . . are lascivious and degenerating to the highest degree." Thunderwater objected, "Here you see men and women, boys and girls, maybe half-drunk, reeling about the floor in a close embrace. The man's arm rests on the girl's waist and hers is around his neck. The atmosphere of the room is stifling with the fumes of liquor and smoke. Seductive, sensuous music completes the disgusting affect. Compare with that the ancient religious ceremonial of my people. . . . Every step is a ceremony, every effort a sacrifice to Manitou."[9]

Once he relocated to Cleveland in 1908, Thunderwater began to take on the role of an unofficial ambassador and host of Native people visiting and living in the city. In July 1908, for example, he was showing visiting Indians around the city when a streetcar accidentally struck the sightseeing wagon in which they were riding. Under the headline "Indians on Warpath—Car Smashes Wagon

Load and Custer Massacre is All but Repeated," the city newspaper described the incident in wildly overblown language. "A street car which crashed into a 'rubber neck' wagon loaded with Indians . . . started a small race war yesterday," the newspaper informed its readers. "The conductor of the car who was the frightened pale face lost first blood. Chief Thunderwater of Cleveland was showing his brothers and sisters of the Osages, Cul-de-Sacs [Sauk?] and Nez Perce around the city. . . . His guests were looking over St. Paul's Episcopal Church when, bang! It was the Euclid Av street car swinging around the corner. Everyone was thrown into the far corner of the big vehicle." Continuing with a description of the chaotic scene, the newspaper reported that the Indians "swarmed angrily" out of their car and two of them "grabbed the street car man and jammed him roughly against the wagon," adding, comically, that a "third went through him and took his notebook and broke his pencil. . . . He might have been burned at the stake if Chief Thunderwater . . . hadn't thrown himself into the breach," the paper concluded its report on the peaceful resolution of the incident. "The chief of the Sacs and Foxes quieted his brothers, restored the notebook to the thoroughly tamed conductor, and herded the crowd back onto the wagon."[10]

Later that same year Thunderwater took an active role in caring for the remains of "No-Wa-Lee-Wa-Get-Ka," a Cayuga-Mohawk from the Grand River reserve in Ontario who had been working in the city as a longshoreman. No-Wa-Lee-Wa-Get-Ka, also known as "Albert Hess," was just thirty-four years old and had died of tuberculosis. Described by the *Plain Dealer* as a simple, working-class man and a member of the longshoremen's union who "shared his last dollar cheerfully with the men of the civilization he did not accept," No-Wa-Lee-Wa-Get-Ka had no family to provide for his burial. Thunderwater, identified in the same newspaper article as a "peace chief of the Sac and Foxes," stepped forward to provide for the funeral and burial. It must have involved considerable effort and expense. According to the *Plain Dealer*, a well-appointed electric car transported the deceased and his pallbearers, six longshoremen, to the burial site at Highland Park Cemetery in Warrensville, fifteen miles southeast of Cleveland. The "strange pageant," as the event was described by the newspaper, was held in the evening, lit by "flaring torches and flames," and attracted several hundred mourners and curiosity-seekers. Thunderwater, dressed in his Native regalia, adorned with a flowing red blanket, and playing a small drum, led a procession of about two dozen Native mourners, many also dressed in regalia, to the grave site. He opened the ceremony with a prayer, apparently delivered in the Lakota language, and then No-Wa-Lee-Wa-Get-Ka was lowered into the ground along with his dog, smoking pipe, and rifle. As reported by the newspaper, at the conclusion of the ceremony Thunderwater addressed the gathered throng and declared, "It is your boasted white civilization that has murdered this man. You have covered Mother Earth with a death bringing cover of cement and brick and tar in place of the health giving green grass. That is what has brought on tuberculosis, the white man's plague—tuberculosis, which has carried off my brother."[11]

Drawing, perhaps, on his own interest and background in entertainment work, Thunderwater also supported locally performed and Native-themed theatrical events. In the summer of 1909 he took an active role in the outdoor staging of a dramatization of Longfellow's poem "Hiawatha" on the eastern outskirts of Cleveland. The play was the project of the city's YMCA and was performed by youths who were members of the local chapter. Reporting on the preparations and promising readers a note of realism, a city newspaper noted that a young man who was the son of a Mohawk chief was to play the part of Hiawatha. "The boys are being coached by Chief Thunderwater of the Sacs and Foxes," the paper explained, and noted that they would perform the songs in the Seneca language. Sometimes, however, Thunderwater's assistance was not welcome. In October 1910 he attempted to involve himself in the care of a troupe of Ojibwe actors from Michigan and Canada who were performing in Cleveland as part of Cuyahoga County's centennial celebration. When they arrived in the city, event officials informed them that Thunderwater had inquired about their accommodations and activities. In reply, Louis Kabusa, a member of the troupe, stated flatly, "Thunderwater has no business interfering with our plans."[12]

Thunderwater was a lifelong advocate for temperance and regularly complained to city officials about local bars and saloons that exploited Indian customers. In April 1910 his efforts made news in the local press when he complained to the U.S. district attorney in Cleveland about unscrupulous establishments that took advantage of Native visitors to the city. Under the headline "Objects to Firewater," the *Plain Dealer*, noting that Thunderwater "takes under his wing all other Indians who venture into Cleveland," reported he was raising concerns about saloonkeepers who were notorious for selling alcohol to visiting Indians and was demanding action against them by the district attorney's office. Recounting one incident that drew Thunderwater's attention, the paper told the story of a company of Native entertainers who had performed at Keith's Hippodrome in March 1910 and had decided to remain in the city for the summer show season.

Evidently, they had taken to drinking frequently, and Thunderwater demanded enforcement of a city law forbidding the sale of liquor to Indians.[13]

During these early years as a resident of Cleveland, Thunderwater began providing lodging and care to Indians working in and traveling through the city, a practice that would become a lifelong commitment for him and one of his most important contributions to the Native community of the city. He was, perhaps, inspired by his parents' friend, Peter Bennett, whose hospitality they enjoyed during their periodic trips through the city in the 1860s and 1870s. In 1910, in addition to his son and daughter-in-law, Thunderwater had two lodgers boarding with him, one of whom was Sherman Charging Hawk, a married, thirty-nine-year-old Lakota from the Rosebud Agency in South Dakota, whose occupation was listed in the U.S. Census for that year as "showman" in a "circus show."[14] Over the course of the next several decades, Thunderwater had numerous Indian lodgers and guests in his home, many of whom were Haudenosaunee. They included Adrian Clark, a Seneca from Cattaraugus; Cephas Hill and Gilbert Peterson, both Senecas from Tonawanda; and Isaac Hill, an Onondaga from Grand River. Another of his lodgers was Louis Blackman, an Odawa from Suttons Bay in Northern Michigan. In 1927 Blackman provided an affidavit in Thunderwater's Louisville libel case in which he stated that Thunderwater "constantly provides for those who call upon him for assistance and he feeds, clothes, gives medical attention through Dr. W. R. Boyd and others when needed and that his home is often used to house Indians in distress. This has been the condition of affairs for many years." "Dr. W. R. Boyd" was William R. Boyd, a forty-five-year-old physician and longtime Thunderwater associate, who was born in Okmulgee, Oklahoma, and may have been of Muscogee (Creek) ancestry. In 1930 Thunderwater had five "Indian" lodgers in his home. One was twenty-year-old "Jacob Sineway" from Oklahoma, who was single and worked— possibly for Thunderwater—as a "retail salesman." Another was "Howard Meter," twenty-six, single, and from Oklahoma, who worked as a machinist. The third Indian lodger was thirty-nine-year-old "Martin Clausen," who was from New York, likely Haudenosaunee, and who worked in the city as a mill laborer. The fourth lodger was a single, twenty-seven-year-old named "Hill," who was also a "laborer," from Canada, and probably also Haudenosaunee. Finally, there was eighty-one-year-old Cyrus Allen from Oklahoma. A widower, he was unemployed and almost certainly was supported by Thunderwater. In 1940 one of his Indian lodgers was Dan Tarbell, a single, thirty-six-year-old Mohawk from Akwesasne who had been unemployed for nearly nine months.[15]

Over the course of the next several years, Thunderwater's political engagement and activism with Native issues would grow and focus increasingly on matters related to the Haudenosaunees in New York and Canada. By 1914 he would establish the Council of the Tribes, a pan-Indian self-help and advocacy organization modeled on the Six Nations Confederacy. And soon he would become an important political force in Haudenosaunee communities in Canada.

CHAPTER 3

THUNDERWATER AND THE COUNCIL OF THE TRIBES

Whereas it is next to impossible for any one person or family of persons among the Indians of the American continent to protect themselves from the infringements of their legal rights. . . . Whereas certain and unscrupulous and selfish persons have, since the coming of foreigners to this continent, been usurping the proper and reserved pleasures of the Native Indians. . . . Whereas it requires strength through united effort, influence and money to comb existing evils and to advance with the times. . . . [I]t now becomes a necessity and a practical fact that this organization named the Council of the Tribes has been organized.

—From the preamble to the constitution and bylaws of the Council of the Tribes, organized by Chief Thunderwater in Cleveland, Ohio, in 1914

Chief Thunderwater's political and humanitarian involvement with Indigenous issues and people soon extended beyond Cleveland to the Haudenosaunees in New York and Canada. The seed of his interest in Haudenosaunee matters may, in fact, have had very deep roots. Later in life Thunderwater would point to the reburial of Red Jacket in Buffalo, New York, in 1884, as a personally and politically transformative moment for him. A well-known Seneca chief and orator, Red Jacket had a complicated history of self-interest, diplomacy with Great Britain, cooperation with the U.S. government, and concern for the impact of Euro-American influence on his people's culture and language. He died in 1830 and was buried at Seneca village in present-day South Buffalo in ground that was then part of the Buffalo Creek reservation. In October 1884, in the wake of the Buffalo Creek dispossession, Red Jacket's remains were exhumed and reinterred in the city's historic Forest Lawn Cemetery. Also reinterred were the remains of several other notable Senecas, including Destroy Town, Young King, Little Billy, and Tall Peter. Hundreds attended the ceremony accompanying the reburials, including a delegation of Haudenosaunees from Grand River; Horatio Hale, the well-known ethnologist; Ely S. Parker, the famed Seneca sachem, attorney, Civil War veteran and military secretary to General Ulysses S. Grant who had served as the first American Indian commissioner of Indian Affairs; and E. Pauline Johnson, the soon-to-be prominent Mohawk poet and performer. Thunderwater, who was then nineteen years old, also attended. He would have heard the orations by Parker and Johnson in which they asserted the importance of Haudenosaunee culture, nationalism, and land rights, and he might have become aware of the ways in which the Six Nations participants used the occasion to renew intertribal connections. He might even have heard the Grand River delegation speak of the efforts in their community and on other reserves in Canada to protect traditional government from the threat of assimilative Indian Act policies. Thunderwater claimed that his experience at Red Jacket's reburial awakened him to the cultural and political aspirations of the Haudenosaunees and marked the beginning of his commitment to activism on behalf of Indigenous people in the United States and Canada (see map 2).[1]

Among the Haudenosaunee matters that concerned Thunderwater was the issue of border crossing between the United States and Canada. In 1908 he wrote to the Office of Indian Affairs in Washington, D.C., on behalf of Haudenosaunees and other Native groups in Canada and asked for relief from taxes or duties on their commercial activities with people in the United States. In the early twentieth century the retailing and wholesaling of locally produced "Indian" crafts and beadwork at places like Niagara Falls and elsewhere was an important source of supplemental income for many families in Haudenosaunee communities in Canada. A decade earlier, beadworkers in Kahnawake had petitioned the U.S. Congress on at least two occasions to protest import duties on their craftwork and to assert their border-crossing rights under the Jay Treaty of 1794. As a traveling salesman who traded in herbal teas and medicines, Thunderwater may have had personal experience with the border-crossing issue and, as a product of his own family history, he almost certainly had an appreciation of the Haudenosaunees as a transnational people. His communication with the U.S. Treasury Department suggests close familiarity with Haudenosaunee communities in Canada, and it anticipated both the Haudenosaunee fight for border-crossing rights in the immigration case of Mohawk ironworker Paul K. Diabo and the establishment of the Indian Defense League of America by Tuscarora chief Clinton Rickard two decades later. Responding to Thunderwater in November 1908, J. F. Horthey of the Treasury Department stated, "All Indians are free of duties passing or repassing the boundary lines of the United States and Canada, and also free of

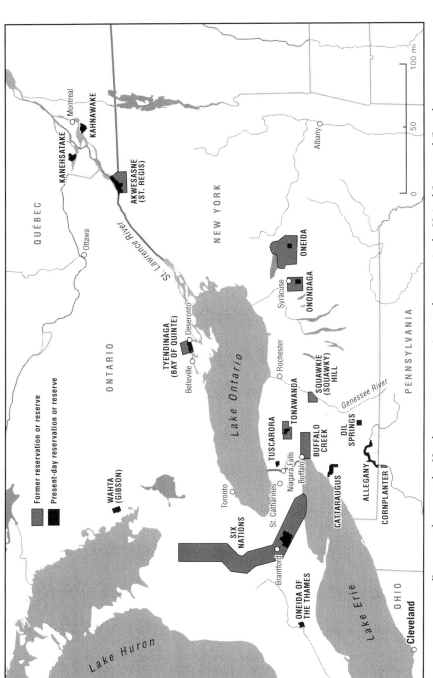

MAP 2. Former and present-day Haudenosaunee reservations and reserves in the United States and Canada.

Map by Erin Greb.

taxes, license in trading and selling bead-work, bark-work, baskets, snow shoes, moccasins, medicines, etc., etc., of their own manufacture in premises."[2]

Thunderwater was likely familiar with a number of other issues affecting the Six Nations during this time period. In 1906 the Cayuga Nation renewed its longtime effort to obtain fair compensation from the State of New York for profits realized from the sale of Cayuga lands it obtained under cessions in 1795 and 1807. The Cayugas argued that the sale of the ceded lands violated the U.S. Constitution and the Trade and Intercourse Act of 1790. Initially, the state resisted the Cayuga petition, but then its attorney general ruled their claim valid, and in 1909 the Cayugas and New York agreed to compensation totaling $270,000. In spite of this, the state's governor refused to pay and requested a new report on the Cayuga claim. That report concluded the Cayuga claim was without legal basis. In 1910 the Cayuga Nation, represented by Rochester attorney George P. Decker, sued New York State, contending that Congress had not ratified the 1795 treaty and sought funds for compensation and damages that would enable them to purchase land in New York for a reservation. A year later the state's attorney general ruled that the suit lacked a legal basis. The matter dragged on for another decade until the report of the Everett Commission in 1922, which concluded that Six Nations land claims, including the Cayuga claim, were valid.[3]

Other Haudenosaunee land claims cases also marked the first decade of the twentieth century. In 1906, the same year the Cayugas initiated their claim for compensation, the State of New York forcibly ejected several Oneidas from land near the city of Oneida, which they claimed was tribally owned. The state supreme court had determined that Oneida Nation title to the land in question had been extinguished in the mid-nineteenth century and had been legally conveyed to the private owners who had sought the Oneidas' ejection. The Oneidas claimed that the original and subsequent conveyances of title to the land were illegal. A decade later the Oneidas succeeded on appeal, and tribal title to the land was recognized and restored. In another case the Seneca Nation and Tonawanda Band of Senecas claimed riparian rights related to a string of islands in the Niagara River, which, they argued, had been sold illegally in 1815. Represented by attorney George Decker, between 1912 and 1914 they appealed directly to Congress for redress but were unsuccessful.[4]

In the midst of these various land claims efforts came rising concerns among the Haudenosaunees in the United States about federal government efforts to end tribal treaty obligations. In this early version of a "termination" effort, the U.S. Congress and the Office of Indian Affairs sought to negotiate written agreements

with tribes that would end perpetual annuity payments due under treaty arrange-
ments. The objective of the effort was assimilation. As the commissioner of
Indian Affairs wrote in his annual report for 1909, "Perpetual annuities form
a strong tribal bond and a bar to individual progress. They keep the eyes of the
Indians turned toward the Treasury of the United States instead of the allotment
of land, on day labor, or on trade." In 1908 the commissioner sent special Indian
Affairs agents to visit a number of tribes identified for termination arrangements.
Among them were the Six Nations of New York, the Oneidas of Wisconsin, and
the Sac and Fox tribes in Oklahoma and Iowa. In 1909 Indian Affairs concluded
agreements with the Oneidas of Wisconsin and the Sac and Fox in Oklahoma,
and the commissioner was preparing to send a special negotiator to the Senecas
in New York to do the same. Most Haudenosaunees opposed termination and
resisted commutation of their treaties. While the Oneidas of Wisconsin initially
agreed to end their annuity, they were deeply divided over the issue, and Congress
did not ratify the negotiated arrangement. The Sac and Fox in Oklahoma, on
the other hand, were not as divided, and they ratified the negotiated agreement
to end tribal annuities in 1910.[5]

It is likely that Thunderwater was familiar with these developments. He was
attuned to the issues of federal Indian policy, as his political activism in Cleveland indicates. His uncle Moses had been a principal and an assistant principal
chief of the Sac and Fox in Oklahoma and had died only a few years before the
"commutation" of their tribal annuities, so it is almost certain that he was aware
of that development and the "termination" effort behind it. With his own Seneca
roots and the network of Indian travelers and workers in Cleveland of which
his home served as a sort of hub, it is reasonable to suppose that Thunderwater
was well aware of the issues regarding land claims and termination among the
Haudenosaunees. These issues would echo in the priorities he set forth in the
establishment of the Council of the Tribes just a few years later.

Thunderwater's involvement with Haudenosaunee communities became more
formalized in 1909 when twelve members of the Tonawanda Band of Seneca
Indians appointed him as an "ambassador" to represent and advocate for their
interests. Identifying themselves as "Chiefs, Firekeepers, Warriors" and "Clan
Women" of the "Six Nations Tonawanda Band," they included Lyman Johnson, a
well-known Longhouse leader at Tonawanda, and twenty-three-year-old Freeman
Johnson, a recent graduate of the Carlisle Indian School who would eventually
become chief of the Wolf clan at Tonawanda. The other "Chiefs, Firekeepers, and
Warriors," included Ben Ground, Sylvester Sundown, William Parker, Arthur

Jones, Emerson Infant, and Perry Smith. The "Clan Women" identified in the written appointment included Emily Logan, Lula Peters, Eva Smith, and Margaret Smith. Together, the twelve stated that they acknowledged "Oghema Niagara, Chief Thunderwater" to be their "duly appointed Peace Chief . . . to act in [their] name, place and stead before executives or other officials as well as the general public." Unfortunately, in their formal charge to Thunderwater as "Peace Chief," they did not define the specific matters on which he was to act on behalf of the Tonawanda Senecas. The choice of Thunderwater for such a role was likely due to some combination of Thunderwater's own Seneca ancestry and connections, his wide travels and network of Native connections, his activism on behalf of Indian people, and his public relations savvy and experience as an entertainer. Thunderwater's growing political ambitions, along with his effectiveness as a self-promoter, perhaps also played a part in his appointment.[6]

Being named an "ambassador" and "peace chief" by the members of the Tonawanda band was undoubtedly significant for Thunderwater. To begin with, it reinforced his claim to political leadership and representation and identification of himself as a "peace chief." In addition, it may have contributed to his familiarity with Haudenosaunee political organization and spirituality. The Tonawanda Band of Seneca Indians formed in 1857 following a division within the Seneca Nation over its sale of reservation lands to the U.S. government and the Ogden Land Company in the Buffalo Creek Treaty of January 15, 1838. The lands sold included the Tonawanda reservation. Maintaining that the Seneca chiefs did not represent them, the Tonawanda Band objected to their inclusion in the treaty and refused to leave their land. The divide widened in 1848 when the Seneca Nation adopted American-style elected government, while the Tonawanda Band preferred to continue with the traditional system of consensus-based decision-making and a council of hereditary chiefs selected by senior clan women. In 1857 the split was complete when the Tonawanda Band signed a treaty with the United States that formally recognized the Tonawanda Band, enabled it to repurchase 7,500 acres of its lost reservation lands back from the Ogden Land Company and recognized their traditional government. The traditional system of hereditary clan chiefs persisted at Tonawanda into the twentieth century, making it one of the few Haudenosaunee communities in which traditional government continued to be officially recognized.[7]

In addition, Tonawanda was the center of the Longhouse religion, which originated in 1799 in a series of prophetic visions experienced by Sganyodaiyoh, "Handsome Lake," a Seneca chief on the Allegany reservation. As it evolved, the

Longhouse religion melded traditional Haudenosaunee spirituality, elements of Christian theology, and Euro-American norms into a set of moral, religious and social beliefs and practices that offered the Senecas a hopeful alternative to the poverty, instability, and despair they were experiencing in the early nineteenth century. Before his death in 1815 Sganyodaiyoh moved to Tonawanda, and over the next several generations the *Gai'wiio*, or "good message," of Handsome Lake spread to other Haudenosaunee communities and was gradually codified. Tonawanda emerged as the "head fire" of the Longhouse religion, the place where Sganyodaiyoh's wampum was kept, where the code was standardized, where Longhouse preachers were approved, and where the annual circuit of Haudenosaunee communities for the recitation of the code began each autumn. If he had not already been familiar with it, through his connection with the Tonawanda Senecas, Thunderwater would have gained some understanding of Haudenosaunee traditional government and Longhouse spirituality.[8]

Thunderwater's connection to the Tonawanda Senecas persisted and extended to Senecas in other communities as well. In 1912 he became involved in the case of Lovina Skye, an eleven-year-old girl from Tonawanda who had been taken from her foster parents by a local constable and sent to a juvenile institution for "wayward" girls. Skye was being raised by her maternal aunt, Molly Skye, and her husband since the young girl's mother had died six years earlier. In June 1912, while her foster parents were working the fields on their farm, the constable visited their home, arrested Lovina for truancy and sent her off to the Hudson Training School for Girls. Lovina's parents and others at Tonawanda were upset by the detention of the girl, and Thunderwater became involved, even to the point of taking her case to a special session of the state supreme court in Buffalo to have her released. Reporting on the case, the *Buffalo Morning Express* referred to "Old Chief Thunderwater's efforts to restore peace among the Seneca Indians on the Tonawanda reservation by securing [Lovina's] return." Through an attorney he had engaged, Thunderwater was able to bring evidence before the court that Lovina's absence from school was related to health reasons and eventually secured her release from juvenile detention.[9]

At the same time the Lovina Skye case unfolded, Thunderwater waged a campaign in Buffalo, just as he had in Cleveland, against saloons and other city establishments that sold liquor to Native visitors, many of whom were from the Tonawanda reservation. City newspapers reported regularly on his efforts. In mid-April 1912, under the headline "To Help Indians—Chief Thunderwater Works to Stamp Out Sale of Liquor," the *Buffalo Commercial* announced the beginning of his efforts. The *Commercial* noted that Thunderwater had "baptized his [granddaughter] in December at Niagara Falls with ancient rites" and reported that he had come from Cleveland to Buffalo to organize "the preliminary work that shall better the conditions of the Indians of the Six Nations." Complaining about the "low-down hangers-on" selling bootleg whiskey to his people, Thunderwater pronounced, "They call it 'squirrel liquor.' They take half a keg of the cheapest brand of red-eye, fill it with rainwater and alcohol, put in some brown sugar and some broken-up plugs of tobacco and my people are induced to buy and drink the concoction. Is it any wonder that we are scourged with tuberculosis?" According to the *Commercial*, Thunderwater had met with Indian bureau officials, had secured the cooperation of the Buffalo Brewers Exchange in his campaign, and was soon to be addressing members of the city's Wholesale and Retail Liquor Association to urge them to "do all in [their] power to prevent the sale of liquor to Indians." The newspaper also indicated that Thunderwater had visited the Tonawanda, Cattaraugus, Tuscarora, and Allegany reservations to gather information about liquor trafficking and enlist local supporters for his efforts. The article concluded by noting that he proposed to take his concerns and campaign to the state capital in Albany.[10]

A month later the *Buffalo Morning Express* and *Buffalo Courier* informed readers that a complaint by Thunderwater to the U.S. commissioner of Indian Affairs led to the arrest of two saloonkeepers for selling liquor to Senecas from Cattaraugus who were in the city to peddle herbs and flowers. In June 1912 the *Courier* again reported on Thunderwater's activities, drawing on a familiar racist trope to emphasize his apparent resolve: "Chief Thunderwater . . . is once more on the warpath. The chief is in the midst of his crusade against the saloon keepers who persist in selling liquor to the Indians. He says he is going to stop the practice if he has to get all the federal authorities in the state to help him." Thunderwater continued his antiliquor campaign in Buffalo through the summer of 1912.[11]

Thunderwater's efforts to fight liquor trafficking to Native people in the Buffalo area may have fostered relationships with like-minded advocates of sobriety in the Seneca communities, where an organization known as the Six Nations Temperance League had an active and influential decades-long presence. Originating as the Tuscarora Temperance League on the Tuscarora reservation in 1830, the organization attracted numerous members, spread to other Seneca communities, and two years later was renamed under the "Six Nations" designation. In the years that followed, the Six Nations Temperance League attracted hundreds of members at Tuscarora, Tonawanda, Cattaraugus, Allegany, and Oil Spring, and eventually at Onondaga as well. Weekly or semimonthly meetings were a regular feature of the local chapters of the organization, as was an annual convention that rotated from one reservation to another. The organization was still quite popular in 1905 and by this time had expanded its presence to Haudenosaunee reserves in Canada as well. In 1910, with Charles Doxon of Onondaga (who a year later would serve on the executive council of the Society of American Indians) as president and Horatio Printup of Tonawanda as vice president, the Six Nations Temperance League held its annual convention in Salamanca, New York. In 1914 one missionary publication hailed the league as the oldest temperance organization in the United States. Thunderwater's temperance work in the area almost certainly brought him into contact and perhaps even collaboration with the leaders and members of the organization.[12]

During that summer of temperance activity in 1912 Thunderwater also joined others from Tonawanda and Cattaraugus in opposing the establishment of Seneca Indian Park in Buffalo on ground that was part of the former Buffalo Creek reservation and which the Senecas claimed was a burial site of their ancestors. In fact, he was very familiar with the ground in question—it was the site from which Red Jacket's remains were removed in 1844. The disputed land had come into the possession of John D. Larkin, a wealthy Buffalo industrialist and business magnate, who then donated it to the city for use as a public park. Larkin and members of the Niagara Frontier Landmarks Association, which assisted in the establishment of the park and placed a prominent boulder and tablet at its main entrance, responded to the Senecas' concerns by emphasizing that all the bodies buried in the old cemetery had been removed and reburied elsewhere. Those bodies included the remains of a number of prominent Seneca individuals, including Mary Jemison, the well-known Scots-Irish immigrant girl who was taken captive by Shawnees in 1755 and eventually traded and adopted into a Seneca family. The Senecas countered that the remains of many of their ancestors were still buried in the disputed ground, and its use as a city park dishonored them and desecrated their graves. At the dedication of the park in late June 1912, Thunderwater and a large group from Tonawanda and Cattaraugus attended the ceremony to protest. They included Chief Thomas Poodry of Tonawanda and Chief Edward Cornplanter of Cattaraugus. According to the *Buffalo Sunday Morning News*, Thunderwater was one of the leaders of the protest and, as a spokesperson, emphasized that for the Senecas it was sacrilege to turn the burial ground into a public park. "I come here with the peaceable intention of entering a public protest," he told the *Morning News.* "This is not right. . . . None of us want the feet of thousands to trample into the dust the bones of our grandfathers and ancestors. What would you people think if we acquire one of your cemeteries and transform it into a place for pleasure and entertainment? Surely it is little enough that we ask. It is one of the rights that really belongs to us, the keeping sacred of the places where our ancestors lie buried." The dedication exercises at the new park featured a recounting of the history of the Seneca Nation and were supposed to include an address by Arthur C. Parker, the noted ethnologist of Seneca ancestry then serving the state archaeologist, who telegrammed at the last moment to say that he was unable to attend. Fearing disruption of the ceremony, police were on hand and kept Thunderwater and the Seneca protesters at a distance from the dedication ceremony. Forced to look on in silence, Thunderwater threatened court action to shut down the park. The plaque placed at the entrance to the park during the ceremony must certainly have been upsetting to him and his fellow protesters and a constant reminder of the indignity that they and their ancestors had suffered. "In this vicinity from 1750 to 1843 dwelt the largest portion of the Seneca nation of the Iroquois league," the plaque read. "In this enclosure were buried Red Jacket and Mary Jemison, the White Woman of the Genesee, and many noted chiefs and leaders of the nation, whose remains have been removed and reburied elsewhere."[13]

Another important influence on Thunderwater's political development at this point may have been the establishment of the Society of American Indians (SAI), the progressive pan-Indian movement of American Indian professionals and intellectuals that originated in Columbus, Ohio. The seeds of the SAI were planted in 1908 in a series of lectures on contemporary American Indian issues given in Columbus by Dr. Charles Eastman (Santee Dakota), Dr. Carlos Montezuma (Yavapai-Apache), and Rev. Sherman Coolidge. The lectures garnered widespread public attention and generated momentum for an Indian-led national conference and pan-tribal organization. That momentum came to fruition three years later in October 1911 with a planning meeting and an inaugural conference at Ohio State University. Key players in the establishment of the SAI included Eastman, Montezuma, Arthur C. Parker, attorney Thomas Sloan (Omaha), BAE supervisor Charles Edwin Daggett (Peoria), educator Henry Standing Bear (Oglala Lakota), and writer and activist Laura Cornelius Kellogg (Oneida). Given Thunderwater's political interests and activism, his proximity to Columbus (about 140 miles southwest of Cleveland), and the widespread press coverage of the lectures and founding conference, it is hard to imagine that Thunderwater was not aware of the development of the SAI. In fact, the Council of the Tribes, the pan-Indian organization he would form in Cleveland just two years after the establishment of the SAI, shared some important similarities with the evolving SAI. There were also some marked differences.

Arthur Parker's role in the development of the SAI is worthy of note because, as a Seneca and a well-known American Indian professional and intellectual, he was almost certainly known to Thunderwater. Also, Parker would eventually play a brief but significant part in the response of Canada's Department of Indian Affairs to Thunderwater and the Council of the Tribes. The son of a Seneca father and a Scots-English mother, Parker was born on the Cattaraugus reservation in 1881. In 1892 his family moved to White Plains, New York, where he attended public schools. After graduating from high school, he worked as an archaeology and anthropology assistant at the American Museum of Natural History in New York, and then from 1900 to 1903 studied for the ministry at Dickinson Seminary in Williamsport, Pennsylvania. Because his mother was not Seneca, Parker did not have nation membership status at birth, but in 1903 he was formally adopted into the tribe as an honorary member. After completing his studies at Dickinson Seminary, Parker worked for a short time as a reporter in New York City before going on to start what would become a career of significant achievement as an archaeologist, ethnologist, and historian, initially with the Peabody Museum at Harvard University and then with the New York State Museum and New York State Library in Albany.[14]

Along with the other founders and leaders of the SAI, Parker was committed to pan-Indianism, was critical of federal Indian policy for fostering the economic and social dependency of Native people, and strongly supported Indian advancement through self-help and formal education. Like them, he hoped to base the new organization in Washington, D.C., and hold its meetings and conferences at academic institutions rather than on Indian reservations. As with the SAI membership in general, Parker supported privatization of tribal lands and ending the reservation system and favored a path to citizenship for American Indians. As he was well aware, many Haudenosaunees opposed these positions. At the same time, he and the SAI leadership intended that the organization would play an active role in supporting their reservation counterparts who sought to investigate and address government wrongdoing and injustices. Parker, like many of the middle class and well-educated members of the SAI, opposed Wild West shows and other forms of entertainment work out of concern that they perpetuated stereotypes of Indians as primitive and savage.[15]

If Thunderwater was aware of the formation of the SAI and was informed about Arthur C. Parker, he might also have been familiar with the growing importance and views of Laura "Minnie" Cornelius Kellogg. Kellogg, an Oneida from Wisconsin, was the granddaughter of Daniel Bread, the principal chief and cultural leader on the Oneida reservation in the middle decades of the nineteenth century. By 1911, at just thirty years of age, she had gained national attention as an educated, experienced, well-traveled, and articulate advocate for the dignity and rights of the Oneidas of Wisconsin and Indian people in general. In the summer of 1911 Kellogg formed part of the organizing committee of the American Indian Association, which was soon to be renamed the Society of American Indians and, in fact, much of its work was completed at her home in Wisconsin. There the committee drafted the SAI's constitution, formulated the general rules of the organization, and planned the October conference in Columbus. Following the meeting in Columbus, she served as secretary of the SAI's executive committee and later as the vice president of the organization's education division.[16]

Though she was a founding member of the SAI and was in firm agreement with the organization's emphasis on Indian dignity and rights and its platform on self-help, Kellogg held views that were not only different from but decidedly at odds with those of Arthur Parker and other founding members of the SAI. She was a vehement critic of the Bureau of Indian Affairs and particularly so of the Indian boarding school system that had produced much of the SAI's leadership. Contrary to the SAI's orientation toward education for assimilation, Kellogg saw education as a means to the end goal of Indian self-government. In addition, in her view Native education should draw on Indigenous cultural traditions as well as the progressive ideas of Euro-American society. Her position that reservations could be developed as places for Indian economic self-sufficiency and as a basis for political autonomy and Indian self-determination took her even further from the mainstream of thought and action in the SAI. At the inaugural meeting of the SAI in October 1911, she famously proclaimed, "I am not the new Indian. I am the old Indian adjusted to new conditions." These philosophical differences, along with her marriage in 1912 to Orrin Joseph Kellogg, a non-Native attorney from Minneapolis, and subsequent legal troubles stemming from their investigation of oil leases and the Indian school on the Osage reservation in Oklahoma, alienated Kellogg from the SAI leadership, and her formal connection with the SAI ended in 1913.[17]

In 1913, two years after the establishment of the SAI, Thunderwater founded his own organization, the Council of the Tribes, as a Cleveland-based pan-Indian advocacy and self-help organization. Like the SAI, the purpose of the Council of the Tribes was to counter the exploitation of Indigenous people and address their economic, social, and cultural concerns through coordinated educational, legal, and political action. As signed by "Oghema Niagara—Chief Thunderwater," the preamble of its constitution and bylaws read,

> Whereas, it is next to impossible for any one person or family of persons among the Indians of the American continent to protect themselves from infringements of their legal and ancient rights, and
>
> Whereas, certain unscrupulous and selfish persons have, since the coming of foreigners to this continent, been usurping the proper and reserved pleasures of the Native Indian and from time to time, taken advantage of the fact that the majority of the Indians have little or no knowledge of the laws and forms of business of the white people, and introduce intoxicating liquors among our people, to the end that they may the more readily defraud the said Indians out of their earnings, pleasures and real estate, and generally so demoralize the Indian that he becomes a nonentity in the public eye, and
>
> Whereas, it requires strength through united effort, influence and money to combat existing evils and to advance with the times to detect and punish those that do evil to the Indians and present with intelligence the cause of the Indian to the Honorable members of society, that they may the more fully appreciate the situation in which the Indian has been placed, and give their aid toward redemption of legal rights usurped, and stop wrongs which are constantly perpetuated against the Indians,
>
> It now becomes a necessity and a practical fact that this organization named the Council of the Tribes has been organized.[18]

Thunderwater's stated aim was to expand the Council of the Tribes to Native communities throughout the United States and Canada. From its outset the council, similar to the SAI, sought to aid Indian people with grievances against the government and advocated progressive goals of temperance, educational advancement, and agricultural modernization. In contrast to the SAI, however, and more in line with the views of Minnie Kellogg and sentiment in Haudenosaunee communities, the Council of the Tribes opposed the sale of reservation land. In addition, and again in contrast to the SAI, Thunderwater envisioned the Council of the Tribes as a reservation-based movement focused on problems of reservation life, especially as these were related to federal Indian policy, and, most important, stressed Native sovereignty and self-government rather than assimilation and integration into the dominant Euro-American and Euro-Canadian societies. This orientation may not have been clear at the very outset, but soon it came to dominate Thunderwater's thinking and the goal of the organization. Thunderwater's experience with Haudenosaunee communities over the next few years, especially those in Canada, was a major factor in this development. Given this, it is also not surprising that Thunderwater and the Council of the Tribes would come to be focused on *Haudenosaunee* problems and grievances and *Haudenosaunee* sovereignty and self-government.

In addition to his family background and growing involvement with Haudenosaunee communities in New York, another important element in the development of Thunderwater's nationalist and Haudenosaunee orientation at this time may have been his familiarity with developments at Onondaga and, in particular, the work of attorney George Decker. Decker is best known for his work with Levi General (Deskaheh) and the hereditary chiefs at Grand River in Ontario in the 1920s to advance the cause of Six Nations sovereignty in Europe and before the League of Nations in Geneva, Switzerland. However, in 1910 Decker began working with the Cayuga Nation, Seneca Nation, and the Tonawanda Band of Senecas on their land claims cases. In 1914 he was serving as an advisor to the Six Nations Confederacy Council at Onondaga in its attempts to fend off persistent efforts by the New York state legislature to expand its jurisdiction over the Haudenosaunees. In November 1914 Decker gave an important address at Onondaga in which he laid out his major concerns and recommendations to the Confederacy Council. A typescript of that address was obtained by Thunderwater and is contained in his personal papers.[19]

Directed to Haudenosaunee people in New York, Decker's address to the Six Nations Confederacy Council emphasized three key points—the "natural" political right of the Haudenosaunees to regulate their own affairs, the importance of federal protection from the "hostility and overreach" of their "white neighbors," and the need for resistance "in all reasonable ways" to attempts by the State of New York to exercise jurisdiction over their reservations. In the address Decker recounted the history of white incursions on Haudenosaunee lands and infringements of Haudenosaunee sovereignty and concluded by arguing for the necessity of "confederate action" by the Haudenosaunees in order to protect their interests and future. As he stated in the typescript of the address obtained by Thunderwater:

> Confederate action can only be secured by the creation of a body of representatives from each tribe. Such [a] confederate body should be given full power to act according to the occasion and without the necessity of calling special councils of the tribes for they must often act forthwith, sometimes on two days' notice, in assertion of your rights at Washington or at Albany or before some court which has been called upon to ignore your rights. . . . Nothing of that sort can be done effectively . . . [u]nless you have a legal advisor. . . . One who knows your history and is in sympathy with you. One who is to be consulted on all important matters of this kind. In that way the steps that you take will be intelligently directed and be most effective because they will always be consistent.

Over the course of the next five years the priorities and efforts of Thunderwater and the council would come to closely resemble Decker's idea of "confederate action."[20]

As conceived by Thunderwater, organizationally the Council of the Tribes consisted of an "Inner Council" of several officers, including "Councillors," a "Supreme Secretary," a "Grand Councillor," and a "Great Councillor," who was Thunderwater himself. In official correspondence, the "Great Councillor" was sometimes referred to as the "Great Counsel" or "Sachem." Linked to the central "Inner Council" was a network of local "Circles," each composed of dues-paying members and headed by its own "Grand Councillor" and several "Councillors." The emblem of the council, which was depicted on official letterhead and membership certificates, consisted of a triangular, teepee-shaped image with the full name of the organization running along its interior upright sides (figure 5). Within the triangle is a second, smaller triangle, at the center of which are the letters "CT," a reference to the Council of the Tribes, and images of a sun and crossed arrow and calumet. Along the interior base of the larger triangle are six horizontally aligned circles. On council letterhead, below or on either side of the emblem, were the words "The Protection of The American Indians' Interests," "Unanimous Agreement," and "Persistency." Some early versions of the letterhead also contained the phrase "Union-Protection-Publicity." Some of these symbols and phrases were featured in the regalia that Thunderwater wore during council events and in public appearances long after the demise of the organization around 1920.[21]

FIGURE 5. Council of the Tribes letterhead. Chief Thunderwater designed the letterhead for the Council of the Tribes in 1915. He used the letterhead in his correspondence with Council of the Tribes members and officials of Canada's Department of Indian Affairs and often signed his letters as "Tehotiokwawakon," ("One Who Builds Up or Supports Us"), the name given to him by his Mohawk supporters at Akwesasne in 1914.
Image courtesy of the Western Reserve Historical Society, Cleveland, Ohio.

The structure and emblem of the Council of the Tribes have been derided as "quasi-Indian" and evidence that Thunderwater was a charlatan and the council an elaborate con. However, a more carefully considered view is that the organizational structure, emblem, and other elements of the organization resonate strongly with and may have been based on important elements of Haudenosaunee political culture and history. To begin with, the six circles prominently featured in the council emblem evoke the Haudenosaunee Confederacy. Thunderwater might have intended this to represent the Six Nations of the Confederacy, or this might be a model of the council's local circles based on the organization of the confederacy. With local councils and representatives linked to a central executive body responsible for the organization as a whole and its external affairs, the Council of the Tribes had a rough similarity with the organization of the confederacy, albeit without the emphasis on its principles of democratic, consensus-based decision-making. At the outset, and more so as it developed over the first year or two of its existence, leaders of local council "circles" also had a place on the "Inner Council" of the organization. In addition, the local "circles," which developed solely in Haudenosaunee communities, often included one or more of the traditional hereditary clan chiefs in those communities. One reason for the success of the Council of the Tribes may have been the way its structure resonated with that of the confederacy.[22]

The connection between the Council of the Tribes and Indigenous political culture and history went deeper. A curious feature of the council was its calendrical system, invented by Thunderwater himself and used to date important council documents, such as the membership certificates of those who joined the organization. Disparaged by one author as "pseudo-Indian" and another as employing "a kind of pan-Indian terminology" and reckoning time "in what was said to be a traditional manner," the council calendrical system is better understood in terms of its consistency with a fundamental element of the organization—the need for Indigenous people to respond collectively to the destructive and assimilationist policies of the American and Canadian governments. Rejecting the Gregorian calendar of Western societies, time was reckoned from 1492, the "Great Sun of Entry," or "G.S.E." This, of course, was a reference to the date of Columbus's "discovery" of the Americas and, thus, the "entry" of Europeans into the territory and lives of its Indigenous peoples. In the council calendrical system a day was referred to as a "Sun," a month as a "Moon," and the date as the number of years from the "G.S.E." As an example, the council membership certificate of forty-one-year-old Wellington Green of Tyendinaga, also identified as a member of the "Iroquois Nation," "Mohawk Tribe," and "Turtle Clan," was dated the "6th Sun of the Buck Moon and the G.S.E. 423," or July 6, 1915 (see figure 6). Like all Council of the Tribes membership certificates, it was signed by Thunderwater as "Niagara, Chief Thunderwater." The certificate of seventy-eight-year-old Peter Teronioton of Kahnawake, "member of the Iroquois Nation, Mohawk Tribe, and Bear Clan," was dated the "6th Sun of the Buck Moon and the G.S.E, 424," or July 6, 1916.[23]

Further, along with the organizational emblem and expressions of pan-Indian orientation and unity, Council of the Tribes letterhead prominently referenced two dates in its system of timekeeping, 1612 and 1720, that resonate strongly with Haudenosaunee political culture and history. "1612" corresponds to the approximate date in Haudenosaunee oral tradition marking the beginning of their relationship with the Dutch, among the first Europeans with whom they had intensive, sustained contact, and the Haudenosaunee-European commitment to *kaswentha*. The notion of *kaswentha* emphasizes the distinct identity and cultures of the Haudenosaunee and Europeans and the agreement by each to coexist peacefully, respectfully, and without interference in the affairs of the other. According to that tradition, the agreement made between the Five Nations and Dutch was marked by material representation of *kaswentha* in the form of a long wampum belt consisting of two parallel rows of purple beads against a

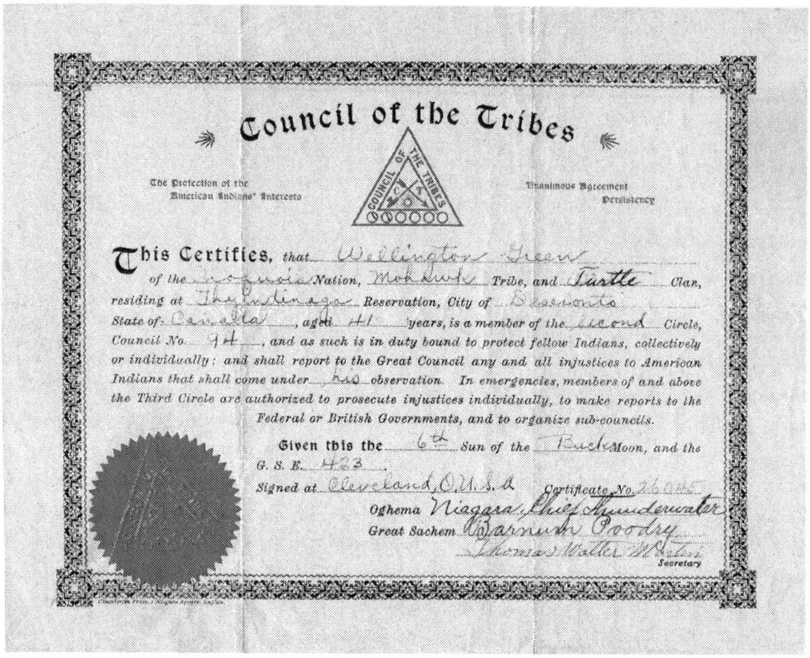

Council of the Tribes

The Protection of the American Indians' Interests

Unanimous Agreement Persistency

This Certifies, that Wellington Green of the Iroquois Nation, Mohawk Tribe, and Turtle Clan, residing at Tyendinaga Reservation, City of Deseronto State of Canada, aged 41 years, is a member of the second Circle, Council No. 94, and as such is in duty bound to protect fellow Indians, collectively or individually; and shall report to the Great Council any and all injustices to American Indians that shall come under his observation. In emergencies, members of and above the Third Circle are authorized to prosecute injustices individually, to make reports to the Federal or British Governments, and to organize sub-councils.

Given this the 6th Sun of the Buck Moon, and the G. S. E. 423.

Signed at Cleveland, O. U.S.A Certificate No. [illegible]

Oghema Niagara Chief Thunderwater

Great Sachem Barnum Poodry

Thomas Walter Martin

Secretary

FIGURE 6. Council of the Tribes membership certificate for Wellington Green, an active member of the Tyendinaga circle of the Council of the Tribes.
Image courtesy of Deborah Greene and Clarence Green.

background of white beads. By the late nineteenth century, *Kaswentha* and "Two-Row Wampum" provided the foundation and orientation for Haudenosaunee political relations with Europeans, Euro-Canadians, and Euro-Americans. "1720" corresponds to the approximate time at which the Tuscaroras were adopted into the Haudenosaunee Confederacy, transforming the "Five Nations" into the "Six Nations." Reflecting this cultural and political background and the influence he would experience as a result of his intense engagement with Haudenosaunee communities over the next few years, it is no accident, or ruse, that Thunderwater would soon be claiming that the Council of the Tribes was an effort to resurrect the Six Nations Confederacy.[24]

At its inception the "Inner Council" of the Council of the Tribes included a diverse group of Native people, many of whom were Haudenosaunees. Besides Thunderwater himself, the officers included Thomas Walter Martin of Grand River as "Supreme Secretary" and Peter Papineau of Akwesasne as "Secretary to the Grand Councillor." Martin, thirty-two years old, was a key player in the Council of the Tribes and over the next few years would become a central figure in the development of the organization at Tyendinaga. Papineau, in his early thirties and a steelworker, was the son of Angus Papineau, one of the "life" (hereditary) chiefs at Akwesasne during this period. Among the "councillors" of the Inner Council was Edward Cornplanter of Cattaraugus. About sixty years of age, Cornplanter was a farmer and leader of the Longhouse religion at Cattaraugus; he had also been present with Thunderwater at the Seneca Indian Park protest in Buffalo in 1912. Barnum Poodry, another Inner Council councillor, about fifty years of age, was a Seneca from Tonawanda, where he grew up as the son of a farmer; in 1915 he was living and working as a machinist in Rochester, New York. Peter Day, nearly seventy years old, was a Mohawk and member of the Wolf clan at Akwesasne; he was a farmer, a band councillor on the Canadian side of the St. Regis reserve, and a key supporter of the hereditary chiefs system within that community. Mitchell Johnson, thirty-five and a laborer, was also from Akwesasne. James Crow, a Seneca, was a fifty-three-year-old farmer from Cattaraugus. Another member of the Inner Council of councillors was Henry Eagle Head, a Lakota from the Pine Ridge reservation in South Dakota. Eagle Head had been an associate of Thunderwater's for more than a decade and someone that he may have met directly or indirectly through his work in the entertainment industry. Though Eagle Head would not remain long as one of the inner councillors, he and Thunderwater would continue to be associated for many years. Other Inner Council councillors included William Muscle, Frank Solomon, Joseph Thomas, and Joseph C. Jacob.[25]

One other Inner Council councillor of the council at the time of its establishment was William R. Boyd, the Cleveland physician who provided care to the Indian boarders and guests in Thunderwater's home. As noted, Boyd was possibly of Muscogee or mixed white and Muscogee ancestry. He was born about 1882 in Okmulgee, Indian Territory, the capital of the Muscogee (Creek) Nation. His father and mother, Mohania Malcome, were born in the Oklahoma Indian Territory as well. The "Boyd" surname is common on the Creek census rolls for this time period, but neither "William R." nor his parents are listed there. Boyd trained as a physician and surgeon and moved to Cleveland in the early 1900s, when he became an associate and friend of Thunderwater. A hint of the close relationship between the two might be seen in the naming of Thunderwater's granddaughter, "Mahoniall," a close approximation of Boyd's mother's given name. After the Council of the Tribes was established in 1914 Boyd held the position of "Supreme Physician and Treasurer."[26]

The first large-scale meeting of the Council of the Tribes took place on the St. Regis reserve in the fall of 1914, with the first "circle" of the organization established there in December of that year. Over the course of the next two years, Thunderwater's following in Haudenosaunee communities in Canada expanded rapidly. In 1915 a second major "convention" of the Council of the Tribes was held in Tyendinaga, a large number of Thunderwater supporters emerged, and the second "circle" was organized. In the fall of 1916 a third "circle" was organized in Kahnawake and major council meetings were held there and at Grand River. The Thunderwater movement was born and quickly became a potent force in local and national Haudenosaunee political development.

CHAPTER 4

THE THUNDERWATER
MOVEMENT

*[Chief Thunderwater] came to Ohsweken as a result of repeated appeals
from many of the Six Nations Indians and lastly on the invitation of the Indian
Council. He thanked the Indians of the Indian Council and especially Asa Hill,
Sec[retary] of the Indian Council for their hospitality. He came also because
he felt that there was great work to be done on the Iroquois reserves in righting
the wrongs that had been perpetuated against the Indians for years and years.
He said that . . . with his help . . . they would be able to get complete control of
their own affairs. He said that they should keep their own councils, transact
their own business. He asked the Indians not to trust the white man, they have
been trying for 300 years to push the Indians back into slavery and they had
partly succeeded. They have passed much legislation with this object in view.
The 'Indian Act' is full of clauses that show this.*

—From an Indian Department report to Duncan Campbell Scott, deputy
superintendent general of Indian Affairs, following a major convention of the
Council of the Tribes at the Six Nations of the Grand River reserve in October 1916

The rapid rise of Chief Thunderwater's popularity and spread of the Council
of the Tribes in Six Nations communities in Canada was integrally related to
a strong current of Haudenosaunee nationalism that had formed during the
last quarter of the nineteenth century, but which was thwarted by government
action and impeded by internal community divisions throughout the period.
Thunderwater was likely aware of these developments prior to the establishment
of the Council of the Tribes and, if he was not, he certainly became familiar
with them as his political message struck chords at Akwesasne, Tyendinaga,
Kahnawake, Kanehsatake, and Grand River.[1]

Beginning with the Enfranchisement Act of 1869, federal Indian policy in
Canada aimed at the political assimilation of First Nations people, and in par-
ticular, of groups considered more "advanced," such as the Haudenosaunees.
One of the key provisions of the Enfranchisement Act was the replacement

of established traditional councils on Indian reserves with an elective system in which the adult male members of the band selected councillors for limited terms of three years. The act could be applied to any Indian band by the order of the governor general, even without the band's consent. The Indian Act of 1876 maintained this objective, with the change that the elective system would be introduced only after an official request for implementation from a band. In 1880 this provision was amended, giving the superintendent general of Indian Affairs the authority to abolish traditional councils and impose the elective system on any band deemed prepared to receive it. The Indian Advancement Act of 1884 was an even more aggressive attempt to transform Indigenous political cultures and institutions. Following the model of Euro-Canadian municipal government even more closely, under this policy, band council elections would be held annually rather than every three years.[2]

Haudenosaunee people in Canada widely and formally opposed the Enfranchisement Act of 1869, in particular its provision for the abolition of traditional councils and the establishment of the elective band council system. Each of their reserves was served by a council of hereditary clan chiefs, males who were selected as representatives by the senior women of their clans and who held their positions for life. These traditional councils of hereditary, or "life," chiefs were all variations of a system based on the core principals of Haudenosaunee political organization and adapted to local cultural and historical circumstances. In all the Six Nations communities there was intense and persistent, but not unanimous, opposition to the 1869 Act and the subsequent Indian Act legislation. Despite this, over the next two decades the Indian Department, typically with some degree of support and assistance from local Indian Act supporters, abolished the traditional councils at Tyendinaga in 1870, Akwesasne in 1888, Kahnawake in 1889 and elsewhere and replaced them with elected band councils.[3]

In each instance, local opposition to the band council system quickly turned to resistance, which took a number of forms. At Tyendinaga, opponents disrupted band council meetings and sought and secured election, then worked to frustrate council activities and question the authority of the Indian Department over their affairs. The Indian Department deposed one of the most obstructionist opponents in 1876, only to see him reelected in 1880 and again in 1882. Supporters of traditional government in Kahnawake used similar tactics. They did so at Akwesasne, as well, and they also actively protested and boycotted band council elections. So few voters participated in the St. Regis election of 1891 that the Indian Department postponed the process for several months.[4]

In each of these communities, local resistance to the band council system included organized efforts to revive the traditional system of hereditary clan chiefs. At Tyendinaga in 1887, supporters of traditional government openly defied the Indian Department by selecting a new council of hereditary chiefs and endowing them with the confederacy titles of the Mohawk clans. Over the course of the next several years they sought official recognition of their "hereditary lords" who, they emphasized, had been installed according to the "ancient Five Nations constitutional ceremony." Supporters of traditional government at Akwesasne pursued a similar strategy. In 1891, at the same time as the heavily boycotted band council elections, they also revived a traditional council and selected chiefs "for life." Subsequently, more than a hundred and forty members of the St. Regis band petitioned the Indian Department seeking acknowledgment of their action and official recognition of the new life chiefs. They persisted in their efforts to select chiefs according to the "old way" and declared that they would "never abandon [their] law to take the laws of white people." At Kahnawake, where supporters of chiefs "for life" regularly outpolled advocates for the elective system, activists for traditional government formally petitioned Indian Department and other government officials in 1890, 1894, 1896, and 1897 to restore "their ancient constitution of government by chiefs."[5]

Only at Grand River did traditional government continue to function, though there, too, it was under significant pressure. The Six Nations Council, which also functioned as the council of the Six Nations Confederacy in Canada, was split between Longhouse chiefs, who supported the hereditary system and opposed efforts to alter the existing council or restrict its authority, and reform-oriented Christian chiefs, who were more amenable to the Indian Act system. This divide existed within the larger Grand River community, as well, but a significant majority supported traditional government and opposed introduction of an elected band council system. During the period in which the Indian Act system was established at Tyendinaga, Akwesasne, and Kahnawake, the reform-minded chiefs succeeded in modifying council processes and procedures along Indian Act lines, leading the Longhouse chiefs to intensify their efforts to resist the Indian Act and support traditional government.[6]

These local efforts to resist the Indian Act system and reestablish and protect traditional government encouraged activists to collaborate with one another around their common goals, eventually leading them to more collective, coordinated action. In 1870 delegates from the Haudenosaunee reserves in Canada attended a grand council at Grand River at which they expressed formal opposition to the Enfranchisement Act, and specifically and unanimously to the section related to elective government. In the years following, the hereditary chiefs and their supporters at Tyendinaga drew on and received support from their counterparts on the Six Nations Council, who urged them to "never forget the ways of old." In September 1890, activists for traditional Haudenosaunee government from Akwesasne, Tyendinaga, Kahnawake, Grand River, and elsewhere gathered at Tyendinaga for a grand council convened to discuss the threats to Six Nations sovereignty and traditional government. Delegates from Onondaga, the seat of the Six Nations Confederacy in the United States, also attended. According to a newspaper report on the plans for the meeting, the Grand River chiefs were attending with "the wampum belts relative to the treaties and the great silver pipe of peace and these will be displayed to show the public that the Indians are a free nation." Several of the petitions from Tyendinaga, Akwesasne, and Kahnawake to restore traditional government followed closely in the wake of this important grand council.[7]

Four years later, in 1894, a second and similar grand council was held on the St. Regis reserve and was attended by more than 1,200 delegates from Akwesasne, Kahnawake, Kanehsatake, and Grand River. In a joint statement addressed to the superintendent general of Indian Affairs, they stated that the elective system of government had an "evil effect" that had "created a bad and ill-feeling among our people." As a unified Six Nations people, they declared, they intended to "hand back" the system of elected councillors and reinstitute their councils of hereditary clan chiefs. At this same grand council, activists at Akwesasne announced that they intended to resume their "systematical constitutional Iroquois government," which they did in late 1894 with the selection of six life chiefs nominated by the clan mothers and confirmed by clan members. Similarly, activists from Kahnawake issued their own statement in which they declared their intention to "free" themselves from the Indian Act system and reestablish their "seven lords appointed by the seven totems according to our ancient custom." Several of the petitions from Kahnawake to government officials soon followed, seeking to suspend the Indian Act system and restore their "ancient constitution."[8]

As these developments, particularly the 1890 and 1894 grand councils, suggest, the local and increasingly collaborative and coordinated movement to resist the Indian Act system and restore traditional government fostered collective Haudenosaunee identity and demands for autonomy and self-government, the articulation of which often drew on key themes and ideas in Haudenosaunee political culture and history. For example, petitioners from Tyendinaga in the

1880s who sought to restore a traditional council of hereditary chiefs typically referred to themselves as the "Six Nations" Mohawks of the Bay of Quinte. Activists for traditional government in other communities did the same. In 1888 one of the Tyendinaga leaders, Joseph I. Brant, wrote a long letter to the governor general of Canada in which he drew on the principle of *kaswentha*, noting the long-established commitment of the British to "remain in their own vessel." He also reminded the governor general of the historic covenant chain relationship of peace, friendship, and support between Great Britain and the Six Nations by emphasizing the need to "polish" the "chain" that had now become "tarnished" by the Indian Act. Brant argued that it was the governor general's obligation to assist the Six Nations in the "preservation of [its] liberties, rights, privileges, and customs." In 1890, just months after the September grand council in Tyendinaga, supporters of the hereditary chiefs there wrote to the governor general, emphasizing that their "original Five Nations government" was long-established and their right to it was "inalienable." They stated, "We wish to maintain . . . our just rights and adhere firmly to our Nationality as . . . subjects of our Confederacy."[9]

In a similar vein, activists in Kahnawake also wrote to the governor general following the 1890 grand council, indicating that by reestablishing traditional government, they hoped to "reform and renew our national rites and ceremonies" and that they were determined to "retain and preserve our nationality as Ro-di-no-Shiou-ni." A separate petition from female members of the Bear clan in Kahnawake expressed precisely the same sentiment. In early 1895, soon after the 1894 grand council and the reconstitution of their hereditary chiefs council, supporters of traditional government in Akwesasne wrote the governor general pointing out not only that the elective council system had undermined the welfare of the band, but that it was "injurious to [our] Nationality."[10]

The ongoing work of Seth Newhouse at Grand River to codify Haudenosaunee traditions regarding the structure of the confederacy, the appointment of hereditary chiefs, and the operation of traditional councils may have facilitated these expressions of Six Nations identity and sovereignty. Newhouse's work was a response to internal efforts at Grand River to adopt the Indian Act system and other changes that he saw as a threat to confederacy autonomy and customs. In the late 1870s he began traveling extensively in the Haudenosaunee communities in Canada for his work, and in 1885 he completed a three-hundred-page draft under the title of "Cosmogony of De-ka-na-wi-da's Government of The Iroquois Confederacy." In 1894 he attended the grand council in Akwesasne as a member of the Grand River delegation.[11]

The intensity of the commitment to traditional government, Haudenosaunee identity, and Six Nations sovereignty was especially evident in developments on the St. Regis reserve in the late 1890s. In 1897 advocates there for the hereditary chiefs system met with an Indian Department official to stress that they should not be subject to the "white man's law" and that they wanted to return to "the old Iroquois plan of electing chiefs by means of women of particular families, totems, or clans." In November of that year they reorganized their chiefs council with the appointment of twelve life chiefs representing four different clans. The hereditary chiefs from Kahnawake, themselves selected in a recent reestablishment of a traditional council in that community, confirmed the Akwesasne chiefs in their position by "laying on of the Wampum on the shoulder as a sign of authority according to . . . Indian custom." A few months later, in June 1898, the clan mothers responsible for nominating the life chiefs, supported by more than one hundred and twenty members of their clans, petitioned the governor general seeking official recognition of their "Constitutional Iroquois Government." When, at the same time, the Indian Department attempted to hold band council elections, activists for traditional government blocked access to the meeting place and forced the Indian agent to cancel the proceedings. They did so a second time several weeks later, resulting in a second postponement. When band council opponents attempted to obstruct the elections a third time in May 1899, they drew a forceful response from the Indian Department. Dominion police arrested the opposition leaders and, in the process, shot and killed one of their supporters. Those arrested were prosecuted, sentenced, and jailed. Subsequently, the Indian Department and the advocates for a hereditary clan system negotiated an agreement that provided for elections to be held, but also for the number of councillors to be set at twelve, the same as the number of hereditary chiefs, without a vote conducted and overseen by a representative of the department. This gave supporters of traditional government the opportunity to select their chiefs in advance and have them appointed as councillors by acclamation during the formal nominating process. In contrast to the previous band council elections, participation was very high.[12]

The commitment to traditional government was also visible at Grand River. In the 1890s the pressure for restructuring the Six Nations Confederacy Council intensified through the efforts of a group of reformers known as the "Progressive Warriors," who petitioned the Indian Department in 1894 and 1898 to establish a fully elected council under the provisions of the Indian Advancement Act.

Lacking community support for such a change, the department denied their petitions. These efforts reenergized support for the hereditary chiefs, traditional government, and assertions of Six Nations sovereignty. The Longhouse chiefs responded by reintroducing the traditional practice of opening council meeting with white wampum to symbolize the legitimacy of its proceedings and by supporting new codifications of the oral tradition of the confederacy.[13]

In short, the final decades of the nineteenth century constituted an early phase in the rise of modern Haudenosaunee nationalism in Canada. During this period, shared opposition to the Indian Act system and the common goal of maintaining and reestablishing traditional government were centripetal forces that drew many in Six Nations communities in Canada together, fostering collaborative and coordinated political activism, enhancing collective Haudenosaunee identity, and energizing demands for Haudenosaunee political autonomy and self-government.

Despite these important developments, the local and collective efforts to reestablish and protect traditional government were not successful. At Kahnawake, in the face of the repeated attempts from 1895 through the early 1900s to gain official recognition for the hereditary chiefs and traditional council, the elected band council system remained firmly in place. Indian Department officials routinely denied or simply ignored the numerous petitions from supporters of traditional government to rescind application of the Indian Act system. The situation was much the same at Tyendinaga. At Grand River the progressive push for reform of the Six Nations Confederacy Council reorganized as the Indian Rights Association, which in 1907 and 1910 petitioned the Canadian government to replace the hereditary council with a full elected band council system. Because of the still deep split within the Grand River community over the Indian Act system, the Indian Department denied the petitions. However, by this point there was considerable friction within the Six Nations Council, as the reform-minded Christian chiefs had gained control of the body and were rebuked and opposed by their Longhouse counterparts for failing to respect and follow the political traditions of the confederacy. At Akwesasne the agreement negotiated for the 1899 council elections unraveled quickly, resulting in a cancellation of the elections for 1902. For the next four years St. Regis remained without a functioning council. In 1906 an agreement similar to that of 1899 was worked out, through which the life chiefs were elected to three-year terms. Though unsatisfactory to the many local activists for traditional government and Haudenosaunee autonomy, this hybrid framework of hereditary chiefs serving within the Indian Act system persisted through the elections of 1909 and 1912 and was still in place at the time Chief Thunderwater appeared on the scene in 1914.[14]

Thus, Canada's Department of Indian Affairs actively and persistently stifled the current of nationalism that was gathering force on Haudenosaunee reserves in the late nineteenth and early twentieth centuries. Charged with implementing a policy aimed at the complete economic, social, political, and cultural assimilation of First Nations people, the Indian Department ignored Haudenosaunee claims to sovereignty, deposed hereditary chiefs, imposed the elective band council system in the face of significant community opposition, and rejected efforts to reestablish traditional government. The split in Haudenosaunee communities over the issue of local government also impeded this current of nationalism. In each instance, alongside local opposition to band councils and support for restoring traditional government, there was also local support for the Indian Act system and elected government. The Indian Department exploited these divisions and used them as a rationale for applying the Indian Act, instituting the elective council system, and rejecting efforts to restore the authority of traditional chiefs. One of the important consequences of the Indian Department's effectiveness in curbing the movement for traditional government and the rise of Haudenosaunee nationalism may have been that it short-circuited the emergence of clear collective leadership beyond the local level. By doing so, it hindered the development of a more formal organizational structure that could have sustained that political energy and facilitated the development of long-term political strategies. Nevertheless, this political current in Haudenosaunee communities in Canada did not dissolve. Rather, it continued to churn and reorganized in 1915 under the influence of Chief Thunderwater and the Council of the Tribes.

In November 1914 Thunderwater held the first recorded meeting of the Council of the Tribes at Akwesasne on the Canadian side of the St. Regis reserve. He followed that with a second, much larger meeting that same month on the American side of the reserve. According to the *Utica Observer*, which reported on the meetings and drew on an interview with Thunderwater for its account, the second "convention" was a "monster" event attended by an estimated two thousand Mohawks and other First Nations people from the United States and Canada. A principal reason for the convention was to address ongoing local dissatisfaction with the elected band council system and the interest of many at Akwesasne in restoring traditional government by hereditary clan chiefs. As the *Observer* noted, Thunderwater and the local convention participants were

planning that the "government of the Mohawks" at St. Regis would be "completely reformed." In reporting on the meetings to his superiors in Ottawa, the
Canadian Indian agent for the reserve described Thunderwater as "somewhat of
an agitator" and noted that "the Indians are flocking to him with all their tales
of long suffering and great injustices."[15]

In mid-December 1914, a month after the "monster" convention at Akwesasne, Thunderwater supporters organized a local circle of the Council of the
Tribes at a meeting on the American side of St. Regis. Organizers recorded the
date of the event in Council of the Tribes reckoning as the "Great Sun of Entry
Four Hundred and Twenty-Two." Hereditary chiefs and their supporters were
prominent among the circle leaders. The officers of the circle included Chief
Louis Solomon as the grand councillor, Loran Swamp as chairman, Peter Herron as treasurer, Michael Solomon as secretary, and Charles Cook as "keeper of
the door." Circle councillors included Silas Gray, J. B. Jacobs, Thomas Garrow,
Joseph Wood, Louis Square, Charles Cook, John S. Herron, and Phillip Wood.
At the conclusion of the convention Thunderwater's supporters named him
"Tehotiokwawakon" ("one who builds up or supports us") and appointed him
as "great sachem, advisor, great counsel."[16]

In the months following the organization of the St. Regis circle, Thunderwater wrote to Indian Department officials on several occasions to inform them
about the purpose and structure of the Council of the Tribes. Soon after the
December 1914 meeting, he sent a copy of a Council of the Tribes membership
certificate to department officials informing them that he and his supporters
intended to organize additional circles on reserves in Canada and the United
States. Six months later, in June 1915, Thunderwater sent a typed, single-spaced,
five-page letter from his home in Cleveland to the superintendent general of
Indian Affairs in which he provocatively noted that a central purpose of the Council of the Tribes was to establish a "league of Indians organized for the purpose
of detecting and exposing crooked methods executed by crooked individuals."
He also detailed the structure of the organization. Emphasizing a theme that
would grow in importance as the council evolved primarily as a Haudenosaunee
movement, he asserted the autonomy of the chiefs at St. Regis and elsewhere:

> [The] chiefs are with few exceptions members of this Council and desire
> that their decisions in any matter pertaining to their reservations, be
> INTELLIGENTLY PRESENTED TO YOUR OFFICE *AND NOT MEDDLED WITH BY*
> *INTERESTED PERSONS BEFORE PRESENTATION.* It appears that such action

has in many instances been impossible and that at least one [Indian] agent has actually endeavoured to intimidate Indian chiefs and to declare that they had no right to hold meetings or to come to conclusions without his presence and approval. If such authority is given to agents, then Indians are little more than slaves under a master.

Signing his letter as "Oghema Niagara, Chief Thunderwater," he noted that his supporters at Akwesasne had given him the name "Tehotiokwawakon" and that he had been "formally adopted into the St. Regis Band of Mohawk Indians at St. Regis, Quebec, Canada."[17]

At about this same time Thunderwater supporters at Tyendinaga also organized a circle of the Council of the Tribes. Among its leaders and most active members were direct descendants of the hereditary chiefs and band council opponents from the 1870s and 1880s. The officers included Michael Claus as grand councillor, Johnson Lewis as vice grand councillor, Isaac Claus as secretary, and George Hill as treasurer. The circle councillors included Andrew Secro (Scero), Solomon Brant, Isaac Brant, William J. Secro (Scero), John Smart, Simon Hill, Peter Bardy, and Cornelius Maracle. In late September 1915 the Tyendinaga circle hosted a major four-day convention of the Council of the Tribes, with Joel Johnson, one of the leaders of the hereditary chiefs movement in the 1880s, serving as chairman. Held over five days and including Thunderwater supporters and delegates from other Haudenosaunee reserves, the convention included an official reception hosted by Thunderwater, speeches by local council leaders, a keynote address by Thunderwater, and drafting of petitions to the governor general of Canada.[18]

While the content of the speeches, address, and petitions of the council convention are not known, subsequent events point to the event as a critical factor in reigniting the hereditary chiefs movement at Tyendinaga. In the band council elections at Tyendinaga soon after the council convention, voters turned out the sitting councillors and elected a new council consisting entirely of Thunderwater supporters. Once in office, the Thunderwater councillors defied the Indian Act by forwarding their minutes and resolutions directly to the Indian Department without first obtaining the approval of the local Indian agent. In doing so, they argued that they were capable of administering their own affairs and that, by virtue of their sovereignty as people of the Six Nations, the Indian Department had no right to impose the Indian agent on them, to require that he attend their meetings, or to demand he approve their minutes and decisions. Often, in action reminiscent of the tactics employed by Indian Act opponents a generation earlier, the "Thunderwater" band councillors refused to conduct official business at all. When they did, in line with Haudenosaunee tradition, they allowed women to vote, an action that concerned Indian Department officials and Indian Act supporters within the community.[19]

Thunderwater supporters were also emerging in Kahnawake, and within a year of the Tyendinaga convention they organized a council circle as well. As with Akwesasne and Tyendinaga, in Kahnawake interest in Thunderwater and the Council of the Tribes was tied to the established but dormant current of opposition to the Indian Act system and support for traditional government. In addition, in Kahnawake this current was complicated and deepened by other local issues.[20] In the early 1900s education for most school-age children in Kahnawake was provided by a Roman Catholic day school in the main village on the reserve; the school was formally run by the Indian Department and informally overseen by the local Jesuit priest at the St. Francis Xavier mission. In the 1890s, with a succession of poorly trained, mostly non-Native instructors teaching in French, enrollment and attendance in the school was extremely low. Desperate to improve this situation, in 1900 the Indian Department turned to Peter J. Delisle, a twenty-three-year-old college-educated member of the band who had been serving as a secretary and interpreter for the local band council. The Indian Department hired Delisle after he wrote to the department secretary to inquire about a teaching position and stated that "Indian children knowing only their own language teach faster with a teacher of their own race who has passed the necessary examinations and who can explain things in their own tongue." Under Delisle's leadership, school enrollment and attendance improved dramatically, with the head of the Schools Branch of the Indian Department soon recommending the hiring of an additional Native teacher from the community. By 1910, nearly three-quarters of the children in Kahnawake were enrolled in school, and daily attendance exceeded 50 percent, nearly double the rate of a decade earlier. Citing their teaching skills and native language instruction, Indian Department officials credited Delisle and other Native teachers for the impressive turnaround.[21]

In 1913 Duncan Campbell Scott was promoted to the position of deputy superintendent general of Indian Affairs, and one of his first official actions was to initiate a plan to "Anglicize" the schools in Kahnawake. To accomplish this goal, he sought to remove the Mohawk teachers from the main schools on the reserve and replace them with nuns from the Sisters of St. Anne, a teaching order active in Native education in Canada. As a government official, Scott had a history of opposition to hereditary council activism in Kahnawake going back more than a decade. While his plan to "Anglicize" Kahnawake's schools stemmed partly from the priorities of cost control and assimilation for which he was well known, he also intended the action to demonstrate Indian Department authority and exert greater control over developments on the reserve. As part of Scott's plan, in 1915 Peter Delisle and the other Native teacher in the main Catholic day school were dismissed and replaced by teachers from the Sisters of St. Anne order, which maintained a provincial house for the training of young nuns in Lachine, Quebec, directly across the St. Lawrence River from Kahnawake.[22]

Many in Kahnawake opposed Scott's plan, and their leader was none other than Peter Delisle. Support within the community for the Indian Department's decision and the Sisters of St. Anne centered within the local band council and, in particular, in its head councillor, or "mayor," Frank McDonald Jacobs. Jacobs, a solicitor, the local postmaster, and a former schoolteacher in Kahnawake, was a strong proponent of the Indian Act and the band council system. Delisle and his supporters determined to make the band council elections of 1915 a point of their opposition and, in a measure of the level of dissatisfaction with the Indian Department's decision and the Sisters of St. Anne, Delisle tallied the largest number of votes, and Jacobs and three other councillors (out of a total of six) were turned out of office. Delisle and the other newly elected councillors then used their official positions within the band council to express and further their opposition to the department and the Sisters of St. Anne.[23]

At the same time, interest in Chief Thunderwater grew rapidly in Kahnawake and a circle of the Council of the Tribes soon formed, probably during the summer of 1916, a year that saw local opposition to the Sisters of St. Anne deepen with the Indian Department's decision to build a permanent residence for the teaching nuns in the main village on the reserve. Delisle, dismissed teacher, Sisters of St. Anne opponent, and Indian Department critic, was appointed by Thunderwater as the grand councillor of the Kahnawake circle. Other officers included John T. Dailleboust as vice grand councillor, F. T. John as secretary, and Peter K. Delorimier as treasurer. The local circle councillors included John T. Canadien, Louis Goodleaf, James Phillips, James Ross, Mitchell Dailleboust, John Dailleboust, and Joseph Martin. All were opponents of the Sisters of St. Anne, and many were supporters of traditional government.[24]

In September 1916, one year after the rally at Tyendinaga, Thunderwater and the local circle of Council of the Tribes held a major six-day convention in

FIGURE 7. Installation of Peter J. Delisle as the grand councillor of the Kahnawake circle of the Council of the Tribes in September 1916. Thunderwater, dressed in regalia, stands at the center of the photograph with his back to the photographer. Delisle may be the man to Thunderwater's left, wearing white shoes and holding his hat in hand.
Image courtesy of Library and Archives Canada.

Kahnawake. The convention opened on a Sunday with the formal installation of Delisle and the other council officers. A picture of that event depicts an outdoor scene in the main village on the reserve. In the background a long wooden stockade borders an expansive open ground; beyond that, the rooftops of homes can be seen, a Union Jack hangs from a flagpole, and high-tension electrical wires stretch off into the distance (see figure 7). Looking on is a crowd of men, women, and children, some dressed in Native regalia and others in formal Western attire. Thunderwater, wearing a feathered headdress and dressed in fringed buckskin and beaded shirt and leggings, stands before those assembled, while Delisle, attired in a dark suit, stands to his side. In the lower righthand corner of the photograph is the notation in Thunderwater's handwriting, "Administering the Oath to the Grand Councillor Caughnawaga Quebec Canada Council of the Tribes."[25]

The opening day of the Kahnawake convention also featured "Agnes Dominick" and "Mother Iro Dominick," who may have been clan mothers, and was marked by a "Green Corn Dance in full Indian costume." The day concluded with a "grand lacrosse match" between teams from Kahnawake and Akwesasne. The program over the next several days included addresses by Thunderwater, local council leaders, and others on such topics as "Indian education," "temperance," and "health and sanitation." The "Big Day" of the convention, its fifth, was devoted to political issues and included speeches by Thunderwater and circle councillors and members. There was also a speech by Chief Michael Montour (Wishe Sakoientineta), who had been the hereditary chief of the Great Bear clan from 1881 until 1889 and was described in the official program of the rally as the "last Chief of the old regime." As the grand councillor, Peter Delisle closed out the "Big Day" with an address on "Indian Treaties and Rights." Reflecting the importance of the convention and his role, Council of the Tribes supporters presented Thunderwater with a black felt cap commemorating the events. Likely produced by a local artisan, the band of the brimless cap was beaded with the name "Chief Thunderwater." The front side of the crown of the cap featured the American and British flags in bright red, blue, and white beads, while the back side of the crown marked out "1916 Kanawake" in yellow beads.[26]

Over the course of the next several years "Thunderwaterism" in Kahnawake continued to be intertwined with local opposition to the Indian Department and manifest itself in the local band council elections. Emboldened by the convention and local development of the Council of the Tribes, which grew to more than two hundred members, Delisle continued his visible and vocal opposition to the Sisters of St. Anne, leading the local Jesuit missionary to write to Deputy Superintendent General Scott with the warning that Delisle was "urging the Indians to rebel against constituted authority." From 1917 through 1920, Council of the Tribes members in Kahnawake completely dominated the local band council, with John T. Dailleboust, the vice grand councillor, garnering the most votes and the position of "mayor" in 1917 and 1918.[27]

The Thunderwater movement emerged quickly in Kanehsatake, as well, though there the circumstances of the establishment of the Council of the Tribes are less well documented than at Akwesasne, Tyendinaga, and Kahnawake. By the summer of 1915 a local circle was established with local officers that included James Moses as grand councillor and Mitchell Cole, William Elien, James Montour, and Abraham Nicholas as councillors. In June 1915 they wrote to Thunderwater to encourage his continued support for their work to curb the sale of alcohol to residents of the reserve at hotels and other establishments in the local village of Oka. In addition, they reported to him on the local circle's efforts to oppose upcoming elections for the local band council. "We will put up a big fight," they informed Thunderwater, "we will try to kill the election down as we know very well there are not very many that are pulling on the election side." Continuing,

Moses and the councillors sought Thunderwater's assistance: "If you have power to help in our work . . . we will be very glad to hear as soon as you can. . . . We always have in our minds that you had told us in some of your letters . . . that whatever trouble we have you will stand forward and fight the cases for us." Closing their letter on a note of support for Thunderwater, they stated, "We Indians stand behind and help you as much as we can."[28]

Thunderwater held a fourth major meeting of the Council of the Tribes at Grand River in October 1916, just one month after the convention in Kahnawake. With growing concern, Duncan Campbell Scott dispatched an Indian Department official, R. H. Abraham, to attend Thunderwater's appearance and directed him to take note of his remarks and activities. In his report Abraham stated that Thunderwater had come to "Ohsweken," a village on the reserve where the Six Nations Council met, "as a result of repeated appeals from many of the Six Nations Indians," suggesting that Thunderwater was well known to many members of that community. He added that Thunderwater had also come to Grand River on the "invitation of the Indian Council." According to Abraham, when Thunderwater opened the meeting at Grand River, he thanked the members of the council, especially Asa Hill, its secretary, for their hospitality. Hill was a strong and vocal advocate at Six Nations Confederacy traditions, rights, and autonomy. In another interesting connection between the Six Nations Council and the Council of the Tribes, and as a reflection of how Thunderwater's organization was adapted to local circumstances and culture, Asa Hill's wife served as the secretary of the Grand River circle of the Council of the Tribes.[29] Abraham went on in his report to indicate Thunderwater's purpose in coming to Grand River, noting his emphasis on the issue of self-government and the malicious intent of the Indian Act system. The parallels with some parts of George Decker's address to the Six Nations Confederacy Council at Onondaga in the fall of 1914 are evident:

> [Thunderwater] came . . . because he felt that there was great work to be done on the Iroquois Reserve in righting the wrongs that had been perpetuated against the Indians for years and years. . . . He said that it was a deplorable condition of affairs that Indians, as intellectual as the Six Nations Indians, should have to be treated as children by the Indian Dept. He appealed to the audience as to whether this was right or not. He assured them that alone they could do nothing to remedy this; but with his help (he had ways and means not at the disposal of any other of forcing

Governments to do his bidding) they would be able to get complete control
of their own affairs. He warned the Indians against the white men and told
of different ways (the white men) had of fleecing the Indians. He said that
they (the Indians) should keep their own councils, transact their own business. He asked the Indians not to trust the white man, [stating] they have
been trying for 300 years to push the Indians back into slavery and they
had partly succeeded. They have passed much legislation with this object
in view. The 'Indian Act' is full of clauses that shows the truth of this.[30]

According to Abraham's memorandum to Scott, Thunderwater went on to
emphasize the importance of formal education for fighting "the white man"
and advised the use of the newspapers to publicize their grievances and further
their actions. He also sought to address an issue with which he had been engaged
in Cleveland and Buffalo, the need for temperance and the use of liquor "by the
white man" to undermine Indian welfare. Thunderwater asserted that he was
"a pagan, not a Christian" and that the Six Nations people "would have to keep
their money and not give it to God for white men to worship," if they wished to
prosper. "The Christian's God is money," he reportedly declared.

Abraham continued his report, focusing on Thunderwater's claims about his
work at Tyendinaga. It is unclear if the overblown rhetoric was Thunderwater's,
in his attempt to magnify his role, or that of the Indian Department official, in
his attempt to mock Thunderwater and convey his contempt:

> He told of the work he had done at Deseronto, he had appointed his own
> council there, placed his supreme [secretary] in the council chambers as
> a safe guard against white treachery and notwithstanding the fact that
> the Indian Dept. and Indian agent did everything in their power to defeat
> his council and remove the [Secretary]. He said the name 'Thunderwater'
> was a power at Deseronto, that the Indian Agent trembled whenever he
> hears the name. . . . He stated that the Indian Dept. had boasted that he
> could not get a following at Deseronto, the same as they had when they
> heard he was coming to Brantford but he had now 400 members there
> and more coming in. He fully expected that the Brantford Indians would
> do much better than this.

According to Abraham, Thunderwater also voiced his opposition to Great Britain's decision to join the war against Germany in 1914, claiming that its "fighting
in Europe" was simply "for gold," and expressed "sorrow that there were Indians

in this fight." Purportedly, he added that "white men" encouraged division within Grand River and other First Nations communities over this and other issues as a distraction "in order that they might steal their lands while the quarrel was going on." He concluded the meeting by reemphasizing a theme that evidently ran throughout his remarks—he could and would "assist [the Six Nations] greatly in securing their rights." Abraham closed his report to Deputy Superintendent Scott with a note of warning: "I sincerely hope that some means will be found to prevent Thunderwater's return to the Six Nations Reserve as it will be sure to have a depressing effect on the work I have planned for the future there."

The rapid growth of the Council of the Tribes and his own popularity encouraged Thunderwater to further "confederate action." Over the course of several months in early 1917 he and his supporters prepared to incorporate the Council of the Tribes in Canada, a legal standing that they believed would enable them to more effectively pursue their goals in the courts and at higher levels within the Canadian government. In a letter to the local council circles and supporters in mid-January of that year, a copy of which he also sent to the superintendent general of Indian Affairs, Thunderwater argued that "Indians have a legal right to organize" and that because of the department's refusal to recognize their concerns, "the only hope that the Indians have for self protection is to do so." In addition, he stated he was convinced that Canadians generally were sympathetic to the concerns of Indian people and that the Council of the Tribes would take its issues to the public through the press. "Act together and make your appeal to the people of the Dominion," he urged council supporters. Thunderwater also responded to the complaints against him by his opponents and explained the purpose and activities of the council. Further, addressing the issue of border crossing, with which he already had some familiarity, he stated that he also intended "to fight the immigration and customs acts as applied to the Indians, as in our opinion it is not in compliance with the treaties and words of the King under which those treaties were made. We feel convinced that both in the Dominion of Canada and the United States, the supreme court will uphold the Indians right to 'pass and re-pass the boundary without molestation.'" He explained that he had hoped to work cooperatively with the Department of Indian Affairs on these matters, but that he and the Council of the Tribes had met only with indifference, obstruction, and lies.[31]

Several months later, in October 1917, Thunderwater, several council officers and others from Grand River, Tyendinaga, and Akwesasne attempted to meet with Deputy Superintendent General Scott at his office in Ottawa to explain the purpose of the Council of the Tribes, protest what they referred to as the "infringements of Indian Rights," and obtain formal recognition of the organization by the Indian Department. Scott flatly refused to meet with Thunderwater. Through a very brief meeting with one member of his group, Scott informed them that he wanted nothing to do with the organization and that Thunderwater was "behind the organization for the purpose of robbing the Indians." Upset by this rebuff and insult, Thunderwater stated that Indians in Canada had a right to organize, just as any other citizen, "more particularly so as their rights were being flagrantly infringed." He declared that they wanted incorporation by a special act of Parliament "so that they could fight in court the unlawful abuse of [Indian] rights." Subsequently, Thunderwater took his story to the *Ottawa Citizen*, which reported on the Council of the Tribes and the attempted meeting with Scott. According to the *Citizen*, the Thunderwater delegation had come to Ottawa at the request of some eight hundred supporters and the Council of the Tribes was a "resurrection of the confederation of the Iroquois founded in 1620." Thunderwater and his supporters also visited the office of Interior Minister Arthur Meighen to register their protest of Scott's treatment and refusal to meet with them.[32]

True to their word, Thunderwater and his supporters moved forward with the effort to incorporate the Council of the Tribes. In April 1918, six months after the snub by Scott, "Bill 30—An Act to Incorporate the Council of the Tribes in Canada," received its first reading in the House of Commons. Introduced by a member of parliament from Belleville, Ontario, near the Tyendinaga reserve, Bill 30 was the official appeal of 175 petitioners, nearly all of whom were from Tyendinaga, Grand River, Akwesasne, Kahnawake, and Kanehsatake. They included many of the leaders of the opposition to the Indian Act system and of efforts to reestablish traditional government. With the head office of the incorporated organization to be located in Deseronto on the Tyendinaga reserve, their stated purposes were to provide material aid for its "distressed" members, to educate them "socially, morally, and intellectually," to encourage their loyalty to "Crown and country," to promote temperance and "hygienic principles," and to foster modern agricultural practices among Indians. In what may have been a related development, at about this time the Confederacy Council at Grand River recognized Thunderwater as a member of the Six Nations with an official certificate signed by Levi General (Deskaheh), the deputy speaker of the Confederacy Council, and stamped with its official seal (see figure 8). As a result of behind the scenes work by Scott and other Indian Department officials, several months later

FIGURE 8. Six Nations membership card for Chief Thunderwater. Signed
by Chief Levi General as deputy speaker of the Six Nations Council and bearing
the seal of Six Nations Council, the membership card probably dates to about 1918.
Image courtesy of the Western Reserve Historical Society, Cleveland, Ohio.

Bill 30 was quietly withdrawn from consideration and never received a second
reading. Thunderwater and his supporters' efforts to incorporate the Council
of the Tribes in Canada were dead.[33]

Despite this setback, over the course of the next two years the Thunderwater-
inspired efforts to revive hereditary chiefs systems in Haudenosaunee communities intensified. In July 1918 "Thunderwaters" at Akwesasne prepared their own
slate of candidates in an effort to take over the local band council, as was done
in Kahnawake and Tyendinaga in 1916 and 1917. The local Indian agent estimated
that roughly two-thirds of the voters at Akwesasne opposed the Indian Act
system, and in response, the Indian Department canceled the scheduled band
council elections.[34] Supporters of the hereditary system, many of whom were
Council of the Tribes members, responded by reaffirming their hereditary chiefs
and announced their intention to "renew and defend old traditions and rights."
Just months later, in September 1918, a grand council was held to formally install
the chiefs and was attended by chiefs and others representing the Mohawks,

Oneidas, Onondagas, Cayugas, Senecas, Tuscaroras, and Hurons. Reporting on the "great convention," *The Gazette* of Montreal described the proceedings, which were opened by participants from Grand River, who, presumably, were hereditary chiefs on the Six Nations Confederacy Council:

> The Oswegans, who are still Pagan Indians, began the ceremony of instal-
> lation by lighting a fire, calling out incantations as they went about it,
> believing that their prayers for wisdom mounted with the smoke of the
> fire to the ear of the Great Spirit which animates and rules all things. . . .
> The Indians sat in different linguistic groups, each nation debating any
> question brought up and then when arrived at a decision, allowing their
> official speaker to announce their decision. As many as six different lan-
> guages were spoken in the Council. The official speaker of each nation
> carried the wampum as he recounted the deeds of the ancestors of the
> tribe, telling off the beads as he did so, describing the formation of the
> great Peace League by Hiawatha and coming down to the present and
> the present problems.[35]

One of the representatives present at the grand council and the installation of the Akwesasne chiefs was Peter Delisle, the ex-schoolteacher and grand councillor of the Kahnawake circle of the Council of the Tribes. According to Delisle, the installation of the chiefs was a "stirring sight to those privileged to witness it." The grand council concluded with a plan to hold another "international council" with the object of "organizing to look after the interests and welfare of the Indian." According to the *Gazette*, "considering themselves still nations who have never given up their Sovereignty . . . they have also a project for choosing an ambassa-dor to represent them at Ottawa and to deal as one sovereign power to another."

In Kahnawake, as already noted, Thunderwater supporters dominated the band council in 1917 and 1918. They did so again in 1919, with the grand councillor Delisle heading it up as the top vote-getter and "mayor." In March of that year the Indian Department charged Delisle with sedition when, at a public meeting, he had encouraged his supporters to obstruct work repairing local church buildings unless the community was given control over its secular affairs. For this he was arrested and tried but found not guilty. In a measure of the level of support for Delisle, he was reelected to the band council in 1920, served as "mayor" again that year, and was elected a third time in 1921.[36]

Developments in Tyendinaga mirrored those at Akwesasne. In November 1918, in the wake of the unsuccessful effort to incorporate the Council of the Tribes, one month after the Akwesasne grand council, and just a few months prior to its scheduled band council elections, opponents of the Indian Act system in Tyendinaga installed nine chiefs and nine subchiefs from three different clans to constitute a new traditional council. Among those installed were several of the elected "Thunderwater" councillors. According to a statement they directed to the Minister of the Interior, "We, the Mohawk Band of Indians of the Bay of Quinte Six Nations Iroquois, . . . have accepted the ceremonies of the Confederation of the Five Nations formed by De-ka-nah-wi-deh. . . . [W]e have declared that there will be no more elections as we have chosen our chiefs by the regulations of the Confederate Ceremonies." Three months later the sitting band councillors approved a motion to "adopt the Life Chief system" and cancel the upcoming elections. Nevertheless, the Indian Department moved ahead with elections and, in action reminiscent of Akwesasne ten years earlier, opponents attempted to block access to the meetinghouse where nominations were to take place. Their action failed. However, participation in the meeting was minimal and ended in the nomination of only five candidates. The Indian agent declared them elected by acclamation, and subsequently the Indian Department confirmed their appointments.[37]

A few months later, in February 1919, nearly four hundred men and women from Tyendinaga, identifying themselves as "chiefs and warriors, women and people of the Six Nations Tyendinaga Reserve" and including the nine hereditary chiefs, sent a petition to the governor general of Canada supporting the December 1918 council resolution to abolish the elective system and institute a council of hereditary chiefs. Their petition was rejected. They followed with another directed to the King of England and signed by 578 men and women, a significant majority of the Tyendinaga's adult population at that time. The petitioners argued that they had a right to select the chiefs for life "according to ancient custom and rites of [the] tribe. . . . [A]lthough a large majority of our band desire to revert to our former and ancient custom of electing chiefs for life," they complained, "this right is refused us by the Department of Indian Affairs." A third petition came five months later, in October 1919. Directed to the superintendent general of Indian Affairs and signed by 116 men and women, the petitioners recalled the earlier council resolution abolishing the elective system and reestablishing the system of hereditary chiefs. They also recalled that "the People" with "legal and full authority and ceremony of and by the Confederation and Confederated Chiefs did confirm the installation of [their] Chiefs" and demanded that they be recognized by the Indian Department as "fully authorized representatives of

the Bay of Quinty Band of Mohawk Indians." The petitioners went on to state
that the majority of the people "seriously and strenuously" objected to the new
councillors appointed by the department in late December of the previous year.
They underscored this point by arguing they were "neither wards nor subjects
of or to the Crown" and that the councillors were installed illegally and had no
authority to represent the band.[38]

In retrospect, it is evident that Thunderwater's political rise and the popularity of the Council of the Tribes were critical factors in the reemergence of
the Haudenosaunee movement for traditional government and Six Nations
sovereignty. That movement had formed during the final decades of the nineteenth century out of widespread discontent with the Indian Act system and
began to coalesce with collective action and an intensification of Haudenosaunee
identity across a number of Six Nations communities. It was cut short, though
not overcome, in the early twentieth century by the policies and tactics of the
Department of Indian Affairs. Thunderwater and the Council of the Tribes
provided both leadership and an organizational structure through which those
deeply held political aspirations resurfaced and reorganized. Haudenosaunee
nationalists were not drawn to Thunderwater because of his political vision.
Rather, the vision was theirs. They were drawn to him and the Council of the
Tribes because both provided a vehicle for the expression and realization of their
goals to revive traditional government and restore Haudenosaunee autonomy
and self-determination. Thunderwater possessed no traditional authority, but
he did have Haudenosaunee roots, had a demonstrated commitment to Native
interests and Six Nations communities, and was a charismatic and perhaps even
inspirational figure with keen oratorical and organizational skills. Combined
with this, Thunderwater was personally and politically ambitious and adapted
his political priorities to reflect those of the supporters he attracted. As this
dynamic developed, the Council of the Tribes, which Thunderwater had established as a pan-Indian self-help organization, evolved to reflect this reorientation
and emphasize the goals of reestablishing Haudenosaunee political traditions
and self-government. As Thunderwater grew in popularity and influence and
revitalized Haudenosaunee nationalism, he became the object of intense concern
for Duncan Campbell Scott and the Department of Indian Affairs. From their
perspective, "Thunderwaterism" threatened the authority of the Indian Department, the implementation of the Indian Act, and the very foundation on which
Canadian Indian policy was based. They resolved to break Chief Thunderwater
and the Thunderwater movement.

CHAPTER 5

THUNDERWATERISM AND THE RESPONSE OF CANADA'S INDIAN DEPARTMENT

I am quite satisfied . . . that [Chief Thunderwater] is stirring up the Indians to an effort to do away with some of the authority of the Department and that promises are made which if carried out, would not be in the interests of the Department and its system of handling Indian Affairs.
—C. C. Parker, inspector of Indian agencies, reporting to Duncan Campbell Scott, deputy superintendent general of Indian Affairs (October 30, 1917)

═══════════════

The principal aim of the [Council of the Tribes] common among these Indians is to create a spirit of Indian Nationalism, "Indian First." They uphold that an Indian was always to continue to retain his identity as an Indian in so far as it affects his aboriginal rights, and that he never intended to assimilate the ways and customs of the white man or to become a subject of his law.
—Charles A. Cooke, Mohawk interpreter in the Indian Department, reporting to Deputy Superintendent General Scott (October 31, 1917)

Chief Thunderwater drew the attention of the Department of Indian Affairs from the moment he appeared on the scene at the St. Regis reserve in late 1914. His activities and the political movement he reawakened in Haudenosaunee communities troubled the department and, in particular, Deputy Superintendent General Duncan Campbell Scott. Scott and the department quickly adopted a policy of ignoring Thunderwater's attempts at communication in an effort to deny him and the Council of the Tribes any credibility or legitimacy. However, as his following and the number of council circles and supporters grew, it worked vigorously and sometimes unscrupulously to thwart Thunderwater, the organization, and local council circles (see figure 9).

FIGURE 9. Duncan Campbell Scott, Deputy Superintendent General of Indian Affairs.
Scott (1862–1947), head of Canada's Department of Indian Affairs from 1913 to 1932,
regarded Thunderwater as the leader of a retrograde movement in Haudenosaunee
communities that threatened assimilationist federal Indian policies. From 1915
to 1920 he worked actively to discredit Thunderwater and defuse the
Thunderwater movement.
Image courtesy of Library and Archives Canada.

When the Council of the Tribes held its first meetings at Akwesasne in November 1914 the Indian agent on the Canadian side of the St. Regis reserve warned
his superiors in Ottawa about the "agitator" Thunderwater and indicated that
the people there were "flocking to him" with their "tales of long suffering and
great injustices." The department's concern heightened when five of the St. Regis
chiefs contributed ten dollars in band funds to Thunderwater and the Council of
the Tribes. As a result of the arrangement made between the Indian Department
and supporters of traditional government in 1906, these five chiefs, as well as the
others who composed the St. Regis band council, were also hereditary chiefs.
Several months later, after Thunderwater had been named "Tehotiokwawakon"

and appointed as "great sachem, advisor, and great counsel" by his supporters in Akwesasne, the department secretary, J. D. McLean, informed several of the chiefs at St. Regis that they had no authority to appoint Thunderwater as an ambassador. He did so again in May 1915, writing directly to chiefs Loren Jacko, Mitchell C. Jacobs, and Angus Papineau. Jacko had been appointed chief in 1911 upon the death of Charlie Leaf; Jacobs had been one of the five chiefs accused of taking band funds to support Thunderwater; and Papineau was a longtime supporter of traditional government and one of the principal "agitators" during the tumultuous events of May 1899 when Dominion police arrested the leaders of the opposition to band council elections and shot and killed one of their supporters. "I have to remind you," McLean stated, "that you have no power to appoint a chief or representative to deal with any matter affecting the Canadian St. Regis reserve. . . . It is hoped that you will not again attempt to create the impression that you have a power that you do not possess."[1]

During the spring and summer of 1915 Thunderwater wrote to the superintendent general of Indian Affairs several times to intercede with the Indian Department on a variety of local concerns at Akwesasne and Kanehsatake. At Akwesasne the issues included the beating of a female student by a local schoolteacher, selling of liquor by the father of the Indian agent, and intimidation of community members by the agent and a local priest. At Kanehsatake the matters involved the behavior of the local priest and seminarians and unknown persons surveying land on the reserve. In his letters to the superintendent general, Thunderwater also indicated his support for the hereditary chiefs and complained that his supporters in these communities were threatened with loss of band membership and privileges. Using the Mohawk name given to him by Council of the Tribes supporters at Akwesasne, he signed his communications to the superintendent general as "Chief Thunderwater–Tehotiokwawakon."[2]

Thunderwater's activities at Akwesasne also drew attention from an unusual quarter—Arthur C. Parker. Parker, of course, was a Seneca, a noted authority on American Indian history and culture, a reformer on behalf of Indian people, and a founding member of the Society of American Indians (SAI). In April 1915 Parker wrote to Deputy Superintendent General Scott to inquire about Thunderwater and his activities, doing so in his official capacity as secretary-treasurer of the SAI and on SAI letterhead. He stated that the SAI had received "extremely uncomplimentary reports regarding this man." Also, Parker emphasized that the SAI was "inclined to believe that his work was that of an imposter," but offered no further evidence or details to support his claim. He inquired if Scott was aware of Thunderwater's activities at St. Regis and if the Indian Department had acknowledged or supported him in any way. He added that he was taking the matter up with the Department of Indian Affairs in Washington, D.C., as well, in order to "protect the St. Regis Indians on the United States side." Scott responded immediately to Parker, indicating that they were well aware of Thunderwater's activities at St. Regis and that Thunderwater had written to the department on a number of matters. "We ignore him altogether, not even answering his letters," Scott noted. Parker replied that he had "advised the Indians on the United States side of the [St. Regis] reservation that [Thunderwater] is not a representative of the Canadian Government." The exchange with Parker heightened Scott's concern over Thunderwater, and he initiated an official inquiry into his identity and the possibility of barring him from Canadian soil.[3]

Scott's concern with Thunderwater deepened with more detailed and direct communications echoing the "extremely uncomplimentary reports" noted by Parker. One Thunderwater opponent from Akwesasne wrote to the Indian Department in June 1915, describing the Council of the Tribes as "distinctly revolutionary" and expressing concern that Thunderwater supporters would take over the band council in the upcoming July elections. He was so alarmed that he asked Scott if the department could bar Thunderwater supporters from holding elected office. At this same time the Indian agent at St. Regis wrote to department secretary McLean with a similar worry and stated that he anticipated trouble from Thunderwater at the upcoming band council elections. In response, Scott dispatched a special department inspector to the reserve to conduct the July elections. No doubt, he was disappointed with the result. In reporting to Scott on the elections, the inspector, referring to the arrangement made in 1906, wrote, "Many were opposed to a poll of any kind; they led one another into the belief that, according to some alleged understanding the St. Regis band had with the Department some years ago, the selection of chiefs were to be made according to clans." The inspector also noted that he told the members of the Council of the Tribes "not to spend their time and substance on the machinations of the agents of one Thunder-water."[4]

Scott received similar reports from Tyendinaga. In mid-September 1915 T. Irvine Brant, one of the elected band councillors, penned an anxious and secretive letter to the deputy superintendent general about Thunderwater, one of his deputies, and the upcoming Council of the Tribes convention. To affirm his own sympathies and reliability, Brant informed Scott that he was well known to J. D. McLean, the Indian Department secretary, and emphasizing the sensitive nature of his communication, stated that the local Indian agent and head of the local band council suggested he write to the deputy superintendent general "in a small detective like way." He added that as an extra precaution, he had posted his letter from Marysville, just off the northern border of the Tyendinaga reserve, rather than Deseronto, where he feared Thunderwater supporters might have discovered his actions. Brant informed Scott that Thomas Walter Martin, Thunderwater's "Supreme Secretary," had been living on the reserve for several months and, even though Martin was known to have been from Grand River, claimed that he "hail[ed] from somewhere no one knows where." Noting Thunderwater's popularity and the level of local interest in the Council of the Tribes, he indicated that "some 600 people" had become members and that Thunderwater and Martin had collected $900 from the "poor people" with "no fair exchange for their money except [their membership] certificates." Brant asked, "Is this not taking money under false pretenses?" According to him, Martin stated that Thunderwater was working to "dispense with the [band] councillors and the [Indian] agent and the Government," to enforce "old treaties," and to "retake" Tyendinaga land surrendered in the past. Brant also stated that Thunderwater claimed he was working at Tyendinaga and elsewhere under Canadian and U.S. government authority and indicated that he had also written to Edgar Meritt, the assistant commissioner of Indian Affairs in the United States, to express his concerns about Thunderwater's aims and activities. "What I wish to know is this," he inquired. "Does the Dominion government permit a foreigner—an American—to carry on such an affair as that or is it just an excuse that he may collect the poor people's money for his own benefit?" Concluding his letter to Scott, Brant proposed a course of action that he had formulated with the local Indian agent: "We suggest that you send a detective to wait on Martin and Chief Thunder with a pair of bracelets for each."[5]

The reply to Brant's letter came from the Indian Department secretary. "The person styling himself as Chief Thunderwater," J. D. McLean wrote, "has no status in Canada with respect to Indian matters, has no connection with nor is he recognized by the Government of Canada." He indicated that arresting Thunderwater, as Brant had proposed, was not possible, but expressed hope that "the Indians would not be foolish enough to part with their money on the representations that this man has been making. . . . So far as the Department can see, there is no one likely to be benefitted by his efforts but himself."[6]

Following the Council of the Tribes convention in Tyendinaga in late September, Brant's suggestion to apprehend Thunderwater with a "pair of bracelets" was offered by another of his local opponents, Solomon Loft, a former band councillor. McLean replied that, with the information at hand, the department could not take such measures against Thunderwater, but added, "if at any time it can be shown that he has rendered himself liable to prosecution, action will be taken." He encouraged Loft in his opposition to Thunderwater and responded to another apparent recommendation he made: "I am pleased to know that the Chiefs [band councillors] and other influential members of the band have declined to associate themselves in any way with this man's activities and I am sure that their attitude will have a very beneficial effect among the members of the band. . . . I have noted your suggestion that it might be well to advise the agents of other bands to be on the look out for this man's appearance on their reserves and will keep it in mind."[7]

While the Indian Department refused to officially acknowledge Thunderwater by ignoring his communications, its mounting concern took it to some unusual lengths. Following the September 1915 convention at Tyendinaga, Scott dispatched C. C. Parker, his inspector of Indian agencies, there to investigate Thunderwater, who had remained on the reserve. The plan devised by Parker was to invite Thunderwater to meet with the local Indian agent while he secreted himself in an adjoining room. His expectation was that Thunderwater would make incriminating statements to the agent, and then he would emerge from hiding and arrest the chief on the spot. The meeting took place as planned in early October 1915, but not with the hoped-for result. As Parker reported to Scott, "There was nothing in what he said that could be considered slanderous or threatening. . . . After having listened to him for some time and being satisfied that he was not going to lay himself open to a breach of the law, I walked into the [Indian agent's] office and had a short talk with him myself. I tried to make him understand that he had no standing as far as our Department was concerned and that he should be careful not to incite or encourage Canadian Indians to act rashly nor over-step the authority of our agents." Parker also reported to Ottawa that while he did not attend any of the meetings Thunderwater held after the convention, from what he could learn there was little to which he found objection. "He preaches temperance, better farming by Indians, and compulsory school attendance," he wrote. Despite this, Parker closed his report to Scott with this warning and recommendation:

> It might be worthy of mention that those whom Thunderwater has obtained
> as his followers are the class of Indians who are always seeking trouble and

FIGURE 10. Chief Thunderwater and Council of the Tribes members at Tyendinaga in October 1917. Thunderwater is seated in the second row, fourth from the left, and appears to be wearing a beaded cap presented to him at the Council of the Tribes rally in Kahnawake in September 1916. Solomon J. Brant, seated on Thunderwater's left, and Andrew S[c]ero, seated at the left end of the second row, were leaders in the Tyendinaga circle of the Council of the Tribes.
Image courtesy of Chief R. Donald Maracle, Tyendinaga Mohawk Council,
Tyendinaga Mohawk Territory, Ontario.

seldom satisfied; at the same time not prosperous and poor farmers . . . The chief trouble that will be realized from [the Council of the Tribes] is that it is dividing the bands and creating two factions who will not work in sympathy and we may yet be compelled to deal with this matter. I submit, as a recommendation, that an amendment to the Indian Act be prepared which would cover such gatherings on Indian reserves and the right of an outsider organizing and holding such meetings.

This was extraordinary. In response to the growing Thunderwater movement and its concern about the political impact on Haudenosaunee communities, the Indian Department was considering a revision of the Indian Act that would limit the right of Native people to peacefully organize and protest (see figure 10).[8]

Over the course of the next year, ongoing events frequently reminded Scott and other Indian Department officials of the problems caused by Thunderwater and the Council of the Tribes at Tyendinaga. In June 1916 eighty-one members of the band petitioned the department to remove Thunderwater's deputy, Thomas Walter Martin, from the reserve. It declined to do so. Also at this time, Michael Claus, the grand councillor of the Tyendinaga circle, wrote to J. D. McLean to inform him that he had resigned from his position because he believed the Council of the Tribes to be a fraud through which Thunderwater was attempting only "to get as much money out of the people as he can." In late July 1916, T. Irvine Brant wrote again to the Indian Department to express his concern about "the workings of one Chief Thunderwater and Society," saying, "I am resolved to either molest or torment the said chief to the best of my ability. Perhaps some are not aware of the fact that the majority of his members are the uneducated class and by his having great fluency of speech it makes them believe that he has supreme power."[9]

As with Arthur Parker a year before, the Indian Department's alarm over Thunderwater and the Council of the Tribes was no doubt heightened by the concern expressed by another well-known Haudenosaunee scholar, Tuscarora linguist and ethnologist J. N. B. Hewitt. In early May 1917 Hewitt wrote to the Office of Indian Affairs in Washington to inquire about Thunderwater, whom he referred to as "the alleged Indian who styles himself 'Chief Thunderwater.'" Hewitt sought information about Thunderwater's work among the Haudenosaunees in New York State and his claims to be able to assist them with various grievances involving the federal government. The reply Hewitt received came from the assistant commissioner of Indian Affairs, Edgar Meritt, who stated that Thunderwater was, indeed, known to them. He noted that Indian Affairs began receiving correspondence from him in 1915, but they broke off all communication after they became concerned that he might be committing mail fraud by raising membership subscriptions for the Council of the Tribes in the United States. Meritt indicated that Indian Affairs had looked into the matter with an eye toward possible criminal charges but found no evidence against Thunderwater and dropped plans to prosecute him. He closed his letter to Hewitt with the observation that Thunderwater was no longer active among the "New York Indians" and the suggestion that if his activities among the "Canadian Indians" violated the laws of Canada, then "the matter should be brought before the proper authorities." While there is no evidence that Hewitt contacted the Canadian Department of Indian Affairs directly, the department somehow obtained a copy of the assistant commissioner's reply to him and placed it in its growing file on Thunderwater and the Council of the Tribes.[10]

Following the developments at Tyendinaga, the Indian Department's concern increased with the growth of the Thunderwater movement in Kahnawake. In the late summer of 1916 J. M. Brosseau, the local Indian agent, informed his superiors in Ottawa that the "Thunderwater Association" on the reserve had elected "chiefs independent of the government," by which he meant the appointment of Peter Delisle and others as the officers of the local circle of the Council of the Tribes. Acknowledging the reports about Thunderwater and the directions he had received from the Indian Department, Brosseau wrote with some consternation about the response from the Kahnawake community:

> On June 13, last, the Dept. informed me that an American Indian named Chief Thunderwater has already caused much trouble among our Indians of Canada, and you ask[ed] to warn my Indians of Caughnawaga to be on their guard, which I did by transmitting to Chief Beauvais a copy of the letter in question. Instead of following the advice of the agent, *the chiefs have carried on propaganda in favour of the said Thunderwater*; and that individual continues to extort money from our Indians. . . . I am informed that about 200 [Council of the Tribes] certificates have already been sold here. . . . I have come to the conclusion that the sum of at least $400 has already been extorted out of the Indians of my reserve. . . . [O]ur Indians are preparing to receive at Caughnawaga the said Thunderwater on Sept. 3 and 4 next. I think it would be good policy to take energetic measures against this individual.[11]

At about this same time, the Indian agent at St. Regis, who had had his own experiences with Thunderwater and was familiar with his activities at Tyendinaga and Kanehsatake, warned the department about Thunderwater's planned visit to Kahnawake, stating that "this man should not be tolerated at all" and proposing that he be deported from Canada by the Immigration Department. Similarly, shortly before the Council of the Tribes convention in Kahnawake in September 1916, an official in the Hastings County Court in Belleville, Ontario, wrote to A. P. Sherwood, the chief commissioner of the Dominion police in Ottawa, about Chief "Underwater" following a recent visit he had made to Tyendinaga. Raising questions about both Thunderwater's intentions and political loyalties, the court officer wrote, "His advice and counsel was of a nature not in harmony with Loyalty to the Crown . . . [and] it would appear from the information I have received that he is endeavouring to get the Indians throughout Canada to co-operate in causing detrimental action to the Government of Canada. . . . It has been intimated to me that the funds he uses so lavishly are furnished from a German Source." It is important to note that there is no evidence anywhere in Indian Department files, Thunderwater's personal papers, or elsewhere that support for his activities came from any "German Source." The court officer also stated in his letter to Sherwood that Thunderwater had addressed his supporters at Tyendinaga "in their own language," though this is unlikely as there is no evidence that he spoke Mohawk or any other Native language. The county court official advised the chief commissioner to send "someone who understands the Indian language to watch this man at the Caughnawaga Convention . . . and satisfy yourself whether he is a safe man to be at large, or not." His concern raised, Chief Commissioner Sherwood forwarded the court official's letter to Duncan Campbell Scott with his own added note, which read, "Forwarded for your information. Perhaps you could arrange with the Indian Agent [at Kahnawake] to get a line on this man's doings with a view to his receiving some further attention if necessary."[12]

A month later, in October 1916, the Council of the Tribes held its fourth major convention at Grand River, and Scott received a detailed report on Thunderwater's activities and statements from Indian Department inspector R. H. Abraham. What he read must have concerned him. Thunderwater had moved from a plan for Indian uplift and self-help to a position that was openly critical of federal Indian policy and defiant of the Department of Indian Affairs. According to Abraham's report to Scott, in his address to his Grand River supporters, Thunderwater charged that they were "treated as children by the Indian [Department], warned them not to trust the white man," and claimed that the purpose of the Indian Act "was to push the Indians back into slavery." Stating that they should "keep their own councils" and "transact their own business," he advocated strongly for Six Nations autonomy and self-government and stated his commitment to assisting the Haudenosaunees in "greatly securing their rights."[13]

Scott soon initiated a more direct response to Thunderwater and "Thunderwaterism." In the late fall of 1916 he requested that the superintendent of immigration look into the possibility of deporting Thunderwater or barring him from Canadian soil. In December the superintendent reported to Scott that unless there was evidence that Thunderwater was advocating the overthrow of the government of Great Britain or Canada, there were no grounds for deporting him or excluding him from entering the country. A month later, in January 1917,

Scott wrote to the under secretary of state to say that while the objectives of the Council of the Tribes seemed innocent enough, its true motive was "to make difficulties for this Department and its agents and to stir up among the Indians distrust of the Department and opposition to the special laws existing for Indians." He continued, "I have been seriously considering the possibility of refusing Thunderwater admission to Canada." By this time Scott had also learned of Thunderwater's plans to incorporate the Council of the Tribes in Canada, and he attempted to head off this effort. As he stated to the under secretary, "I understand that this society is to apply for incorporation this year, but I do not think it is in the best interests of good administration to allow its incorporation. I thought it well to bring this matter to your attention."[14]

Scott's concern was no doubt heightened by Thunderwater's stance on Canada's and Britain's efforts in the First World War, a position he had been aware of since at least the previous October, when Thunderwater had been invited to speak at Grand River. According to Inspector Abraham's report of those remarks, Thunderwater had "maintained that Great Britain was 'fighting in Europe for gold'" and had "expressed sorrow that there were Indians in this fight." In the early months of 1917 Scott was confronted by the problem in a more serious way when Thunderwater-supported resistance threatened to obstruct the government's plans to build an airfield on the Tyendinaga reserve. C. C. Parker, inspector of Indian agencies, was assigned by the department to implement the plan, which was supported by the Tyendinaga band council. According to Parker, the principal opponents of the airfield plan were the "Thunderwater element," who were opposed to the forced leasing of individual landholdings and against any aid to the war effort. He added that with the development of the Council of the Tribes in the community over the previous two years, the Indian Department was underestimating the number of Thunderwater supporters. In the end, their resistance caused only a minor delay in the development of the airfield, which was completed by the summer of 1917. Nevertheless, the events added to Scott's concern with Thunderwater and the Council of the Tribes.[15]

These circumstances may explain Scott's refusal to meet with Thunderwater and his supporters when they visited his office in Ottawa in late October 1917 to advise him about the purpose of the Council of the Tribes and discuss their plans for incorporation. Three days after the attempted meeting, Charles A. Cooke, a Mohawk and a clerk and interpreter in the Indian Department, wrote to Scott to share his perspective on Thunderwater, his supporters, and the Council of the Tribes. Cooke, who was born "Thawennensere" in Kanehsatake in 1870, had family ties to Akwesasne and Grand River, spent part of his boyhood at Wahta (Gibson) and was one of the first and longest-serving Indigenous employees in the Canadian civil service. He was also a Haudenosaunee scholar in the mold of Arthur C. Parker and J. N. B. Hewitt. Cooke began his memorandum to Scott by referring to Thunderwater's followers at Kahnawake, Akwesasne, and Kanehsatake. "It is safe to say," he stated confidently, "that about 75% of these Indians are more or less actively identified with the movement known as the Council of the Tribes." He also pointed out, "It includes women, for they have a special work in the organization." Cooke continued, outlining the ultimate goal of Thunderwater, the council, and its supporters, and the roots of this development in the political conditions in Haudenosaunee communities in the late nineteenth and early twentieth centuries:

> *The principal aim of the organization common among these Indians is to create a spirit of Indian Nationalism, "Indian First."* They uphold that an Indian was always to continue to retain his identity as an Indian in so far as it affects his aboriginal rights, and that he never intended to assimilate the ways and customs of the white man or to become a subject of his law. . . . It is no wonder that a movement with such a racial slogan, among illiterate people living under false prejudices against white people, found many disciples. The minds of these people were in an exceptionally congenial mood to receive any such teaching. [From] about 1900 at St. Regis several of the chiefs, smarting under the ban of deposition, began a campaign against the Government for what they termed heightened interference with their rights and a cry was 'Life Chiefs for the Indians.' *This campaign spread to the other Iroquois Reserves and for some years after there was considerable correspondence with the Department on the subject. It subsided, however, almost to normal conditions excepting among the few, and the forerunner of Thunderwater found it to be a splendid field for the organization of such a society as the Council of the Tribes.*[16]

Cooke went on to suggest that Thunderwater and his "agents" took advantage of other local matters concerning the Haudenosaunees besides the dissatisfaction with the Indian Act system and the intent to return to traditional government. These included commercial duties imposed on the Haudenosaunees at the international border when entering the United States, Roman Catholic control of reservation day schools, the residence of non-Natives on reserves, and loss of reserve lands. He concluded his memo to Scott with the prediction that the Thunderwater movement would soon unravel, mainly as a result of his somewhat surprising view of the character of his fellow Haudenosaunees. "It is my candid opinion," Cooke wrote, "that . . . enthusiasm . . . will die of failure, for the Indian is not endowed with magnanimity of spirit to continue very long to give his ready cash to some cause which gives him no immediate, personal return. . . . [A]gents and local officers of the organization, who are principally men of aggressiveness, blinded by local prejudices, have gone beyond the bounds of reason in their efforts and are responsible for much of the disaffection existing today against the Government."[17]

When Scott refused to meet with Thunderwater and his followers in October 1917, they took their story to the *Ottawa Citizen*. They also registered a protest at the office of Arthur Meighen, the interior minister and superintendent general of Indian Affairs. Meighen knew little about these matters, and his office requested that Scott provide some explanation, which he did. In his memorandum to the minister, Scott reviewed his objections to Thunderwater and the Council of the Tribes, characterizing him and the organization as unprogressive and antagonistic toward the government and "loyal" Indians and noting the Indian Department's tactic of ignoring Thunderwater so as not to bolster his standing or the organization in any way.[18]

Six months later, in April 1918, Edward Guss Porter, the MP for the Hastings West district, introduced Bill 30, "An Act to Incorporate the Council of the Indian Tribes of Canada," in the House of Commons, and Scott and the Indian Department worked quickly to block the effort. Porter was from Belleville, Ontario, near the Tyendinaga reserve and appears to have been a strong supporter of efforts by Native people to exercise their political rights. At the same time that he presented Bill 30 for its first reading, department officials in Ottawa instructed their agents on Haudenosaunee reserves to organize formal petitions from Thunderwater opponents to protest incorporation of the council. In due course, it received petitions from Tyendinaga and Akwesasne. In their appeal to the Indian Department, the 140 petitioners from Akwesasne stated, "We most heartily disapprove of this society and we are adverse to its incorporation, as it will only tend to create division and be a detriment to our best interests." These efforts to thwart incorporation of the Council of the Tribes drew an immediate response from Thunderwater supporters. In Kahnawake they met and petitioned the government, stating, "We the undersigned members of the Iroquois Nation of the Mohawk Tribe of Indians, located on the Caughnawaga Reservation, do hereby respectively and vigorously protest against the action of the Indian

Department at Ottawa in endeavouring to obstruct passage of the Bill to incorporate 'Council of the Tribes' of Canada, of which we are members. . . . [We] beg that the Government will not deny the right of Indians to help themselves, which the passage of the Bill will confer."[19]

It is clear that a major concern within the Indian Department about incorporation of the Council of the Tribes was that it had become a major channel for continued Haudenosaunee claims of political autonomy and demands to reestablish traditional government. From its point of view, incorporation of the council would only serve to fortify these positions. In a memorandum to Minister Meighen ten days after the first reading of Bill 30, Scott summarized the activities of Thunderwater since 1914, the Indian Department's growing concern with the Council of the Tribes, and the department's efforts to defuse the movement. "The Indians flocked to hear him [at Akwesasne]," Scott wrote, "and that element of the Indians in particular that is unprogressive, shiftless and complaining readily joined the organization. . . . The same thing subsequently took place on the reserves at Oka, Caughnawaga, Tyendinaga and the Six Nations with the same results." He continued,

> *The Indians have been led to believe that they will be able to repudiate the Government and take their affairs into their own hands.* They have been told that the Indian Agent, the representative of the Government, had no right to sit in their council and that it is their intention to oppose the immigration and customs laws and certain provisions of the Indian Act. . . . *Whatever the ostensible objects of this organization may be the real object or result of the organization among its members is to have them revert to former conditions as much as possible:* to look forward to the recovery of their alleged lost privileges and rights rather than to take their places in civilized communities; *to conduct their own affairs in their own aboriginal way, absolutely independent of and in defiance of the Government.* . . . In view of the above facts, the Department would greatly regret the passing of [Bill 30].[20]

Scott's alarm and the supporting evidence he provided to the interior minister had the desired effect. Following the first reading of the bill, Edward Porter consulted with Meighen and Scott and became aware of their strong opposition to the incorporation effort. Nevertheless, he moved for a second reading of the bill, but then withdrew the motion when it became clear that he lacked sufficient support for it in the House of Commons. Porter's intention was to reintroduce the bill after the recently passed Military Voters Act of 1917 had begun to take effect. The Military Voters Act extended the voting franchise to Indians in the armed forces, and he reasoned that this might improve the prospects for passage of Bill 30. However, Porter did not follow through on this commitment, and the effort to incorporate the Council of the Tribes died.[21]

Despite this setback, "Thunderwaterism" persisted, and Haudenosaunee activists and council supporters pressed forward with efforts to reestablish traditional councils and advocate for self-government. One result, in July 1918, was the effort by "Thunderwaters" at Akwesasne to take over the band council, affirm their hereditary chiefs, and announce their commitment to "renew and defend old traditions and rights." Another was the grand council at Akwesasne in late September of that year, attended by representatives and Thunderwater supporters from a number of Haudenosaunee communities and at which the supporters of traditional government at Akwesasne formally installed twenty-four hereditary chiefs. That council ended with a commitment to deal with the Canadian government "as one sovereign power to another." In Kahnawake, Thunderwater supporters continued to dominate the band council, and their leader, Peter Delisle, was tried for sedition. At Tyendinaga, as at Akwesasne, in the fall of 1918 Thunderwater activists installed hereditary chiefs, formed a new council, and announced that they had "accepted the ceremonies of the Con-federation of the Five Nations formed by De-ka-nah-wi-deh." Through a series of protests and petitions the following year, they recommitted themselves to disrupting upcoming elections and abolishing the band council system. Nota-bly, it was during this period that the Confederacy Council officially certified Thunderwater as a member of the Six Nations. Scott and the Indian Department now prepared for a more direct and determined response to Thunderwater and the Council of the Tribes.

CHAPTER 6

DIRTY TRICKS AND THE END OF THE THUNDERWATER MOVEMENT

*I am enclosing herewith two communications from Mrs. Mary Ann George
and her son Mitchell Benedict.... I would like very much, if at all possible,
to get a hold upon Thunderwater, and if I can get a more comprehensive
statement from this woman and boy, I propose to submit them through the
Commissioner of the Dominion Police to the Chief of Police in Cleveland.*
—Duncan Campbell Scott, deputy superintendent general of Indian Affairs,
writing to Gordon J. Smith, Indian superintendent, Brantford,
Ontario (January 15, 1919)

———————————

*Where he was born, I don't know, but I think he should be sent back
to his home in Africa, where all the Negroes belong.*
—William Cree of Elyria, Ohio, writing to Indian Department secretary
J. D. McLean (February 8, 1919)

———————————

*You will perhaps recall the trouble that this Department had with
an Indian of Cleveland, Ohio, styling himself 'Chief Thunderwater,'
and the efforts made a couple of years ago to have him denied entry
to Canada.... Since that time Thunderwater has continued his
agitation among the Indian of Ontario and Quebec.... I am most
anxious that Thunderwater should be refused entry to Canada.*
—Duncan Campbell Scott writing to W. D. Scott, superintendent
of immigration (February 14, 1919)

After successfully thwarting the attempt to incorporate the Council of the Tribes, the Department of Indian Affairs responded to the continued vibrancy of Thunderwaterism and the efforts to restore traditional government and reclaim political autonomy by conducting a "dirty tricks" campaign against Thunderwater designed to undermine his credibility and break the Thunderwater movement once and for all. Duncan Campbell Scott, the deputy superintendent general of Indian Affairs, was the principal architect of this campaign.

One part of the effort by Scott and the Indian Department to discredit Thunderwater involved an accusation of child abuse. The case involved a teenage boy from the Canadian side of the St. Regis reserve by the name of Mitchell Benedict, whom Thunderwater had adopted in 1916 and had been raising at his home in Cleveland. The boy, twelve years old at the time, had been given up for adoption by his mother, Mary Ann (Benedict) George, who at the time was a single parent living in St. Catharines, Ontario, about fifteen miles west of the international border at Niagara Falls. According to the signed and witnessed agreement between Thunderwater and the mother in late September 1916, George consented to the adoption because she was "unable to maintain, support, and educate" her son "in a proper and suitable manner." In exchange for Thunderwater's promises of care and the payment of one dollar, she granted him custody and control of her son until he married or reached the age of twenty-one. For his part, Thunderwater agreed that until that time he would "maintain, board, lodge, clothe, and educate" the child in "a manner suitable to [his] station" and "in the same manner as if the said Mitchell Benedict were his own lawful child." The adoption agreement also stipulated that George would not interfere with Thunderwater's custody, control, or care of the boy. According to testimony Thunderwater offered when the matter of the adoption arose in his libel case in Louisville ten years later, the boy had been severely neglected by George, and his health was poor, a condition also testified to by a number of Thunderwater's Cleveland neighbors who were familiar with the boy at the time of the adoption.[1]

In late 1918 George reconsidered her decision and attempted to regain custody of her son. On Thunderwater's invitation, George, along with her daughter, Mary, visited Mitchell at his home in Cleveland in late December of that year. After a stay of several days at Thunderwater's home, they returned to Ontario, taking Mitchell with them without Thunderwater's knowledge or consent. Angered, Thunderwater accused the mother and daughter of kidnapping and sought the boy's return, going so far as to threaten legal action and even to come to Canada and take him back by force if necessary. Subsequently, George and her daughter countered that Thunderwater had been mistreating young Mitchell and that they had taken him away to save him from further harm.[2]

Thunderwater expressed his concerns and warnings to Mary Ann and Mary George through a letter to her second husband, Gilbert George, shortly after they had left Cleveland with Mitchell and returned to Canada. Complicating matters, Gilbert George was a member of the Council of the Tribes. Writing to him in early January 1919 and addressing him as his "dear fraternal brother," Thunderwater recounted the visit of George's wife and stepdaughter to Cleveland two weeks earlier and his version of what had taken place. He stated that Mary Ann and Mary had come to his home on the pretense of a visit, but that their real objective was to take custody of Mitchell. He indicated Mary George had gone so far as to indicate that she wanted to remain in Cleveland and work at the Cleveland Hotel, but that it was only a ruse to disguise their plan and wait for an opportune time to take his adopted son away. Thunderwater expressed particular disdain for Mary George, the stepdaughter, stating that she was "very deceitful and untruthful. . . . Mary must never again pass through my door." Thunderwater demanded that Mary Ann return his adopted son immediately, noting that if she did not, the boy would miss important school examinations at home in Cleveland. He stated that before the boy came under his care, he stole, "drank whiskey, smoked and did many other things that [were] astonishing for a little boy of his age" and stressed that "the boy has a fine record here and he must continue along these lines." Citing Canadian criminal statutes, he suggested that George hire an attorney for his wife if she did not return the boy, and he urged him to inform her "in very strong language as to the mistake she has been making." Citing the possibility of prison time for his wife if convicted, Thunderwater emphasized that he was prepared to cause her and her daughter "much sorrow." He closed his letter to Gilbert George stating, "I will push the matter to the limit of the law. . . . This means I will have your wife extradited from Canada and returned [to Cleveland] for trial."[3]

Following Thunderwater's threat of legal action, Mary Ann George contacted the Department of Indian Affairs claiming that Thunderwater had mistreated her son and seeking its assistance. Writing from St. Catharines on January 11, 1919, she stated that she was seeking the department's help in keeping custody of her son because Thunderwater had broken his promises. "He is abusing the child," she wrote, "and I don't want no body to buse this child." She stated that during the Christmas-season visit, Thunderwater "punched her son in the face" and choked him "till he was all most blue." She claimed that after these incidents, she went to the "humaine society" in Cleveland, and an official there encouraged her to take her son away and return to Canada. Since George appears to have been illiterate and her communication does not bear her signature or mark, it is not clear who authored the letter she sent to the Indian Department.[4]

The Indian Department received a similar communication from Mitchell Benedict himself on January 11, and it was even more inflammatory. "I thought I would write you few drops today," Benedict began his signed letter, "telling you the curelty [*sic*] I got at Chief Thunderwater's home. . . . Chief treaded [*sic*] me good for about 6 months than he started to whip me . . . [and] he would lock me in the cellar and made me sleep there over night . . . having nothing to eat nor drink. . . . He would choke and punch me with his bar fist," the letter went on in a scrawling hand, "and one day, . . . he grabbed me and rubbed his private up against me and said why don't you say ouch like the girls does. . . . He call me a son of a bich and son of a hoer and he says if I ever disobey him again he would kill me. . . . He says that he has killed three men and that I'll be the fourth one to be dead." Benedict wrote that Thunderwater had stripped and whipped him on a regular basis and that as a result he had "big scars" and "god knows how many little ones." He concluded his letter to the Indian Department by reiterating his mother's claim that she had visited the "humaine society" in Cleveland and had been advised by officials to bring him back to Ontario.[5]

Oddly, there is a third letter in Indian Department files accusing Thunderwater of child abuse, seemingly from Benedict as well, and also dated January 11, 1919. Unsigned and written in a much neater and more legible hand, this letter does not appear to have been written by Benedict himself, though it could have been dictated by him. In the letter many of the claims stated in Benedict's signed letter are repeated and new accusations are made. "I was helping him fit gas pipes," the letter states, "and the pipe made a tight fit and he said to me when you have a wife do you think your cock will fit that tight in her." Later in the four-page letter another threat of violence was introduced: "He once said that he is going to disappear and will take me along with him and no one will ever know where I will be. . . . I am afraid of that man and don't want ever to go into his house again." Duncan Campbell Scott had sought to get a grip on Thunderwater and now, with the letters from Mary and George and her son in hand, he thought he had his man.[6]

From the beginning, Scott appears to have had concerns about the veracity of mother's and boy's accusations against Thunderwater, so he moved quickly.

In mid-January 1919, within days of receiving the letters from Mary Ann George and her son, he directed Gordon J. Smith, the Indian superintendent at Brantford, to travel to St. Catharines and obtain official statements from them. "I would like very much to get some hold on Thunderwater," he wrote, "and if I can get a more comprehensive statement from this woman and the boy, I propose to submit them, through the Commissioner of the Dominion Police, to the Chief of Police of Cleveland." He continued, "It is likely that the boy's story will weaken under examination and I wish you would take the earliest opportunity of going to St. Catherines and interviewing both mother and son. You should obtain from them a signed statement, giving such detail as you think advisable. . . . I do not think it necessary to say anything further by way of instructions," Scott added, "as I know you will appreciate the nature of the information that I wish to obtain." Smith made the trip to St. Catharines within the week and obtained depositions from Mary Ann George, her son, and also her daughter, Mary.[7]

Seeking "more comprehensive" and detailed statements against Thunderwater, Scott must have been disappointed with the results. In her statement to Smith, Mary Ann George testified to the circumstances of the Christmas visit to Thunderwater's home and Thunderwater's physical treatment of her son, but this was described in less extreme and more cursory form than her original letter to the Indian Department. Her sworn statement made no reference to a visit with officials at the humane society in Cleveland or their advice to take the boy from Thunderwater's home and return with him to Canada. The sworn statement from Mitchell Benedict included nearly all the allegations made in his original letter, but nothing more. His deposition, too, left out any mention of the visit to and advice of the humane society officials in Cleveland. The sworn statement from Mary George was also relatively brief, but it did include some graphic details.

> I was present with my mother Mary Ann George when Chief Thunderwater caught my brother by the throat and choked him and punched him in the face. I saw no reason for this treatment. I have seen Thunderwater ill treat my brother about four times. I protested and Thunderwater said neither I nor my mother has anything to do with the boy, that he could do so as he wanted to and could kill him if he wished. I heard him call the boy a son of a bitch and a bastard. He is always swearing and all of that. . . . On the Sunday after Christmas he took the boy upstairs [and] choked him and punched him in the face. . . . On New Year's Eve I heard him say to [my brother], 'If you ever make me mad I will whip you till the blood runs out

of your body and put some salt on it and make you feel it.' I also heard him tell the boy he would disappear someday.[8]

When Thunderwater learned of the accusations, he denied the charges against him and obtained the notarized testimony of two neighbors in Cleveland stating that he had always taken good care of the boy and provided him with proper schooling. One of those neighbors, Minnie Eaton, stated that in her personal experience Thunderwater had always properly fed, clothed, and educated young Mitchell, treated him with kindness, and had never physically mistreated him. She added that Thunderwater had a reputation within his Cleveland community of being a courteous and considerate neighbor.[9]

Even though Scott had doubts about the reliability of the stories of the mother, daughter, and adopted son, with the accusation in hand he returned to his effort to have Thunderwater barred from Canadian soil. In mid-February 1919 he wrote to the superintendent of immigration, reminding him of their earlier communications about Thunderwater and informing him about the case he now had against him. Scott stated:

> You will perhaps recall the trouble that this Department had with an Indian of Cleveland, Ohio, styling himself 'Chief Thunderwater' and the efforts made a couple of years ago to have him denied entry to Canada. We were unsuccessful owing to the absence of statutory grounds. Since that time Thunderwater has continued his agitation amongst the Indians of Ontario and Quebec in different places and at different times. . . . Recently, I received a complaint from a young St. Regis boy . . . who without the knowledge or consent of this Department was adopted by Thunderwater and taken by him to his home in Cleveland. I am most anxious that Thunderwater should be refused entry to Canada, if such action can be at all justified.[10]

The superintendent answered Scott a short time later, but with a disappointing reply. "I should be delighted," he wrote, "if we had some good legal ground for stopping Chief Thunderwater on the Boundary, but I am afraid such ground has not yet been discovered. . . . If [he] were not a citizen of the United States we could deal with him or if he had been convicted of a crime involving moral turpitude we could shut him out . . . but . . . so far as I can see he . . . has not been convicted of any criminal offense." He added that the best he could do at this time was to inconvenience Thunderwater when he entered Canada. "I suppose he enters at Niagara Falls, Bridgeburg or Windsor," the superintendent wrote, "and I am writing to our Inspectors and asking them to give him a thorough overhauling every time he applies for entry to Canada and it may be that such stiff examination will discourage him in his attempts to visit this country. . . . If we intercept him on the Boundary, I will let you know."[11]

It is not clear why, in his communication with the superintendent of immigration, Scott did not share the sworn depositions of Mary Ann George, Mary George, and Mitchell Benedict or detail the behavior of Thunderwater alleged in their letters to the Indian Department. Also unclear is why he did not contact the chief of police in Cleveland with the allegations made against Thunderwater, as he had initially planned to do, or why he did not seek some verification of the charges against Thunderwater by contacting the humane society officials in Cleveland with whom George had supposedly consulted before returning to Canada. If he had undertaken an independent investigation and corroborated the charges against Thunderwater, Scott might have prompted his arrest and conviction, and there would have then been grounds for barring him from Canadian soil. Several years later, when Thunderwater was embroiled in his libel case in Louisville, Kentucky, Scott went to great lengths in his eagerness to work with local authorities to raise questions about Thunderwater's character and credibility. It is not clear why he did not do so in this instance.

Perhaps, as Scott had feared, the allegations made by Mitchell Benedict, his mother, and his sister against Thunderwater did not hold up under close examination. When the charges of child abuse arose again a decade later in his libel case in Louisville, Thunderwater produced numerous witnesses testifying to the good care and treatment he had provided to his adopted son. They included lodgers, neighbors, associates, and even Cleveland police officers. At the trial in the case, Thunderwater testified that during the stay at his home to visit Mitchell, his sister, Mary George, had engaged in "immoral conduct," and he had demanded that both she and her mother leave. He contended that the real reason behind the accusations of physical and sexual abuse was retaliation for having kicked them out of his home. As part of the libel case, Thunderwater's attorneys also obtained the testimony of a witness from Akwesasne who suggested that others had dictated Mitchell Benedict's story of the abuse he experienced at the hands of Thunderwater and that Benedict had perjured himself in his sworn deposition to Indian superintendent Smith in January 1919. Though Scott's efforts to indict Thunderwater as a child abuser and have him barred from Canadian soil fell short of his goal, the experience must have had an intimidating effect on Thunderwater, and the Indian Department may have used the allegations a year later as part of a smear campaign designed to bring down him and the Council of the Tribes.

Another part of Scott's effort to discredit Thunderwater and defuse the Thunderwater movement rested on a claim that he was an impostor, that he was, in fact, of African American and not American Indian ancestry. The possibility that Thunderwater was such an impostor came to the Indian Department's attention initially in 1914 with Arthur Parker's letter to Scott warning him about Thunderwater's activities at St. Regis. Their suspicion deepened with developments in the case concerning the accusations of child abuse against Thunderwater. When Scott and others in the Indian Department sought defamatory evidence against Thunderwater, they contacted and subsequently received a letter from a "William Cree" of Elyria, Ohio. Also known as "Chief Cree," William Cree was in the same business as Thunderwater—selling "Indian" herbs and medicines. Among other things, he also sold "Indian curios," acted as an agent for Indian entertainers and beadworkers, and was a professional wrestler. Given this, and that Elyria was just thirty miles west of Cleveland, it is not surprising that Cree and Thunderwater had encountered each other. In 1918 Thunderwater initiated a plan to supply books and magazines to libraries on Indian reservations in the United States. As part of this effort, he enlisted Cree to assist in soliciting reading materials from the public. In an article on Thunderwater's initiative, the *Evening Telegram* of Elyria encouraged its readers to support Cree's effort: "William F. Cree . . . has been commissioned by Chief Thunderwater . . . Tehotiokwawakon . . . to solicit and collect books, magazines or other literature to be sent to Cleveland and thence to reservation libraries such as are decided on by the Oghema. . . . Drop a card to Mr. Cree if you have anything in the garret that would tickle or enlighten an Indian." With a mocking and heartless note, the *Telegram* added, "We have most of their lands and it is no more than right that they should have some of our literature."[12]

In February 1919 Cree wrote to Indian Department secretary J. D. McLean and suggested in a short but disparaging letter that Thunderwater was really a man named "Palmer" and accused him of using the money he raised to support the Council of the Tribes for his personal purposes. He also suggested, in brief and cryptic words, that Thunderwater's book collection drive was a scam. He did not explain how Thunderwater might have personally benefited from a collection drive to send books to Indian reservations. But strangely, Cree did not offer any information about his involvement with Thunderwater's plan, details that would have lent credibility to his claims. Cree stated that he did not know where

Thunderwater was born, but closed his communication to McLean by stating, "I think he should be sent back to his home in Africa where all the Negroes belong." Cree soon followed up with a second letter to McLean in which he referenced the accusations of child abuse against Thunderwater and Thunderwater's efforts to retrieve his adopted son. "Now this *coon* wants to take him back," he wrote, "but I hope the Canadian Government will not stand by to see a little boy misused."[13]

If Thunderwater was black and not Indian, it would, of course, be damning evidence against him and the Council of the Tribes. Thunderwater held no formal organizational office prior to the establishment of the Council of the Tribes, nor did he occupy any position of traditional authority recognized by his supporters in Haudenosaunee communities. To be sure, his unconventional background as an entertainer and entrepreneur, his experience as a political activist, and his apparent oratorical skills were important ingredients in his popularity and influence. However, an essential element of Thunderwater's legitimacy as a leader and spokesman was his Native background, and his Sauk and Seneca ancestry in particular. This was crucial not only to his supporters, but also to the public at large, especially the newspaper press, which he used so effectively to promote himself and his causes. To be exposed as a fraud would undermine his credibility and confirm the allegations of his opponents and Indian Department officials that he was nothing more than a self-interested con man. Moreover, to be exposed as a *black* man would have been especially damaging. In the early twentieth century, blacks, along with Asian immigrants, occupied the bottom rungs of the racial and ethnic hierarchy of Canadian society, and the dominant racial ideology held that blacks were inferior and incapable of assimilating. As a result, they faced significant prejudice and discrimination across the economic, social, and political spheres of Canadian life. To be revealed as a black man would not only discredit Thunderwater as an impostor, it would assign him to an outcast group, undermining his credibility with the Haudenosaunees, other Native groups, and the public at large.

The Indian Department's case against Thunderwater was informed by additional evidence, but that evidence also appears to have been used selectively to bolster the claim that Thunderwater was an impostor. In May 1919, several months after the Indian Department received the letters from William Cree asserting that Thunderwater was black, it received another communication from Ohio from "Alex Orchard," who identified himself as an "Osage Indian." Orchard directed his correspondence to J. D. McLean and stated that "upon investigation of this man's origin we find that he belongs to the Black race and his right name is Peter Sands. I am writing the Commissioner of Indian Affairs [in] Washington for information as regards this man who claims [Cleveland] to be the headquarters of [the Council of the Tribes] throughout the United States and Canada." Orchard did not indicate the other individuals he was working with, nor did he provide any evidence supporting the claim that Thunderwater was in reality a black man whose true name was "Peter Sands." He closed his letter with the assertion that Thunderwater was a "disgrace to the Indian Race" and that he and his associates were prepared to provide proof of their claim against him. If Indian Department officials were perplexed that one informant identified Thunderwater as a man whose real name was "Palmer" and another who claimed he was "Peter Sands," there is no evidence of it in their extensive file on Thunderwater.[14]

One of the associates referred to by Orchard may have been yet another informant who posted a letter to Secretary McLean just one day later. Identifying himself as "D. S. Edwards" and a resident of Cleveland, he claimed to be of Mohawk descent. Edwards implied that he had known Thunderwater for some time, but subsequent correspondence would indicate that he had been familiar with him for only about six months. He stated that he had "some good information in regards to the man who styles himself as 'Chief Thunderwater.'" Specifically, Edwards indicated that he was personally acquainted with a "colored" undertaker who buried Thunderwater's "foster mother," described her as "a negroe," and had personal knowledge of the "Old Ladies Colored [Home]" where she died. Edwards made additional incriminations. Referring to Thunderwater's claim to be the son of the daughter of Chief Keokuk, he stated that he had information from the Sac and Fox Agency in Oklahoma that "they know nothing of this man. . . . Living relatives of Keokuk in Oklahoma no [*sic*] him not." Even if true, this might not be surprising. As the son of one of Chief Keokuk's later wives and perhaps some forty to fifty years removed from any direct contact between them, it is entirely possible that Thunderwater would have been unknown to Keokuk descendants in Oklahoma. Edwards closed his letter emphasizing his availability to meet with Indian Department representatives if they would visit him in Ohio. Several days later McLean wrote to Edwards to acknowledge receipt of the letter and welcomed any additional information he could provide about Thunderwater, "as he has been a source of trouble in connection with some of our Indian bands in Canada."[15]

Edwards followed with a more detailed letter to McLean and even more specific and damaging claims. He shared his suspicion that Thunderwater misused the funds he collected from Council of the Tribes members and offered second-hand evidence that Thunderwater was not an Indian. "A Chippewa Indian that had lived with Thunderwater for some time," he wrote, "told me that an old Indian told him that Thunderwater was a negro. And I tell you that everybody that knows him says the same thing." He repeated the accusations that some had made about Thunderwater's abuse of his adopted son, reiterated his story that Thunderwater was not known to anyone in the Sac and Fox Tribe or any other Native group in Oklahoma, and claimed that he changed his name from "Peter Sands" to "Palmer" in 1904. Edwards added what he clearly expected would be more damning evidence of Thunderwater's true identity and character: "I also have proof that there are other negroes in the [Council of the Tribes] . . . [and] he also has several Jews in the organization." Edwards then introduced a wholly new and highly inflammatory accusation against Thunderwater—that he was the father of two illegitimate children by the wife of another adopted son. Regarding the first of those two children, Edwards stated, "The mother is white and the father ('the adopted son') is white, but the child looks just like Thunderwater and is brown in color." It is important to note that there is no evidence in Indian Department files, court records, vital statistics records, Thunderwater's personal papers, or in any other source that Thunderwater had another adopted son or that he had fathered any children other than his son Louis. Edwards closed his letter to Secretary McLean by stating he had written with the "hope it may benefit my people in some way sooner or later. Let this be a lesson to the Indians of Canada, they ought to know a faker when they see one."[16]

Six months later, in mid-November 1919, Edwards sent one last letter to the Indian Department. Astonishingly, he retracted all his previous accusations against Thunderwater and offered an apology:

> Not long ago there was an investigation made of Thunderwater by my wife and myself as to whom [Thunderwater] was. . . . We were a bit hasty in sending you the information collected in the above investigation, for we have found things to be a little different now. The undertaker who my wife got the information from has made a great mistake in taking Chief Thunderwater for another party by the name of P. Sands. . . . I have also found that the Council of the Tribes organization is chartered in the State of Ohio. I believe this man to be what he claims and a law abiding citizen, and a protector of Indians and Indian rights. He was elected peace chief of the Iroquois on the St. Regis reservation in 1915. . . . As I have seen my

mistake and the wrong I have done this man, I wish to apologize for all
that has been said against this man. Hoping you will accept my apology.

He received no official acknowledgment or reply from the Indian Department
to this final letter.[17]

Thunderwater was unaware of Scott's scheme to tar him as an impostor and
a black man, and so he had no opportunity to rebut the claims made by others
about his identity or ancestry. The charge that he was in reality a black man
named "Palmer" or "Peter Sands," along with the charge of child abuse, arose
again a decade later in his legal case in Louisville, Kentucky. In that case, which
is discussed in greater detail in the following chapter, Thunderwater marshaled
significant evidence supporting his claims about his identity, family history, and
ancestry. His lawyers also provided sworn testimony from a variety of witnesses,
including Indian associates and lodgers, white neighbors, and African American
residents of Cleveland that he was not an impostor named "Palmer" nor a black
man named "Peter Sands." In addition, at the trial and on the witness stand
Thunderwater offered an entirely plausible explanation for why some residents
of Cleveland knew him by the surname "Palmer."

As he compiled what he hoped would be a damaging case against Thunder-
water, Scott and the Indian Department were reminded, once again, of their
concerns about his activity and influence in Haudenosaunee communities.
Just two weeks before Edwards's final letter to the Indian Department in which
he retracted all his claims about Thunderwater as an impostor, Chief Solomon
Brant of Tyendinaga sent a "Notification" to the superintendent general of Indian
Affairs in the name of the "Six nations Mohawk Chiefs and the People situated at
Tyendinaga Bay of Quinte" to inform him that "Oghema Niagara, Chief Thun-
derwater had been appointed as an 'Embassador for this tribe of Indians.'"[18]

It is about this time, in 1920, that Postal suggests the Thunderwater movement
came to an abrupt and dramatic end with Thunderwater's exposure as a fraud
at a public meeting in Kahnawake. Based on interviews in 1963 with several
surviving Thunderwater supporters, she suggested that one of his detractors
accused him of being an impostor before a large gathering in the local town
hall. She identified the accuser as a "Caughnawagan" and a "lawyer" who at the
time was running for a position on the local band council. These details suggest
that the incident took place in February or March, around the time that council
elections were held, and that Thunderwater's accuser was Frank McDonald
Jacobs. Jacobs was a solicitor, the local postmaster, and, of course, the former

"mayor" of the Kahnawake band council who had been voted out of office in 1915 for his support of the Sisters of St. Anne. In the wake of events in 1915 he had become an ardent Thunderwater adversary and opponent of Peter Delisle and the other local leaders of the Council of the Tribes. According to Postal, the lawyer's accusations led to a confrontation between Thunderwater supporters and opponents that ended only after being broken up by local constables. She stated that soon after this incident Thunderwater disappeared from the reserve, and his cultural and political movement ended.[19]

There are a number of reasons to doubt Postal's story of the sudden unraveling of the Thunderwater movement. The files of the Department of Indian Affairs, which document Thunderwater's activities and the development of the Council of the Tribes in great detail, almost certainly would have contained information about a confrontation such as that described by Postal had it actually occurred. There is no evidence of this sort in Indian Department files. In addition, there is no evidence of such an incident in Thunderwater's personal papers or elsewhere. Further, according to testimony provided by Frank McDonald Jacobs in Thunderwater's legal case in Louisville in the late 1920s, an incident similar to the story related by Postal may have actually taken place at the time of the Council of the Tribes convention in Kahnawake in September 1916. During his court appearance in that trial, Jacobs recounted that he confronted Thunderwater when he arrived in Kahnawake for that convention. "His followers wanted to mob me," he testified. "I told them I would fight them one at a time, but they rejected the proposal." Perhaps Postal or those she interviewed were confused about the timing of the confrontation between Jacobs and Thunderwater. Further, in the summer of 1920, several months after the supposed confrontation in Kahnawake that brought his political movement to an end, Thunderwater received a strong endorsement from his backers in Tyendinaga. In July of that year Solomon J. Brant, hereditary chief of the Bear clan, and seventeen others, identifying themselves as "chiefs and firekeepers" of the "Six Nations Mohawk Band of Indians situated at Tyendinaga" once again formally appointed Thunderwater as their "true and lawful embassador." In a document stamped with the seal of the "Six Nations Council [at] 'Thayendinaga,'" they granted him "full power and authority to do and perform all and every act and thing whatsoever requisite and necessary to be done in and about the affairs and rights of this band of Indians."

Finally, Thunderwater did not disappear. Unfortunately, there is nothing in Thunderwater's personal papers or his correspondence with the Department of

Indian Affairs to indicate what he made of the department's dirty tricks campaign against him. Testimony in his legal case in Louisville suggests that he remained an active, though less influential, presence in Haudenosaunee communities until at least 1922. Moreover, he maintained positive, supportive relationships with many in those communities for another decade or more after the supposed dramatic end to the Thunderwater movement. If Thunderwater was credibly exposed as an impostor and a con man in 1920, it is doubtful that he would have been able to maintain such relationships after that time.[20]

A more likely scenario for the demise of the Thunderwater movement after 1920 is that Thunderwater's influence gradually waned and that "Thunderwaterism" was supplanted by new forms of Haudenosaunee political activism and revitalization. While it seems that the dirty tricks campaign conducted by Duncan Campbell Scott and the Indian Department did not lead to any dramatic confrontation such as that described by Postal, the circulation of the accusations against Thunderwater might still have eroded support for him in Haudenosaunee communities. On numerous occasions between 1915 and 1920, Scott and the Indian Department had used their agents in the field and their network of Thunderwater opponents in Haudenosaunee communities in the campaign to undermine Thunderwater and the Council of the Tribes. They did so again, eagerly, in Thunderwater's libel case in the late 1920s. There is every reason to think that they might have done so as part of their efforts to discredit him in 1919 and 1920.

Another important factor in the decline of Thunderwater's popularity and influence after 1920 may have been his inability to effect real political change. His supporters must have been keenly disappointed, given his promises and the extent to which he put himself forward as an agent of political transformation. While Thunderwater and the Council of the Tribes had become a vehicle for the expression of Haudenosaunee discontent with the Indian Act system and their aspirations for political autonomy and self-government, neither had produced tangible results. The Department of Indian Affairs had not recognized Thunderwater as a credible representative of Haudenosaunee activists. His political positions and rhetoric aside, he had not been successful in communicating or working with Indian Department officials in terms of addressing the local problems that had contributed to the development of the Thunderwater movement. His and his supporters' effort to incorporate the Council of the Tribes in Canada in order to exercise greater political influence in support of Haudenosaunee interests had failed. The restoration and official recognition of traditional government, one of the main political objectives of Haudenosaunee activists and a critical reason for their interest in Thunderwater and the Council, was no closer to reality in 1920 than it was in 1915.

With the disappointment of the Thunderwater movement, Haudenosaunee nationalism expressed itself in new forms and directions. In Kahnawake the withering of Thunderwater's influence did nothing to dampen the political energy that he had mobilized between 1915 and 1920. Peter Delisle and others who formed the core of the Thunderwater movement in the community continued to agitate for Haudenosaunee political autonomy and self-government, although they did so mainly through their positions within the band council system. Along with the hereditary chiefs, they protested the Compulsory Enfranchisement Act of 1920, and in 1922 they were among the many Haudenosaunees from across Quebec and Ontario who gathered at Grand River to express their opposition to forced enfranchisement, an action that contributed to eventual repeal of the act. In addition, the political momentum and connections generated by "Thunderwaterism" in Kahnawake gave rise to Longhouse activism, which was furthered by the community's 1923 visit of George Thomas, the Tadadaho of the Six Nations Confederacy Council at Onondaga. By the late 1920s, that activism led to formal establishment of the Longhouse on the reserve. In a related development, Kahnawake's traditional system of seven hereditary clan chiefs evolved to a system based on three clans (Turtle, Bear, and Wolf), which carried forward within the newly established Longhouse. At Akwesasne, Thunderwater supporters had been at the core of the hereditary chiefs movement and the opposition to band council elections between 1915 and 1920. After 1920, "Thunderwaters," as the St. Regis Indian agent referred to them, continued to press for official recognition of their hereditary chiefs and succeeded in thwarting the Indian Department's efforts to hold band council elections until 1928.[21]

Along with the Indian Department's dirty tricks campaign and loss of confidence in Thunderwater and the Council of the Tribes, the weakening of the Thunderwater movement in Kahnawake, Akwesasne, and elsewhere may also have been related to the emergence of Laura "Minnie" Cornelius Kellogg as a political leader and advocate of Haudenosaunee nationalism. After her break with the Society of American Indians in 1913, Kellogg had gone on to develop her ideas concerning sustainable economic, cultural, and political revitalization of reservation-based Indigenous people. Though her plan for developing economic self-sufficiency was modeled on non-Indigenous sources, she also drew on Native cultural and political traditions for her inspiration, orientation, and ultimate goal. Kellogg set her ideas out more fully and formally in *Our Democracy and the American Indian* in 1920, about the time that the Thunderwater movement began to wane. She soon became committed to applying her vision to her own people and, in coordination with particular sachems on the Six Nations Confederacy Council at Onondaga, advocated a plan for Haudenosaunee cultural and political revitalization based on the legal reclamation of millions of acres of land in New York taken illegally by the state and by land speculators in the late eighteenth and early nineteenth centuries. With the prospect of reclaimed land and its resources as a basis for economic self-sufficiency, Kellogg envisioned a sustainable spiritual and political revitalization of the Haudenosaunees and, ultimately, the revival of a fully reconstituted, fully functioning and autonomous Six Nations Confederacy. Kellogg drew support for her ideas primarily from her fellow Oneidas in Wisconsin and from Haudenosaunees in New York State; however, her vision resonated with Mohawks at Akwesasne, Kahnawake, and other Canadian reserves as well. It would have resonated particularly strongly with Thunderwater supporters. The political movement she had begun to lead, along with the local political and cultural developments, may have absorbed some of the stalled political energy that Thunderwater had generated and harnessed between 1915 and 1920.[22]

At Grand River, "Thunderwaterism" may have been absorbed or replaced by the pan-Indianism of F. O. Loft and the nascent "League of Indians of Canada" and the nationalism of Levi General (Deskaheh) and other militants on the Six Nations Confederacy Council. Loft, a Mohawk from Grand River and a World War I veteran, sought to capitalize on the developing pan-Indian consciousness of returning Native war veterans by organizing a national movement of Indigenous people intended to address common economic, political, and cultural concerns. Following a trajectory similar to the development of the Thunderwater movement, Loft initiated his effort in December 1918 (just months after the failed effort to incorporate the Council of the Tribes) with a grand council of Indians in Ontario on the Six Nations reserve. With a successful meeting and the formation of the League of Indians of Canada, Loft began to build participation and expand the reach of his organization by holding a series of conventions on reserves across Canada. There were also interesting personal parallels between Loft and Thunderwater: they were about the same age, both were colorful characters and charismatic speakers, and both were effective at self-promotion and using the press to generate interest and build their organizations. As deputy superintendent general of Indian Affairs, Duncan Campbell Scott viewed Loft the same as

Thunderwater: he considered Loft's pan-Indian and nationalist goals regressive, viewed his organization as an obstacle to the implementation of federal Indian policy and a ploy designed to defraud Native people, and concluded that the movement he led threatened the necessary assimilation of Native people into Euro-Canadian society. Scott's response, as with Thunderwater and the Council of the Tribes, was to defuse the League movement by using the resources and bureaucratic apparatus of the Indian Department to gather information, discredit Loft, and undermine his influence. Scott even threatened to enfranchise Loft—to make him a Canadian citizen—as a way to compromise his position and his work. Nevertheless, during the 1920s Loft had a good measure of success, though much more so among tribes in western than in eastern Canada or among his own people at Grand River. Eventually, events in Loft's personal life and later his own declining health, along with persistent pressure from Scott and the Indian Department, led to a loss of political momentum and the end of the League of the Indians of Canada.

Loft's accomplishments, however, were significant. The League of Indians is generally considered to be the first national aboriginal political organization in Canada and the forerunner of the National Indian Council (NIC), which was organized in 1961, and the National Indian Brotherhood (NIB), which emerged from the NIC a few years later. The NIB, in turn, led in the 1980s to the development of the Assembly of First Nations, which today is the principal political organization of Indigenous peoples in Canada. By reigniting and providing an organizational structure for the demands of sovereignty, self-government, and self-determination across a number of Haudenosaunee communities in Quebec and Ontario between 1915 and the early 1920s, the Thunderwater movement and the Council of the Tribes can be seen as a precursor to and a foundation for Loft's League of Indians and the important Indigenous organizations that followed.[23]

The sovereignty movement at Grand River led by Deskaheh (Levi General) in the early 1920s may also have absorbed some of the energy of the Thunderwater movement, especially in that community. At that time, the increasing internal community pressure to institute elected government, the allotment of reserve lands to returning World War I veterans by the federal government, and the Compulsory Enfranchisement Act of 1920 challenged traditional government and confederacy autonomy at Grand River. In response, the hereditary chiefs on the Six Nations Council pursued independence from the Canadian government by seeking international recognition of confederacy sovereignty. They hired attorneys, raised funds, and in 1921 sent Deskaheh, the Speaker of the Six

Nations Confederacy Council, to London to make their case before the British Crown and to do the same in 1923 before the League of Nations in Geneva, Switzerland. With a strategy that he seems to have perfected in his efforts targeting Thunderwater and the Council of the Tribes and F. O. Loft and the League of Indians of Canada, Duncan Campbell Scott carried out a persistent and aggressive campaign to discredit Deskaheh and the efforts of the Confederacy Council. Deskaheh and the council failed to achieve the international recognition they sought for the confederacy, but their efforts generated strong local support for the sovereignty position.

Amid these developments and the face of considerable opposition, Scott obtained government approval to abolish the hereditary council system at Grand River and establish an elected council on the reserve. In October 1924 the Six Nations Council was formally abolished, the Royal Canadian Mounted Police confiscated the traditional wampum used to sanction council meetings, and the Indian Department set the date for the first band council elections. With circumstances that mirrored events in other Haudenosaunee communities four decades earlier, traditional government at Grand River was dead. Deskaheh, who had remained in Europe during these developments, returned to North America in poor health in early 1925 and died in June of that year. Despite these developments, the sovereignty movement at Grand River remained alive and continued to move forward, though haltingly, in the late 1920s and 1930s. Two generations after his death Deskaheh emerged as a revered patriot and inspirational role model for many young Indigenous political activists in Canada and the United States who revived those efforts to pursue Six Nations sovereignty—efforts that reverberate strongly in Haudenosaunee communities to this day.[24]

Chief Thunderwater should be recognized for playing a crucial role in this history of modern Haudenosaunee nationalism. Through his charisma, leadership, responsiveness to Haudenosaunee political interests and demands, and his willingness to take on the Department of Indian Affairs, the political movement he led and facilitated revitalized Indian Act opposition and Haudenosaunee political aspirations that had built in the late nineteenth century but had become dormant in the early 1900s. Thunderwater's efforts and hopes on behalf of the Haudenosaunee interests and Six Nations sovereignty were not fully realized; however, the political energy and momentum generated by the Thunderwater movement can be viewed as critical to the important developments that followed, including the League of Indians of Canada of F. O. Loft and the Six Nations sovereignty movement led by Deskaheh and others. Thus, Thunderwater, the

Council of the Tribes, and the Thunderwater movement served as a vital link connecting the rise of Haudenosaunee nationalism in the late nineteenth century and the development of Indigenous political organizations and the Six Nations sovereignty movement in Canada during the second quarter of the twentieth century and beyond.

Though Thunderwater was gone as an influential player in the scene of Haudenosaunee political and cultural revitalization by the early 1920s, his story was hardly at an end.

CHAPTER 7

LIBEL IN LOUISVILLE

*"Records Call Him Many Things, But Not Indian"; "Indian Officials
Tell of 'Chief's' Shameful Treatment of Boy Ward"; "Resident of
Cleveland Blackbelt in Louisville Public Schools"; "Makes Attack
on Government Upon Visit to Schools"*
—Headlines from the *Louisville Times* in an exposé on Chief Thunderwater
in March 1927

Back in Cleveland, Thunderwater lived life much as he had before his rise to
political notoriety and influence among the Haudenosaunees in Canada in 1914.
He continued his herbal medicine business, eventually taking on a partner in
the enterprise, a white man by the name of Charles Rose from Michigan. He
continued his humanitarian activities on behalf of Native people. He assisted
the son of a Council of the Tribes member in securing monetary compensation
after he was badly injured in a motor vehicle accident in Detroit. He continued
to make his home in Cleveland available to needy and traveling Indians. Lodgers
in his home included Jacob Sineway, an Odawa and recent graduate of the Mt.
Pleasant Indian Industrial Boarding School in Michigan, and Howard Meter, a
young Native man from Oklahoma; both worked for Thunderwater as "medicine
salesmen." Others included Martin Clausen, a thirty-five-year-old machinist from
New York, Isaac Hill, a thirty-five-year-old mill worker from "French Canada,"
and Cyrus Allen, an eighty-one-year-old widower from Oklahoma, who was
not employed and was being cared for by Thunderwater.[1]

Thunderwater also remained active in Native affairs and kept abreast of
important political developments related to the Haudenosaunees in Canada.
In the early 1920s he attempted to revive and raise funds for the Council of the
Tribes among First Nations groups in New Brunswick, an effort that drew the
attention of both the Indian Department in Canada and the Bureau of Indian
Affairs in the United States. A few years later he signed agreements with a number
of Lakota people from the Pine Ridge reservation to serve as their agent in various

business transactions in Cleveland. Contained in his personal papers from this time period is a copy of "The Redman's Appeal for Justice," Deskaheh's address to the League of Nations in Geneva in 1923, in which he argued for international recognition of confederacy sovereignty. Reflecting his continuing interest in the border-crossing issue, Thunderwater followed the case of Paul K. Diabo, the Mohawk ironworker from Kahnawake who was arrested as an illegal immigrant in Philadelphia in 1925. With the support of the Six Nations Confederacy councils at Grand River and Onondaga, and that of Haudenosaunee people across Quebec, Ontario, and New York, Diabo contested his arrest on the basis of the Jay Treaty of 1794, which he argued recognized the right of the Haudenosaunees to pass freely across the border between Canada and the United States. Diabo won his case in U.S. District Court in Philadelphia in 1927 and prevailed in a subsequent appeal of that decision by the U.S. Department of Immigration in 1928. Following the initial trial, Thunderwater wrote to the presiding judge, Oliver Dickinson, to commend him for his ruling and indicated that he hoped to put a copy of his decision "in the hands of every Iroquois."[2]

Following Diabo's successful appeal in March 1928, Haudenosaunee nationalists at Grand River issued a declaration of independence from the Canadian government and organized border-crossing demonstrations at Niagara Falls. Thunderwater responded to these events with an announcement of plans for a "legal battle" to win "complete self-rule" for Indian people and stated he intended to enlist famed attorney Clarence Darrow in the effort. Thunderwater's announcement was first reported in Cleveland and was then picked up by newspapers across the country and as far away as Hawaii. "The time has passed when we can deal with the Indian bureaus of either the Canadian or American governments," Thunderwater is quoted as saying. "We shall ignore them and defy them in all future activities. . . . The Indian has always maintained that he is not a subject of Great Britain or any other government." Referring to the American Indian Citizenship Act passed in the United States four years earlier, he declared, "In this country the government has forced a meaningless citizenship upon us and yet continues to herd 240,000 of our people on reservations as virtual prisoners. . . . The [Indian] wants his rights. These rights were promised in treaties with both English and American governments. We have won our first battle in the courts with the decision that there is no international boundary line as far as Indians are concerned. Now we strike again." Thunderwater never followed through with his ambitious plan. It is unlikely that he had the political weight and support to effect the sort of legal battle he had proposed, especially given the decline of his political influence after 1920. Nevertheless, his intended effort indicates that he remained attuned to important developments in the Haudenosaunee political world and especially the continued efforts for Six Nations sovereignty and self-government.[3]

A new chapter in Thunderwater's already extraordinary life opened about this time when he became embroiled in a fraud and libel case in Louisville, Kentucky. The case stemmed from a business venture involving a Cleveland entrepreneur by the name of Frank S. Burr, the owner of a printing and publishing company. The venture involved a plan for promoting newspaper subscriptions through membership in "Indians," a yet-to-be-established youth-based organization that was intended to tap into popular interest in Native people and values-oriented organizations such as the Woodcraft Indians and the Boy Scouts of America. In what was clearly a commercial venture, through "Indians" the children of potential newspaper subscribers would be offered honorary adoption and membership in various American and Canadian Indian tribes, assigned "Indian" names and clans, and have the opportunity to learn about Native cultures and history through educational and recreational activities and quasi-Indian cultural experiences. Burr appears to have been the main originator of the "Indians" plan. Thunderwater's role in its conceptualization is less clear, but, given the elements of the plan, it is difficult to imagine that he did not play a part in its development or that he would not have an important role in its execution.[4]

Designed to promote newspaper subscriptions, the "Indians" plan also aimed to raise awareness and understanding of Native history and cultures and the problems of contemporary Indigenous people in the United States. Under the plan, the children of newspaper subscribers would earn free membership in the "Organization of Indians," through which they would receive a weekly periodical titled *The Indian Corner*. *The Indian Corner* was to include stories on Native history, an illustrated comic strip depicting the positive contributions of Native people to American society, outline drawings for coloring, instructions for making Indian costumes and crafts, news items concerning Indian reservations and federal Indian policy, essay contests, and photographs and articles about local chapters of the organization. In addition, the Organization of Indians would offer its members and their parents opportunities to participate in hikes, camping trips, and outdoor activities such as archery and canoeing, perform in Indian-themed theatrical activities, compete in lacrosse, baseball, and other team activities, and visit Indian reservations. Competitions against "full blood" Indian teams were intended to be an especially attractive opportunity.

A key element and selling point of the "Indians" plan was to offer honorary tribal adoption and membership to newspaper subscribers' children, who would be recognized with special certificates and badges. From the outset, it was clear that the honorary memberships offered would carry no tribal rights and privileges. Geared toward expanding newspaper subscriptions, tribal adoption and membership would be offered only to those children who secured new applicants to the Organization of Indians and, thus, new subscribers to participating newspapers. In addition, any child who secured new applicants and received tribal adoption and membership would be given an "Indian" name, assigned a "clan," be permitted to wear distinctive clan regalia, have an opportunity to win "merit feathers," and participate in special clan activities, such as parades, craft-making, and athletic events. As an additional incentive, children were to be offered the opportunity to earn multiple honorary tribal adoptions and memberships and, by doing so, to earn membership in three "secret organizations." Beginning with the Mohawk tribe, children would be able to earn adoption and membership in as many as fifteen different tribes. Those who earned five tribal memberships would become eligible for the "Wigwams of the Five Tribes," those who earned ten memberships would be eligible for the "Lodges of the Ten Tribes," and those who earned fifteen honorary memberships would be eligible for the "Council Fires of the Fifteen Tribes." Each secret organization would have its own unique signs, signals, passwords, and "mysterious rites and ceremonies." To allay any parental concerns about the welfare of their children, the activities of the "secret organizations" would not be "secret so far as the mother, father, teacher, and minister are concerned, but are to be secretly and mysteriously operated so as to arouse the interest of the children to the highest pitch." According to Burr's plan, to build and sustain newspaper subscriptions, a new tribal adoption and membership could be won only once every six months. Thus, eligibility for the "Wigwams of the Five Tribes" would take two and a half years, and for the "Council Fires of the Fifteen Tribes," it would take seven and a half years.

Thunderwater was to have a major role in promoting and implementing the "Indians" plan. Many of the children's activities for the Organization of Indians were to be planned and overseen by Thunderwater, and he had the major responsibility for securing individuals and connections that would make them possible. In fact, in legal papers filed by Burr in early February 1927 to license a business agent to promote "Indians" to potential clients, it was stipulated that Thunderwater "shall have the sole right to deal with . . . securing lecturers, guides, instructors, groups of Indians for public ceremonies, archery, and athletic

Indian teams, and in securing exhibits of Indian manufactured articles, and all other matters pertaining to Indians as a factor in the . . . organization known as 'Indians.'" He probably was also responsible for providing much of the content of *The Indian Corner*.[5]

Thunderwater was also central to the honorary tribal adoption and membership component of the "Indians" plan. This involved several elements. First, he was to secure agreements with Indian tribes that were willing to offer honorary adoption and membership. According to another licensing agreement Burr signed in February 1927, Thunderwater was to have "the sole right to deal with the Indians in the matters of adoption of whites by Indians." It appears that he planned to create honorary tribal adoption and membership agreements with dozens of tribes, including the Mohawks, Oneidas, Onondagas, Cayugas, Senecas, and Tuscaroras. In addition to securing the agreements, he was charged with assigning "Indian" names to the children who joined the Organization of Indians and applied for honorary adoption. To this end, he prepared typed and handwritten lists of hundreds of boys' and girls' "Indian" names, often in Native languages along with English translations. The lists included names in Mohawk, Seneca, Cayuga, Tuscarora, Ojibwe, Odawa, Cheyenne, Cherokee, Sioux, Osage, Coos, Blackfoot, and Delaware. For sources of the names and translations, Thunderwater relied on his own knowledge, personal associates, and sources such as a Bureau of American Ethnology report titled *Circular of Information Regarding Indian Popular Names*, which the agency had issued in 1915.[6]

Finally, Thunderwater was responsible for preparing the official certificates of honorary tribal adoption and membership by dating, signing, and endorsing them as "Oghema Niagara, Chief of the Supreme Council of the Tribes." The Supreme Council of the Tribes was the U.S. counterpart of Council of the Tribes, which Thunderwater had legally chartered in Ohio in 1917. The official certificate, which was designed and printed by Burr, included a forest-green, nature-themed border featuring images of Niagara Falls, an Indian in war bonnet regalia, a bear, and a grazing buffalo. The certificate also bore the emblem of the Supreme Council of the Tribes, which was identical to the emblem for the Council of the Tribes. The text of the certificate identified the tribe into which the child was to be adopted and contained blank spaces for the individual's given name, their assigned "Indian" name, its English translation, and the date of honorary adoption. The calendric system used to date certificates was the same as the one that Thunderwater had developed for the Council of the Tribes and had used to date council membership certificates between 1915 and 1920.[7]

To initiate the honorary adoption and membership program, Thunderwater secured the cooperation and endorsement of more than two dozen members of the Tyendinaga band. In their written agreement signed sometime in 1926, they identified themselves as the "Chiefs, Councillors, or both, of the Thayendinaga Band of Mohawk Indians" and stated that they "do hereby indorse any and all HONORARY MEMBERSHIPS to this band of Mohawk Indians . . . that are indorsed by our Oghema Niagara, Chief Thunderwater." Those who signed the agreement also referred to themselves as "members of the Supreme Council of the Tribes," and many had been prominent in the Tyendinaga circle of the Council of the Tribes a decade earlier. They included Johnson Lewis, Wellington Green, William J. Scero, Isaac Brant, and Isaac Claus. The agreement was also signed by several hereditary council activists and former Council of the Tribes members from St. Regis, including Loran Swamp, Peter Herron, and Angus Papineau. The agreement they signed also stipulated the following: "It is understood and hereby agreed that the Honorary Memberships shall carry with them . . . none of the rights to participate in the distribution of land, money or goods or other benefits allowed by the Federal Government to the Mohawks." The agreement did not include any monetary or other compensation for the "Chiefs" and "Councillors."[8]

As part of his effort to promote the "Indians" plan, Burr produced a publication, also titled *Indians*, the content of which almost certainly was developed with assistance from Thunderwater. *Indians* appears to have been intended as the first issue of a periodical through which they intended to educate the adult public about Native people and promote membership in the Organization of Indians. Dedicated to the theme of the "Tragedy of the Indian: The Story of Indian Wrongs as Written in the Records of Congress," the thirty-seven-page publication, with a bright red cover and detailed sketch of an Indian decked in Native regalia, was pan-tribal in orientation and decidedly pro-Indian and antigovernment in its tone and content. The "Introduction" focused on the inequities of the Indian treaty process in the second half of the nineteenth century and the cruelties and desperation it had produced on Indian reservations in the United States; it sought to arouse public sentiment, responsibility, and action. With words that signaled Thunderwater's eventual activities and troubles in Louisville, it proposed that the "Indian side of the story" be widely taught to schoolchildren. An excerpt from congressional testimony on the "present-day status of the Indian" noted the dramatic decline in the Indigenous population of the country and pointed to four principal causes: "the introduction of disease, by the white man; the introduction of whiskey, by the white man; tribal wars and warfare with the white man; [and] the housing of the Indian upon inhospitable reservations, by the white man." Other articles in "The Tragedy of the Indian" included information on American Indian service during World War I, federal Indian policies, and the conditions of Indian life in the United States. There was even a piece on the "black curse" (oil) of the Osage Nation and an ongoing series of murders on their Oklahoma reservation. It also included a "Book References" section to encourage "everyone—young and old—to read the *Indian side* of the history and growth of our country." Among the books recommended were Helen Hunt Jackson's *A Century of Dishonor* and Seth K. Humphrey's *The Indian Dispossessed*. Finally, the publication provided detailed information about the "Organization of Indians" and encouraged readers to "Join the Indians and Organize the Clans!" Those interested were directed to contact the Burr's "Indians" office in Cleveland.[9]

As a profit-making venture, Burr's intention was to sell the rights to his "Indians" plan to agents who would market it to newspapers across the United States and Canada. In the one licensing agreement he signed in early 1927 with an agent in Louisville, Kentucky, Burr was to be paid a minimum of $10,000 or 25 percent of the net profit derived from the sale of the plan, whichever was greater. Adjusted for inflation, this was the equivalent of at least $140,000 in today's currency. As detailed as it was with regard to Thunderwater's responsibilities, Burr's plan did not specify any salary or percentage of the profits to be paid directly to him. However, the licensing agreement did stipulate that 5 percent of the net profit derived from the arrangement would be directed to the Supreme Council of the Tribes. Of course, Thunderwater *was* the Supreme Council of the Tribes and the funds would support him in his role as "Oghema" of the organization and in his educational and advocacy work on behalf of Native people. The potential financial and political benefit of the "Indians" plan for Thunderwater were substantial: it would provide his organization with an important source of funds and, with Burr's intention to market his newspaper subscription plan nationwide, it meant that the Organization of Indians, the Supreme Council of the Tribes, and Thunderwater himself would have the national, pan-Indian presence.

The one and only agreement Burr signed for the "Indians" venture involved the *Herald-Post* of Louisville, Kentucky, which was owned by James Buckner Brown, a wealthy financier and powerbroker in Louisville. In 1925 Brown purchased the *Louisville Herald* and *Louisville Post* and merged the two papers to serve as a conservative alternative to the more liberal *Louisville Times* and *Courier-Journal*, sister newspapers that were owned by Brown's political rival,

Robert Worth Bingham. An "Indians" promotion was intended to be part of the newly merged newspaper's effort to compete with the *Times* and *Courier-Journal*. In early February 1927 Burr signed a legal agreement with the representative of a group of investors from Louisville whose intention was to contract with the *Herald-Post* to promote subscriptions and incorporate a company that would take the "Indians" scheme for newspaper promotion nationwide. Subsequent to the signing of this legal agreement, the representative of the Louisville investors signed a contract with the *Herald-Post* to promote subscriptions through Burr's "Indians" plan. The anticipated circulation catchment area of the *Herald-Post* extended throughout the state of Kentucky, north into Indiana, and east into Ohio. The contract was in force for six months and could be renewed upon mutual agreement; it stipulated a minimum payment to Burr of $500 every six months and twenty-five cents for each honorary adoption certificate issued.[10]

The plan to promote *Herald-Post* subscriptions was put into effect almost immediately, and a series of promotional appearances in Louisville by Thunderwater were planned. Thunderwater was to be paid $150 per week for his promotional work, a substantial sum of money at that time. In late February the *Herald-Post* announced to the public that it had completed negotiations with Thunderwater, "the Great Counsel of the Supreme Council of the Tribes," for granting "the membership usually reserved for visiting royalty and other persons of high rank." Honorary adoption into the "Mohawk Indian Tribe," it promised potential customers, was available to "any white child or adult of good standing."

Thunderwater visited Louisville in early March 1927, initially with a good success. His appearance was announced in the "Photo Gravure Color" section of the *Herald-Post* on March 6 with a full-page colorized photograph of him dressed in Native regalia, including his personal feathered headdress, beaded moccasins, and beaded Council of the Tribes waist belt and arm bands. In the photograph he stands erect and faces forward, a geometrically patterned blanket draped over his right shoulder and arm. The caption reads "OGHEMA NIAGARA (Chief Thunderwater)—Great Counsel of the Supreme Council of the Tribes—Chief Thunderwater comes to Louisville under the auspices of the Herald-Post to adopt officially into the Mohawk Tribe the boys and girls of Louisville and vicinity." His activities in Louisville kicked off a few days later with the granting of an honorary membership in the Mohawk tribe to Kentucky governor William J. Fields, a meeting with city mayor William B. Harrison, and a chauffeur-driven tour through the city. Then, with the enthusiastic support from the Louisville's board of education, he appeared at local public schools, again dressed in his Native regalia, to promote honorary adoptions, "Indians," and *Herald-Post* subscriptions with schoolchildren and their families. The total number of honorary adoptions Thunderwater secured as a result of this one and only appearance in Louisville is not known, but in his personal papers there are more than two dozen completed adoption certificates, all for the "Mohawk Tribe," that went undelivered to their intended recipients. Included were certificates for Frederick Lee Davis (named "Nee-wah Wee-goon-gah-lah"/Little Snake), Harry Krebs ("Mah-to-skah"/White Bear), John Nicolai ("Pe-tay Wash-tay"/ Good Buffalo), Vard Phillips ("Wonkee Pah-ta"/Flaming Arrow), Harry Louis Ruffner ("Asuh Otno-wellah"/Three Turtles), and his brother, George Ruffner ("Gua-pah Hanspa"/Four Moccasins) (see figure 11).[11]

The success of Thunderwater's promotional tour was brief, as he was soon embroiled in controversy and the plan from "Indians" was brought to a sudden halt. Concerned about the competition from the upstart *Herald-Post*, the *Louisville Times* and *Courier-Journal* followed Thunderwater's activities closely. Initially, their reporting was favorable. "Thousands of School Children Meet and Hear Chief Thunderwater," the *Times* declared, picturing him with groups of school-children and local dignitaries. At the same time, however, the *Times* city editor contacted the Bureau of Indian Affairs in Washington, D.C., about Thunderwater and learned that he was not a registered Indian in the United States. He followed up by telegramming the Department of Indian Affairs in Ottawa, and suddenly Duncan Campbell Scott was back in Thunderwater's life.[12]

In a brief telegrammed reply to the *Times* editor, Scott stated Thunderwater was not a Canadian Indian, that he was an "imposter," and that he had given the department "much trouble" in the past. The managing editor of the *Times* responded to Scott with a request for any information he could provide about Thunderwater's "parentage and racial classification," urging him to reply as soon as possible for "early exposure of [Thunderwater's] representations here." Scott followed up with an immediate, substantive reply. "Styling himself Chief Thunderwater," he telegrammed, "claiming to be American Indian operated on Canadian reserves between nineteen fourteen and nineteen twenty-two." Casting doubt on the purpose of the organization he headed and completely misrepresenting the high level of Native participation in it, he informed the *Times* editor that Thunderwater's offenses "consisted of inducing Indians to subscribe to thousands of dollars in worthless membership to alleged Council of Tribes" and that the council, "which was to deal with all their grievances," in reality "consisted of himself alone." In addition, Scott charged Thunderwater with

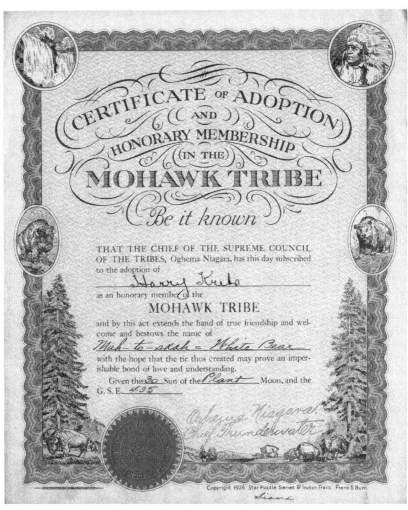

FIGURE 11. Certificate of Adoption and Honorary Membership in the Mohawk Tribe signed by Chief Thunderwater. In 1926 Thunderwater and a Cleveland business partner created an organization known as "Indians" to sell newspaper subscriptions and promote public understanding of Native history, cultures, and contemporary issues. A part of the business plan involved offering honorary adoption and membership in the Mohawk tribe, an arrangement that involved support of former Council of the Tribes members in Tyendinaga.

Image courtesy of the Western Reserve Historical Society, Cleveland, Ohio.

"interfering with the administration of Indian affairs" by "purporting to appoint chiefs on various reservations." He added, "Thunderwater is not a Canadian, spoke no Canadian Indian languages." With regard to his Native identity and the charge of child abuse, Scott was direct: "Thunderwater an imposter. . . . A young Canadian boy who was adopted by him made a sworn declaration as to cruel and shameful treatment he received." Notably, Scott did not include any of the information in the Indian Department's file that would have cast doubts on those allegations.[13]

Following the communications with Scott, and with the damaging information from the Indian Department files in hand, on March 15, 1927, the *Louisville Times* ran a front-page article and full-page exposé on Thunderwater under the banner headline "Thunderwater Takes Advantage of Board of Education." Additional headlines said it all. In bold type the front page blared "Records Call Him Many Things, But Not 'Indian'" and "Sells Worthless Herbs in Cleveland Black Belt," while the exposé shouted "Makes Attack on Government Upon Visit to Schools," "Resident of Cleveland Black Belt in Louisville Public Schools," and "Indian Officials Tell of 'Chief's' Shameful Treatment of Boy Ward." Accompanying photographs drove the indictments home. Under the title "Thunderwater's Great Council 'Wigwam,'" one series of photographs and captions pictured Thunderwater's Cleveland home, described as located "in the heart of the city's negro district," and several of his "Negro neighbors." To emphasize the potential danger to which Louisville schoolchildren were being exposed by the alleged child abuser, the spread also included several photographs of Thunderwater's school visits with him greeting and in close physical contact with the young boys and girls. A third set of photographs depicted the governor, mayor, and a police band that celebrated Thunderwater's visit and described them as "dupes of Thunderwater."[14]

The contents of the articles were devastating for Thunderwater. Drawing substantially on information provided by Scott and the Department of Indian Affairs, the *Times* stated that Thunderwater had been a "continuous source of annoyance to the Canadian government," that his Council of the Tribes was "exceedingly questionable" and had failed to be granted a charter of incorporation by Canada, and that he had personally benefited from the membership fees collected by his organization. Based on information obtained from the Bureau of Indian Affairs in Washington, D.C., the *Times* also stated that in 1917 the U.S. postal service had investigated Thunderwater for mail fraud and that even though no evidence of a crime was found, "the inspectors reached the conclusion that Thunderwater had resorted to misrepresentations in direct dealing with individuals in soliciting funds." Thunderwater was characterized as the "head of a medicine peddling outfit" that sold "worthless herbs." In a clear effort to cast doubt on both Thunderwater's racial identity and his "herbal medicines," the *Times* stated, "The negroes in his neighborhood . . . knew him and speak a good word for his herbs." In his school visits, Thunderwater was accused of a variety of inflammatory, unpatriotic statements. "We know the Indian bureau is a cesspool of iniquity," the *Times* quoted him as saying. "The Government never rights a wrong until the people demand it. . . . Washington leaders have their claws on Indian money, offering the Indian only a small interest of what is his." The *Times* went on to say that the U.S. and Canadian governments considered the certificates of honorary Mohawk adoption and tribal membership promoted by Thunderwater as "worthless" because he had no authority to offer them. In an effort to add weight to this point, the paper stated, erroneously, that "the Mohawk tribe, though it may have some remnants in northern New York, is not officially existent."

The article on Thunderwater's alleged treatment of his adopted son cited Duncan Campbell Scott as one of its sources and Charles Burke, the U.S. commissioner of Indian Affairs, as another. Scott was quoted as saying that Thunderwater's treatment of the boy was "shameful and cruel." Noting that the details of the case were "almost unprintable," the *Times* nevertheless referenced the letter in the Canadian Indian Department's "Thunderwater" file, supposedly written by the boy himself, in which "all kinds of horrific charges" were made. "Thunderwater," the paper reported, "told [the boy] he would kill him and that he would not be his first victim; that Thunderwater's house has all sorts of secrets and secret corridors; that Thunderwater attempted certain approaches toward him and asked why he didn't yell 'like the girls did.'" Before the day was out, Thunderwater hired two local attorneys and initiated a $250,000 libel suit against the *Louisville Times*.

Thunderwater detailed his charges against the *Times* in a letter to the *Courier-Journal* the very next day. The *Times*, he stated, "had printed scurrilous, libelous, and false statements concerning me, my history, nationality and work." He denounced the statements about "his private character" as "false and untrue." Regarding the legitimacy of his "chieftainship," Thunderwater referred to documents appointing him as an ambassador of the Tyendinaga and St. Regis bands and emphasized he had "duped" no one. Stating that the reporting on his speeches to schoolchildren was "malicious," he noted that the critical statements he made about the U.S. government were taken out of context and that they were, in fact, quoted from the federal government's own reports. "An innuendo that I am of negro blood instead of Indian blood," Thunderwater wrote, "is untrue and false. . . . Your photograph of my residence in Cleveland, in which it appears you have framed up the scenery for the occasion, is misleading and maliciously perpetrated by you to do me harm in name, fame and reputation." Signing his letter as "Oghema Niagara—Chief Thunderwater," he demanded that the paper retract its "scurrilous, false and malicious statements." The paper issued no such retraction.[15]

Over the course of several days after the initial *Times* exposé, the *Courier-Journal* published a series of articles intensifying the charges against Thunderwater. On March 16, the same day it published Thunderwater's letter, it ran several articles whose headlines reiterated the themes of the *Times* pieces: "Indian Called Trouble Source," "Not Registered in U.S. or Canada," and "'Chief' is Fake." Perhaps the most inflammatory and racist piece was a photograph depicting Thunderwater in profile under the headline "'Thunderwater' is Bald 'Indian' and Shy of Indian Nose," with a caption that read as follows: "A picture of Thunderwater taken in the rain on Saturday is shown above. The aquiline nose, termed by the dictionary as characteristic of Indian races, did not register in the picture. Thunderwater is bald." On March 17 the *Courier-Journal* ran an article in which it countered the comments by Thunderwater about his school speeches with eyewitness testimony from teachers and newspaper reporters. "I was sorry that he had been permitted to address the children or our school," stated one teacher. One reporter "emphatically refuted" that Thunderwater had been misquoted in the inflammatory statements attributed to him. On March 18 the paper reported on Thunderwater's libel suit against the *Times*, which was filed on his behalf by attorneys W. G. Dearing and J. L. Richardson of Louisville. According to the *Courier-Journal*, the filing claimed as "false" and "willfully malicious" the *Times* statements about his ancestry, business, school speeches, political credentials and work, and treatment of his adopted son. "He states that he is not of negro origin and has no negro blood in his veins and that he is an Indian and at the present time is peace chief and ambassador, Tyendinaga, Deseronto, Ontario, Canada, and St. Regis, Band of Mohawk, Hogansburg, N.Y." Eventually, Thunderwater would file a second libel suit, against the *Courier-Journal*, also for $250,000. His preparation for the suit and the eventual trial would prove to be a disheartening experience for him, but, ironically, it would also produce independent evidence that supported his claims about his identity, character, and political work.[16]

CHAPTER 8

TRIALS AND TRIBULATIONS

For about three hours Thunderwater was on the stand late Monday,
denying the statements concerning his career and activities which were
published in The Times *and* The Courier-Journal *in March 1927 while [he]*
was in Louisville under the auspices of The Herald-Post, *speaking in schools*
and other places and offering certificates of adoption into an Indian tribe
in return for subscriptions to The Herald-Post.
—From the *Louisville Times*, reporting in October 1928 on the first day of
Chief Thunderwater's six-day libel trial in Louisville, Kentucky

Thunderwater prepared for his libel case against the *Louisville Times* and *Courier-Journal* mainly by obtaining depositions that would offer proof of his ancestry, identity, and good character and serve to refute the charges and insinuations made against him by the two newspapers. This included visits by him, his attorneys, his former Council of the Tribes deputy, T. W. Martin, and others, to interview witnesses in Tyendinaga, Kahnawake, Akwesasne, Grand River, Tonawanda, Tuscarora, Cleveland, Montreal, Buffalo, and Detroit. It also involved purchasing books, obtaining reprints of photographs and newspaper articles, and hiring attorneys to take legal affidavits. In February 1928, when he initiated the second libel suit against the *Courier-Journal*, Thunderwater engaged a third attorney, William Marsteller, of Cleveland. In all, over the course of a year and a half until his case went before the court in Louisville in October 1928, Thunderwater racked up nearly $2,500 in expenses, a substantial amount of money at the time, especially for someone of his rather limited resources.[1]

While Thunderwater and his attorneys assembled their case, so too did the *Louisville Times* and *Courier-Journal* and its lead attorney, Charles H. Tabb. Tabb was one of the partners in the prestigious Louisville law firm of Peter, Lee, Tabb, Krieger, and Heyburn. In planning for their defense, Tabb and his associates received significant assistance from Duncan Campbell Scott and the Department of Indian Affairs in Canada. Two days after the *Times* exposé in mid-March 1927, the city editor of the *Courier-Journal* contacted Scott to inform him that he had instructed a representative in Ottawa to obtain officially certified photostatic copies of the incriminating evidence on Thunderwater in the Indian Department's files. A month later Scott provided Tabb with a notarized statement in which he affirmed his concern about Thunderwater's Council of the Tribes, stating that the organization "invariably became hostile to the Department of Indian Affairs and obstructed its administration" and that its members "were no longer amenable to the Indian Act and were going to have absolute control over their own affairs as they did before the white man came." Scott also explained Thunderwater's failed effort to incorporate the council in Canada in 1918, doing so without mentioning that incorporation had widespread support in Haudenosaunee and other Native communities. In addition, he failed to indicate that he and other government officials had worked behind the scenes to scuttle the incorporation initiative because of their concern about Thunderwater's political objectives and the nationalist agenda of the Council of the Tribes. Finally, in his notarized statement Scott reviewed the details of the child abuse charge against Thunderwater, but without noting the backstory of the accusations or doubts that he and other Indian Department officials had about the veracity of those charges. Over the course of the next eighteen months Scott, other Indian Department officials in Ottawa, and Indian agents in the field worked with the legal team for the *Times* and *Courier-Journal* to provide them with copies of key documents in the department's Thunderwater file and arrange for depositions from Thunderwater opponents in Akwesasne, Kahnawake, and Tyendinaga. They also assisted Tabb and his associates with determining the whereabouts of Thunderwater's adopted son and in obtaining his cooperation to testify in court. Finally, Scott arranged for several department officials to appear in court, including one on his behalf because he was not available to testify in person.[2]

Despite his impending court case, Thunderwater continued his political activities and agitation. It was in the midst of preparing for his trial that he closely followed the Paul K. Diabo immigration case and wrote to Judge Oliver Dickinson to express support and thanks for his decision. It was also during this time that Haudenosaunee nationalists at Grand River declared independence from Canada and organized border-crossing demonstrations at Niagara Falls, leading Thunderwater to respond with his announcement of plans for a "legal battle" to win "complete self-rule" for Indian people. Though his plan was extremely ambitious and would have been difficult to accomplish under the best of circumstances, his legal problems no doubt prevented him from following through on any efforts in this direction.[3]

Thunderwater's libel cases against the *Times* and *Courier-Journal* went before the U.S. District Court for the Western District of Kentucky in Louisville in late October 1928, with Judge Charles I. Dawson presiding. The trial lasted six days and was reported on in detail by both newspapers. On the opening day of the trial, Monday, October 22, the two cases were combined into a single one against both newspapers, and a jury was impaneled. In his opening argument W. G. Dearing reviewed Thunderwater's complaints against the two papers and added that the exposé and subsequent articles were motivated by the "intense rivalry" with the *Herald-Post*. For the defense, Charles Tabb countered that the *Times* and *Courier-Journal* stood by their reporting and that the papers had performed "a real public service" in publishing the articles that were the subject of Thunderwater's suit.[4]

Thunderwater's own testimony and cross-examination took up much of the proceedings on the first day of the trial. Dressed in his Native regalia, he testified about the details of his birth on the Tuscarora reservation in 1865 and the background and ancestry of his parents. He also told the story of the development of his political activism on behalf of Indian people, dating it to his attendance at the reburial of Seneca chief Red Jacket in Buffalo in 1884. He explained that he belonged to the "Confederation of Six Nations Indians," that the Supreme Council of the Tribes was a continuation of the "Confederation," and that he was formally made an "Indian chief" by the Mohawks at St. Regis in 1914. He detailed the arrangements with the *Herald-Post* under which he had visited Louisville in March 1927 and denied the numerous claims and accusations about him that were published in the *Louisville Times* and *Courier-Journal*. In response to questions from attorney Tabb about the membership fees that funded the Supreme Council of the Tribes and that were intended to raise concerns about his fiduciary actions, Thunderwater denied that he received any of the collected funds and insisted that they were used to support the activities of the local circles of the organization. In an effort to expose him as an impostor, Tabb also questioned Thunderwater about the charge that his real name was "Palmer," an accusation that reckoned back to the suspicions of Duncan Campbell Scott and the Indian Department in 1919. In reply, Thunderwater recounted that during his boyhood he lived for an extended period in Cleveland with his godmother, "Mrs. Palmer," and that since then, some of his friends and associates there referred to him by that surname.

The remainder of the first day of the trial was taken up with the testimony and depositions of witnesses vouching for Thunderwater's character and providing details of his ancestry, family history, business activities, and humanitarian and

political activities. One witness was Waunetta Griffin, who had known Thunderwater since their days together as performers in Buffalo Bill's Wild West Show.
Born in Oklahoma about 1879 to a Comanche mother and an English father,
Griffin had toured the United States and Europe with the Buffalo Bill show,
performing as an expert rifle shot and horseback rider under the show name of
"Princess Nita." Griffin testified that she became associated with Thunderwater
around 1900 when both were traveling with Buffalo Bill and that Indian people
had addressed him as "Chief."[5] Another character witness for Thunderwater
was Minnie Peck, whose deposition in the case was previously quoted at length.
Peck's deposition provided important details about Thunderwater's identity and
family history and supported the veracity of Thunderwater's claims and records
concerning his ancestry and the circumstances of his birth. The depositions of
two Cleveland police officials were also read into the record. Both stated that
Thunderwater was known in the city as an Indian and not a "Negro" and that
he had good standing in the community. Both also stated they had used his
medicines with positive results. Regarding Thunderwater's treatment of his
adopted son, one of the two police officers testified that he was an immediate
and longtime next-door neighbor of Thunderwater and that while in his care,
Mitchell Benedict was "well fed, cleanly well dressed, sent to church and public
school and given many luxuries and generally treated as a father would his child."[6]

The second day of the trial produced additional witnesses and depositions
in support of Thunderwater. One witness was Carl Mueller, also a Cleveland
neighbor. Mueller testified to Thunderwater's good treatment of his adopted
son and stated that the section of Cleveland in which Thunderwater lived was
not known as the "Negro belt," as claimed by the *Journal* and *Courier-Times*.
Another neighbor stated that their area of the city had not been a "Negro section," but that "some Negroes live there now." The neighbor indicated that he
"knew and had played ball" with Thunderwater's adopted son and that Thunderwater disciplined the boy by "bawling him out," but was never physically
abusive with him. Another deposition read into the record, but not reported on
in the newspapers, came from James McCauley, yet another of Thunderwater's
Cleveland neighbors. McCauley stated that he had known Thunderwater for
more than fifteen years and that Thunderwater had personally cared for him
for several months when he was ill with pneumonia and had refused to accept
any payment for the extensive attention he had given. According to McCauley,
over the years Indians from many different tribes had visited Thunderwater, and
they "in many instances lived with [him] for several months at a time. . . . Chief

Thunderwater has for years paid for food, clothing, lodgings, laundry, tobacco, and other necessities and luxuries for the sick, stranded, and generally helpless Indians that have called on him for aid."

McCauley also provided testimony concerning Thunderwater's care of his adopted son. "He was in a fearfully deseased [*sic*] condition when the Chief brought him from Canada," he stated. "The boy's face, arms and hands were covered with dried pusy scabs, his skin was cracked and he was in an emaciated condition. . . . When the boy . . . arrived at the Chief's home he was a very bad boy. He systematically stole, lied, smoked tobacco, drank whiskey when he could get it and he was only about 12 years old at the time." Emphasizing that he knew the boy well and was often at Thunderwater's home, McCauley continued in his deposition: "[The] boy received the attention and care of a rich man's son. This boy was sent to school, to church regularly. He received toys even to a twenty five dollar train, a pool table, a swimming pool, skates and in fact about everything a boy could wish for. The boy was well fed and clothed. . . . The boy rapidly became better under the Chief's training and the assistance of school teachers." Referring to the circumstances under which the boy's mother and sister had charged Thunderwater with child abuse, he testified, "I know that the Chief put Mary Benedict out of his house [when they came to visit] because of immoral conduct." Over the course of the day, a total of fourteen depositions in support of Thunderwater from Cleveland residents were read and entered into the court record; each was similar in tone and content to those of Peck, Mueller, McCauley, and the Cleveland police officers.[7]

The witnesses appearing on Thunderwater's behalf on the second day of the trial also included a dozen or more men and women from Haudenosaunee communities, including Tyendinaga, Grand River, and Akwesasne, many of whom testified with the use of interpreters. According to the *Louisville Times*, most were dressed in "Indian regalia," which was a point of fascination for Judge Dawson. Dawson asked one of the witnesses, William Scero of Tyendinaga, if he wore his regalia on the reservation. Scero replied that he did not and did so only on special occasions. "What is the idea of all you people coming down here in these clothes?" Dawson inquired. "To prove our nationality," Scero answered. Scero had been an ardent supporter of Thunderwater and the Council of the Tribes as well as an activist in support of traditional government at Tyendinaga. He had been a councillor in the Tyendinaga circle of the council, had signed the petition to incorporate the council in 1918, and was installed as hereditary chief of the

Wolf clan at Tyendinaga that same year. He had signed several of the petitions from Tyendinaga calling on the federal government to abolish the band council system and recognize hereditary chiefs. With a wife, son, daughter, and brothers and sisters who had also signed the petitions, and a mother and father who had signed a similar petition in the 1880s, Scero was part of a family that represented three generations of support for traditional government and Haudenosaunee sovereignty. He had also signed the agreement with Thunderwater endorsing the "Indians" plan for honorary Mohawk tribal adoption and membership. Scero stated in his testimony that Thunderwater had been appointed as a chief at Tyendinaga, but not in the same way as himself. Thunderwater's position was an honorary one, he explained, "empty of power," without traditional authority, but with responsibilities to "look after things" at Tyendinaga.[8]

Solomon J. Brant, another witness from Tyendinaga, had a pedigree and commitment to traditional government and the Council of the Tribes similar to Scero's and had been installed as life chief of the Bear clan at Tyendinaga in 1918. Brant described Thunderwater as an "ambassador" who had been appointed by members of the band after the Council of the Tribes convention in 1915. A third Native witness for Thunderwater was eighty-two-year-old Isaac Hill, who described himself as a "second line chief" on the Six Nations reserve. In fact, Hill was a pine tree chief at Grand River and a member of the Six Nations Confederacy Council. According to the *Times*, Hill stated that Thunderwater "helped out the Indians [on] any matter that came before them."[9]

T. W. Martin, the former general secretary of the Council of the Tribes, also testified on Thunderwater's behalf. Martin identified himself as a Mohawk and noted that he had been present at Akwesasne in 1914 when Thunderwater had been adopted and appointed as a "chief." On cross-examination, Martin stated that he had charged fees for council memberships and that he had used some of the collected funds to support himself. He made no such statement regarding Thunderwater. Peter Papineau, a former Council of the Tribes officer and supporter of traditional government at Akwesasne, confirmed Thunderwater's ambassadorial appointment at St. Regis in 1914, adding that he "was not elected a chief in accordance with Canadian law." Other reported witnesses for Thunderwater included Mrs. Johnson Lewis, Louis Solomon, Peter Brant, and R. J. Barnhart, all from Tyendinaga. Notably, in late September 1928, just a month before Thunderwater's libel case went to trial, Barnhart, along with several of the Tyendinaga hereditary chiefs and former Council of the Tribes members, authored a letter testifying that at the council convention in the fall of 1915 a majority of the members of the Tyendinaga band had appointed Thunderwater as their "chief and embassdor."[10]

A number of other Haudenosaunee witnesses provided depositions in support of Thunderwater and may also have appeared as witnesses. In each instance they made clear that they and other Haudenosaunee people regarded Thunderwater as Indian, testified to the good work he had done in Haudenosaunee communities, and affirmed that Haudenosaunee people had appointed him to represent their interests. One deposition was from Mike LaBorne of Kahnawake, who stated that he had known Thunderwater for a dozen years and that he was recognized as a "citizen chief." Another deposition was from Mike Kaine, also a Kahnawake Mohawk, who referred to Thunderwater as "Tehotiokwawakon" and testified that he was, indeed, an Indian and "honorable in all of his dealings with Indians." Adrian Clark, a Seneca from Cattaraugus, stated that he had known Thunderwater for nearly twenty years, that he had been "elected chief in the Iroquois Confederacy," and that "the Indians of the Iroquois Confederacy have the greatest respect for him and he enjoys among the Indians a reputation of the highest honor and integrity." Clark also noted that on numerous occasions he had seen Thunderwater working at Cattaraugus in the interest of the reservation residents. Cephas Hill, a Seneca from Tonawanda, testified that he had known Thunderwater for only five years, but that he had "heard the old folks tell of his splendid service for many years past." He also stated that he had visited Thunderwater's home in Cleveland a number of times and had enjoyed his hospitality. He indicated that Thunderwater was "universally known to Indians over the United States and Canada as an Indian chief of the Six Nations and in all manner honorable." Gilbert Peterson, another Tonawanda Seneca, stated that he had stayed at Thunderwater's home several times and that Thunderwater had "done effectual work on [his] reservation and vicinity toward the betterment of conditions for the Indians and that his father and many other Indians spoke highly of him for the work that he had done at Tonawanda."[11]

Thunderwater also obtained depositions from several of his Lakota associates. They also acknowledged his Indian identity, good character, and the importance of his political work. One was "Makes Mad," who identified himself as the son of "Ben Charging Hawk of the Tribe Oglala and Lacota Nation" at Rosebud. Makes Mad stated that Thunderwater had been known to the Sioux as "Minniwakyon" since 1876, that he personally knew him to be "a full blooded Indian," and that he and others recognized him as a "citizen chief." Henry Eagle Head of the Pine

Ridge reservation in South Dakota also referred to Thunderwater as "Minni-wakyon" and testified that he was a "full blooded Algonquin Indian" and was recognized as a "citizen chief." Eagle Head also stated that Thunderwater had transacted business for him and that he had always done so "honestly, faithfully and without charge." He concluded his deposition by stating that during the thirty years he had known him, Thunderwater was "trusted, admired by and [had] the full confidence of hundreds of Sioux Indians." Harry Coe, whose deposition was taken in Los Angeles, stated that he was present at Akwesasne in 1914 when Thunderwater was made a "peace chief" and that he personally knew that Thunderwater "worked hard for the Indians, especially the Sioux Indians and Indians of the six nations in New York and Canada." Louis Blackman, an Odawa from Suttons Bay, Michigan, testified that he had known Thunderwater for ten years, had stayed at his home in Cleveland many times, and recognized him to be a "full blood Indian chief." Of his care for other Indians, he stated that Thunderwater constantly provided for "those who call upon him for assistance and that he feeds, clothes, gives medical attention through the services of Dr. Wm. R. Boyd and others when needed and that his home is often used to house Indians in distress."[12]

Additional testimony on behalf of Thunderwater on the second and third days of the trial focused on presenting evidence that the *Times* and *Courier-Journal* had relied on false information and had, in fact, manufactured evidence to support the claim that Thunderwater was a "Negro." One basis for this claim was that Thunderwater was really a black man by the name of "Peter Sands," a charge that originated with information provided by the Department of Indian Affairs and which department officials had good reason to believe was incorrect. Nettie Edwards, a black woman from Cleveland, testified that she knew two men from Cleveland named "Peter Sands," one younger and the other older than Thunderwater; she stated that neither looked like Thunderwater and that both had died some years before. Another black Cleveland resident provided similar testimony.[13] In addition, to support this testimony, Thunderwater's attorneys introduced into evidence the death certificates of two "colored" men from Cleveland, thirty-four-year-old "William Peter Sands," who had died of pneumonia in Chicago in 1905, and eighty-three-year-old "Peter Sands," who had died in Cleveland in 1884.[14]

Thunderwater's attorneys also charged that the *Times* and *Courier-Journal* had doctored and staged the photographs they published to suggest he was a "Negro." Specifically, they argued that the *Courier-Journal* had altered the profile picture of Thunderwater in its March 16, 1927, edition to emphasize his baldness and other supposedly non-Indian physical features. In addition, they argued that newspaper photographers had hired black adults and children to pose in front of Thunderwater's home to create the impression that he lived in Cleveland's "black belt" and regularly associated with "Negroes," and therefore must be black himself. To this end, the attorneys introduced the testimony of Gabriella Morrow, a "colored" woman from Cleveland, who stated in her written deposition that on March 12, 1927, "certain white men" approached her and "offered her the sum of $1 to pose in front of the premises 6716 Baden Court, said premises occupied by Oghema Niagara." Morrow also stated that the men offered her an additional payment of one dollar to pose in front of her own residence, which was, in fact, several blocks away from Thunderwater's home. She added that neither she nor any members of her family were acquainted with Thunderwater. Affidavits relating similar details were also introduced from Morrow's daughter, Elizabeth, and Blanche Willingham, another "colored" Cleveland resident. In a fourth affidavit, Jesse Staples, also a "colored" woman from Cleveland, testified that her three children were paid five cents each to pose for a picture in front of Thunderwater's home. "[The photographer] . . . walked the children over on the next street in front of the house of an Indian chief known as Thunderwater and snapped a picture," she stated in her deposition. "The children told me they had never known Chief Thunderwater and did not know where he lived until told so by this man. I never had anything to do with Chief Thunderwater." Taking a page out of the Department of Indian Affairs playbook, the *Times* and the *Courier-Journal* had conducted their own "dirty tricks" campaign against Thunderwater.[15]

Thunderwater's attorneys concluded their case against the newspapers in a bizarre incident that involved recalling Thunderwater to the witness stand to testify about the *Times* and *Courier-Journal* articles' impact on him. During the course of the questioning, Thunderwater became upset, shouted, "Let me out of here, just a few minutes please!" and ran screaming from the courtroom. He eventually returned to the stand to complete his testimony. Incredibly, this moment was used by the lawyers for the defense in their closing argument as additional evidence that Thunderwater was a fraud and could not possibly be an Indian.[16]

Attorneys for the *Louisville Times* and *Courier-Journal* began their defense in the afternoon of the third day of the trial. They focused a great deal of their attention on the testimony of A. S. Williams, a solicitor with Canada's Department of

Indian Affairs, who had been delegated by Duncan Campbell Scott to appear on his behalf. With the Indian Department's "Thunderwater" file in hand, Williams asserted that Thunderwater was a "Negro" and that he held no title as "chief" recognized by the Canadian government. In a clear reference to the band council system, he explained that in Canada under the Indian Act, "chiefs" were elected by the adult male members of a band for specified terms and that "no election or ceremony [approved of by the Canadian government] making Thunderwater a chief has ever been held." Williams went on to testify that Thunderwater "had sold thousands of worthless memberships in his organization among Canadian Indians." Asked to elaborate on a statement in the *Times* that Thunderwater had caused a great deal of trouble for the Indian Department, he replied that after Thunderwater visited the St. Regis reserve in 1914, "the Indians refused to elect a tribal council and did not elect one until [1927]." Williams followed with what may have been an intentional falsehood aimed at further tainting Thunderwater. In a clear reference to the tumultuous events at Grand River surrounding the abolishment of the Six Nations Confederacy Council and the imposition of the band council system in 1924, which was not connected in any direct way with the Council of the Tribes, he testified that as a result of Thunderwater's work at the Six Nations reserve, "it was found necessary to send a detachment of mounted policeman there and to keep it there ever since, taking away the right of a tribal council."[17]

Williams was also a key defense witness in the matter of Thunderwater's treatment of his adopted son. As part of his testimony Williams began to read the letter Mitchell Benedict purportedly wrote to the Indian Department in January 1919 in which he alleged a string of abuses by Thunderwater. Dearing, one of Thunderwater's attorneys, objected to the reading of the letter, claiming that the story it told was fabricated. It may also be that Dearing argued that the words of the letter were not Benedict's own. However, Judge Dawson allowed Williams to continue. In overruling Dearing's objection, Judge Dawson explained that the contents of the letter did not prove the truth of the youth's charges against Thunderwater, but that he was permitting the letter to be read only to assess the newspapers' claim that such a letter had been written. As already noted, Benedict's letter was highly inflammatory, and the *Courier-Journal* repeated the claims that Thunderwater had whipped, choked, and punched the boy, locked him in an earthen cellar, made "improper advances," and threatened his life. The defense also introduced a new deposition from Thunderwater's adopted son, now twenty-three years old, the reading of which carried over to the morning of the fourth day of the trial. According to the *Times*, the young man "charged mistreatment at the hands of Thunderwater while living with him in Cleveland" and stated that he had been "choked and beaten by Thunderwater." The adopted son's statements were supported and corroborated by the deposition of his sister, who, according to the *Times*, indicated that she "stayed at Thunderwater's house two or three weeks and that he choked, beat, and locked up her brother."[18]

There is good reason to question those allegations. To begin with, the Indian Department never shared with the *Times* and *Courier-Journal* editors its own doubts about the veracity of the boy's story when they first learned of it in 1919. In addition, there are the accounts, at the trial in person and by means of legal deposition, of the many neighbors and associates of Thunderwater who testified to his commendable treatment and care of his adopted son. Further, in preparation for the libel case in June 1927, Thunderwater's attorneys obtained a deposition from Mitchell Arquette of Akwesasne, who claimed that he was a cousin of Mitchell Benedict. Arquette, a Mohawk, was born and raised on the St. Regis reservation, graduated from the Carlisle Indian School, and had competed as a marathoner in the 1912 Olympics. He testified to the great care Thunderwater had given the boy and stated he "positively knows that the said Mitchell Benedict was never abused nor neglected by said Chief Thunderwater while under his jurisdiction nor at any other time." It is not known if Arquette's deposition was ever entered into the record at the libel trial. If so, it was never reported by the *Times* or *Courier-Journal*. In 1929, after the conclusion of the case, Arquette gave a second deposition in which he reiterated the claims made in his first deposition and provided new details. He testified that he had been at Thunderwater's home "for months at a time" when Mitchell Benedict lived there and repeated his claim that Thunderwater had treated the boy well. "He was treated as the son of a very rich man notwithstanding the fact that the Chief is a poor man," Arquette stated. With regard to the charges Benedict had made against Thunderwater in his statement to the Indian Department in January 1919, Arquette testified that he was present in St. Catharines, Ontario, with the boy and his mother and sister after they had left Thunderwater's home in Cleveland and that the letter the boy wrote was actually dictated to him by his mother, father, and sister. It is quite possible that Duncan Campbell Scott was aware of these circumstances of the boy's written account in January 1919 and may have been the reason he was concerned his story would "weaken under examination."

Arquette went even further in his 1929 deposition, suggesting that Benedict was bribed and had perjured himself in his testimony submitted in the Louisville trial. He charged that "Battling Mikey," as Benedict had become known, "was paid a large sum of money by persons from Louisville Kentucky interested in the case of Oghema Niagara vs. The Louisville Times and the Courier Journal." As Arquette explained, he was at the home of Benedict's mother, Mary Ann George, on the St. Regis reserve in early July 1927 when three men drove up and asked for "Battling Mikey." According to Arquette, after being introduced, the men invited Benedict into their car, where he talked to them "for over half an hour." His deposition continued: "He saw one of the men whom he can identify at any time put into the hand of Mitchell Benedict a large roll of yellow bills, most of the roll was Gold notes. . . . Mitchell got out of the car and said that he was going with these men to Malone and told his sister . . . to get ready to go with them. . . . When he came back he had purchased valuable clothing and had paid as much as twelve dollars for a silk sweater." Arquette went on to state that later that evening Benedict was with the three men at a dance, which they "had set up [for] the people of the reservation . . . at which a large quantity of drink of intoxicating nature was consumed." Adding further details about Benedict's contact with the three men just prior to the start of the libel trial in late October 1927, Arquette noted in his deposition that they returned to St. Regis in the "latter part of September or early in October and were with Benedict." Arquette's deposition stated one other important detail. "Why don't you tell the truth and stand by Thunderwater who did so much for you," he claimed to have asked Mitchell. "Benedict answered that it was too late. That if he told the truth now, Thunderwater would have him arrested for perjury."[19]

Much of the activity on the remainder of the fourth day of the trial, and the next day as well, focused on Thunderwater's status as a "chief" and the difficulties he had caused the Department of Indian Affairs in Canada. Some of the testimony came from C. C. Parker, Duncan Campbell Scott's inspector of Indian agencies, who had closely observed Thunderwater's activities on the Haudenosaunee reserves, and G. M. Campbell, the Indian agent for the Tyendinaga reserve. Parker stated that Thunderwater was not a "chief" in the Indian Department's sense of the term. He also stated that Thunderwater had "stirred up trouble among the Indians," one result of which was that the children of many of his followers at Tyendinaga had stopped attending school. "We had to jail the parents," he testified, "to compel them to send their children to school." Parker added that the Canadian government did not recognize Thunderwater's organization and that Thunderwater had "gathered up the worst among the Indians." In an attempt to raise questions about Thunderwater's true identity,

Parker stated, without explanation, that he had "no Indian characteristics, either in feature, character or manner" and that he neither belonged to any Indian tribe nor spoke any Indian language. Agent Campbell stated that Thunderwater had "made a split in the [Tyendinaga] band" and that those who joined him were "shiftless, nomadic or illiterate." He also attested that Indians in Canada had no right under the Indian Act to elect or appoint Thunderwater as a "peace chief," representative, or any other position claimed by him. After hearing this and similar testimony, Judge Dawson ruled that enough evidence had been presented to conclude that Thunderwater was not a "chief" by Canadian government standards and, therefore, that he had no authority to certify tribal adoptions. He declared that these points of Thunderwater's libel case were to be removed from consideration by the jury. In effect, however, Judge Dawson's decision confirmed Thunderwater's claim that he had been appointed as a "peace chief" and "ambassador" by his supporters in several Haudenosaunee communities. That claim was supported by the testimony given by Thunderwater's Haudenosaunee witnesses and was not countered or contested by the defense. Judge Dawson's decision acknowledged that Thunderwater's supporters had appointed him as a "chief" and representative of their interests. But, he ruled, under Canada's Indian Act system they had no right to do so and that under that system Thunderwater held no *officially* recognized political position.[20]

Other activity on the fifth day of the trial included entering depositions from several Thunderwater opponents into the court record. One was from John Walker of Tyendinaga, who stated that Thunderwater's "chiefs" had locked the council house on the reserve and that band councillors had to break in to conduct business. William Arthur John, also from Tyendinaga, reported that Thunderwater had "created much ill-feeling" within the community and that he, as truant officer, had experienced a great deal of difficulty as a result of his followers refusing to send their children to school. Mitchell Laughing and Julius Herne, both from the American side of the St. Regis reserve and identified as elected councillors, claimed in their depositions that Thunderwater had never been a chief in the Mohawk tribe and that there was no such thing as "ambassador of the tribe." Herne also stated that Thunderwater had no authority to adopt anyone into the Mohawk tribe.[21]

On the fourth and fifth days of the trial, the defense also focused attention on the matter of Thunderwater's racial identity. C. C. Parker of the Indian Department had already raised questions about this in his testimony. Also, the defense attorneys had attempted to raise similar questions during Thunderwater's testimony when it cross-examined him about being known in Cleveland as "Palmer." In this regard, an unusual amount of attention was given to the photograph of Thunderwater published by the *Times* that depicted him as a "bald Indian" with the intent of raising questions about his claim to Indian ancestry. The photographer and a photographic expert testified that the picture had not been retouched. Discounting the claim that the defamatory articles about Thunderwater by the *Courier-Journal* and *Times* were motivated by its rivalry with the *Herald-Post*, several representatives of the papers testified that its intent was honorable and proper. "This was a news matter to which the public was entitled," stated one. "We made an investigation. We had found that this man wasn't what he was represented to be and we thought the public ought to know who he was."[22] In addition, the defense countered Thunderwater's claim and evidence that he was not the black Cleveland resident known as "Peter Sands." It presented evidence in the form of several depositions repeating the old allegations from 1919 that Thunderwater was a "colored" man named "Peter Sands" who in 1904 had arranged a funeral for his "Negro" foster mother. Undoubtedly, the original source of this story was the Department of Indian Affairs and two letters it had received in May 1919 from D. S. Edwards, the Cleveland resident who claimed to be of Mohawk descent. It appears that Thunderwater's attorneys were not aware of—nor did the Indian Department share—the third letter it received from Edwards, in which he stated that he had misidentified Thunderwater and recanted all the claims he had made against him.[23]

One final noteworthy moment of testimony in the trial came from Frank McDonald Jacobs of Kahnawake. Jacobs, of course, was the Kahnawake postmaster and former "mayor" of the Kahnawake band council who had been voted out of office in 1915 because of his support for the Sisters of St. Anne and who had become a fierce opponent of Thunderwater and the Council of the Tribes. If the tumultuous public meeting in Kahnawake in 1920 at which Thunderwater was exposed as a fraud did, in fact, occur, as Postal claimed in "Hoax Nativism," it was probably Jacobs that did so. Having traveled to Ottawa several weeks before the trial to give a deposition, Jacobs had eagerly assisted the Indian Department in its preparation of evidence for the *Times* and *Courier-Journal* defense. He had also traveled to Louisville to testify in person. In his testimony Jacobs related details about the beginning of the Thunderwater movement in Kahnawake, the collected money that was supposedly sent to Thunderwater, the events of the Council of the Tribes convention in September 1916, and the appointment of Thunderwater's local councillors. According to the *Times* report of his testimony,

Jacobs claimed that "[Thunderwater] urged the Indians to form their own government . . . encouraging them to take matters in their own hands." He recounted a
confrontation with Thunderwater at the 1916 convention in Kahnawake, saying
that he publicly questioned Thunderwater's tribal background and was threatened by his supporters. Jacobs argued that Thunderwater's Council of the Tribes
memberships were worthless and that at one point he "audited" the books of
the local post office and found that more than thirty money orders had been
sent to him, the largest being $400. Thunderwater's visit, he said, left a "great
disruption" and added that "the chiefs Thunderwater made have been a great
detriment to my race." According to the *Courier-Journal*, Jacobs stated that
Thunderwater considered the Haudenosaunees to be "allies" of the Canadian
government and spoke about "forming a government for the Indians alone."
To stress the unsavory nature of Thunderwater and his followers, he noted that
when Thunderwater arrived in Kahnawake for his convention in 1916, he was
celebrated "by a brass band, which played in front of [the] church during the
sermon." Asked if Thunderwater's meetings and his organization provided any
assistance to the Indians, Jacobs replied that "there was no benefit . . . they only
benefitted Thunderwater himself." Under cross-examination Jacobs stated that
"no individual Indian has the power to adopt persons into the tribe and that all
adoptions by tribes are only honorary." Thunderwater, of course, was offering only
honorary adoptions and was doing so not on his own, but with the cooperation
and endorsement of members of at least two Mohawk bands. On the matter of
Thunderwater's racial identity, Jacobs, who was himself of mixed Native and
white ancestry, reportedly stated without providing supporting details that
"so far as he knows, Thunderwater is not an Indian and that he has none of the
features and manners of an Indian."[24]

Closing arguments in the case were presented on the afternoon of Friday,
October 26. For the defense, Tabb argued that in publishing their articles about
Thunderwater, the *Louisville Times* and *Courier-Journal* had sought only to
inform the public about a man they believed to be an impostor and that they
had a conducted "a very careful investigation" before doing so. Tabb asserted
that Thunderwater was not a chief and that he and his organization had done
no good for Indian people. He argued that his medicines were worthless and
that he had made unpatriotic statements about the U.S. government. Reviewing
the claim of child abuse and raising new doubts about Thunderwater's character
by intimating he was a homosexual or pedophile, he posed this question to the
jury: "Did you ever hear of any man having as many men or boy friends hanging

around? I cannot understand this household of Chief Thunderwater's." Tabb also reviewed the presented evidence that suggested Thunderwater had "Negro blood in his veins." To bolster his point, drawing on racist stereotypes of the time, he referred to the incident earlier in the trial when Thunderwater had been recalled to the stand and ran upset from the courtroom. "Indians are very stoical," he stated. "Can you conceive of an Indian getting up and running out of the courtroom the way that fellow did?"[25]

Representing Thunderwater, attorney Dearing countered Tabb's contention that the *Times* and *Courier-Journal* had been motivated only by its duty to inform an unsuspecting public and argued that the true source of its actions was the newspapers' rivalry with the *Herald-Post*. He pointed out that several witnesses, including Native ones, had testified that Thunderwater's herbs were "good medicine" and that he had never used funds collected for his organization for his personal use. When Dearing attempted to criticize the U.S. Bureau of Indian Affairs and support Thunderwater's views on federal Indian policy, Judge Dawson interrupted and prohibited him from continuing with that line of argument before the jury. Dearing reviewed Thunderwater's and others' testimony about his ancestry and family history, raised doubts about the authenticity of the "bald Indian" photograph of him, and argued that he did not live in the "black belt" of Cleveland. Refuting the accusations that Thunderwater had mistreated his adopted son, he pointed out that he had taken in a sick boy and made him well and that many witnesses had attested to his good treatment of the boy. He noted that Thunderwater had never been prosecuted for the alleged offenses. In referring to the incident in which Thunderwater fled from the witness stand, Dearing, too, drew on racist stereotypes, but to argue a different point. "[He] has the same impulsive character of an Indian," he noted.[26]

Following the closing arguments, Judge Dawson instructed the jury in its charge, emphasizing that he had already ruled on the matter of Thunderwater's claim that he was a chief or ambassador of the Mohawk tribe. "[Thunderwater] was not and is not an Indian chief in the sense in which that word is understood by the public," he stated to the jury. What he meant, of course, was "in the sense" understood and recognized by the Canadian government. "[He] was an imposter, falsely pretending to be an Indian chief," Dawson declared. In reality, he was not. Thunderwater never claimed to be an elected nor a hereditary chief among the Haudenosaunees. In fact, Thunderwater, like his Haudenosaunee supporters, rejected the Indian Act system and the authority of the Canadian government to create or recognize Haudenosaunee chiefs. On this basis the judge also concluded that Thunderwater had no power to adopt white children into the Mohawk tribe. He informed the jurors that they were not to consider Thunderwater's claim that he had been defamed in this regard. Dawson also informed the jury that he did not consider the newspapers' reports about Thunderwater's incendiary statements concerning the U.S. government and the Bureau of Indian Affairs to be libelous and, therefore, also should not be considered for judgment. He did allow them to consider as libelous the published statements that Thunderwater had cheated Indians by collecting Council of the Tribes membership fees, had sold worthless herbal potions as medicine, was guilty of "cruel and shameful" treatment of his adopted son, and was "Negro" and not Indian.[27]

After receiving their instructions, the jurors deliberated for an hour late on the afternoon of Friday, October 26. They resumed their deliberations the next morning, and after just a few hours of discussion they returned to the courtroom to announce that it was deadlocked at ten to two in favor of the *Times* and *Courier-Journal*. In what would seem to be a rather hasty decision, Judge Dawson announced that he was satisfied the jurors were unable to reach a unanimous verdict and dismissed the case. He scheduled a new trial for the March 1929 term of the court. A. S. Williams, the Indian Department inspector who had testified against Thunderwater, sent a brief telegram to Scott informing him of the outcome: "Jury disagreed. Leaving for home on Monday."[28]

While the outcome of the case must have been a great disappointment to Thunderwater, he nevertheless began preparations for the second trial and continued his effort to clear his name and prove his identity. With the retrial moved to October 1929 and then postponed again until the fall of 1930, over the next fifteen months, he gathered additional depositions to support his case. One of those depositions was from Louis Terrance of St. Regis, who stated one of his fellow Mohawks had been paid to testify against Thunderwater in the Louisville trial. Thunderwater also obtained a large number of signed statements, perhaps nearly a hundred, from men and women in Akwesasne who indicated that he was made a chief and given his Mohawk name at St. Regis in 1914 and, generally, that he was an "honest," "capable," and "upright" person who had done good work for the Mohawk people at St. Regis. In June 1929 Thunderwater obtained the second deposition of Mitchell Arquette of Akwesasne in which he suggested that Thunderwater's adopted son had knowingly given false testimony against him in the libel case and that he may have been bribed by representatives of the *Louisville Times* and *Courier-Journal*.[29]

Perhaps the most important deposition secured by Thunderwater was from Chief Isaac Hill ("Skyendockyeh"), the octogenarian pine tree chief from Grand River who had testified in person as a character witness for Thunderwater in the Louisville trial. In 1930 Chief Hill signed a sworn affidavit in which he provided crucial details about Thunderwater's ancestry and family history, as well as information about his political activities. Previously quoted at length, he testified that he was associated with Thunderwater's father when both were young men, confirmed his father's and mother's names and tribal affiliations, and stated that he had known Thunderwater since his early childhood. Hill also stated that "Oghema Niagara" was a "duly elected chief of the Iroquois Nation and had many times had been called into the Council of the Tribes of the Iroquois Nation on occasions of moment." Noting that he had visited and lodged at Thunderwater's home numerous times, he emphasized the importance of Thunderwater's work in caring for destitute Indians in Cleveland and collecting and coordinating relief for "children and the aged" on Indian reservations.[30]

The defense attorneys for the *Louisville Times* and *Courier-Journal* also prepared for a second trial and in this again received eager assistance from the Department of Indian Affairs. Soon after the conclusion of the first trial, J. D. McLean, the department secretary, contacted the Indian agents at Tyendinaga and St. Regis and Frank McDonald Jacobs in Kahnawake requesting their assistance in arranging for new depositions against Thunderwater. In the first trial Thunderwater had produced a number of witnesses who stated that they had paid nothing for the certificates and other materials that they had received from Thunderwater as members of the Council of the Tribes. McLean was especially anxious to counter the impression that Thunderwater did not take money from his supporters and specifically asked the agents and Jacobs to "secure . . . some evidence as to the fact that the people who became members of the Council of the Tribes did pay for the certificates, constitutions and medals that they received." That McLean made his request for depositions from Kahnawake to Jacobs rather than to the local Indian agent, as he did for St. Regis and Tyendinaga, speaks to the high level of cooperation that the Indian Department received from Jacobs in its efforts to discredit Thunderwater. Shortly after receiving the request, Jacobs replied helpfully and with a note of sarcasm, "I have already five people to make depositions regarding payments to our famous Thunderwater." Later, while the arrangements for the new depositions were still under way, Jacobs wrote to McLean again, adding a note that suggests Thunderwater had remained especially popular at Akwesasne. "I am glad to know that the St. Regis Indians are ready to testify," he wrote, "because that is [where] the strongest Thunderwater followers [are] today." Eventually, with the assistance of its agents and Jacobs, the Indian Department provided the *Times* and *Courier-Journal* attorneys with nearly a dozen new signed affidavits testifying against Thunderwater.[31]

In late January 1929 Thunderwater's attorney, W. G. Dearing, attempted to reach an out-of-court settlement with the *Times* and *Courier-Journal*. Charles Tabb, still the lead attorney for the newspapers, supported this idea, but in the end no agreement was reached. With opposition from Tabb, Dearing succeeded in having the date of the second trial moved to October 1929. For reasons that are not clear, that trial never took place, and the case languished for a full year before coming to an end without any resolution in early December 1930. Thunderwater's personal papers and Indian Department files are silent on the uneventful ending of his two-year ordeal and offer no explanation for why the second trial never took place. Even the Louisville newspapers, which reported in such detail on the first trial, had little to say. In a brief article the *Courier-Journal* simply stated, "Chief Thunderwater's two libel suits were dismissed by Judge Charles I. Dawson . . . on motion from W.D. Dearing, counsel of Thunderwater."[32]

CHAPTER 9

AN UNEXPECTED INDIAN
IN UNEXPECTED PLACES

*[T]here were and are significant numbers of Indian anomalies, enough
that we must rethink familiar categories. . . . They suggest a secret history
of the unexpected, of the complex lineaments of personal and cultural identity
that can never be captured by dichotomies built around crude notions of
difference and assimilation, white and Indian, primitive and advanced.
Those secret histories of unexpectedness are . . . worth further pursuit,
for they can change our sense of the past and lead us quietly,
but directly, to the present moment.*
—Philip J. Deloria, *Indians in Unexpected Places*

Following his legal battles in Louisville in the late 1920s, Thunderwater passed the remaining two decades of his life in relative quiet. In many ways, he lived a very conventional life. In the late 1920s he took out a mortgage for $1,000 to purchase the rambling home at 6716 Baden Court that he had rented for so many years. He paid off that loan with regular quarterly payments over the next thirteen years. He drove a used Packard sedan, purchased an Irish Hospital Sweepstakes ticket, and paid monthly premiums on two life insurance policies, naming his business partner Charles Rose as the beneficiary on one. He continued to operate his herbal medicine business with Rose, taking orders from customers in Cleveland and beyond for his elixirs and teas used to treat asthma, digestive problems, and other ailments. Perhaps as a sign of the changing times, in March 1942 he was charged and tried in Cleveland for practicing medicine without a license. Under the headline "Ugh, Medicine Heap Bad, Lands 'Chief' in Court" and a racist caricature of Thunderwater, the *Cleveland Press* told the story. The head of the city's food and drug administration became suspicious about Thunderwater's "homemade medicines and herbs," and in a scenario that must have seemed all too familiar to Thunderwater, he sent one of his inspectors in disguise to his home with a feigned illness. Thunderwater "concocted" a remedy on the spot and was eventually charged with preparing a medical prescription without a license. He was eventually charged in court and released on a $200 bond. Several months later a jury acquitted him of the charge. Though in gradually failing health, as late as 1945 he was ordering the botanical bases for his medicines from suppliers such as the Wilcox Drug Company in Boone, North Carolina. In 1948, when his partner Rose died, he was still receiving orders for their herbal medicines.[1]

By the 1930s Thunderwater's family had fallen apart. His son, Louis Keokuk, who had been working and living with him in the Baden Court home as late as 1920, cut his ties with Thunderwater, abandoned his wife, Blanche, and their daughters, Mahoniall and Marion Wanda, and was never heard from again. In 1930 Blanche was living in Cleveland as a single mother with Marion, then sixteen years old. Marion married the following year and eventually moved with her husband to Willoughby, Ohio, about twenty miles northeast of Cleveland, where they raised three daughters. Blanche remarried in 1932 at age forty-two and remained in the Cleveland area. Thunderwater did remain close to his granddaughter, Mahoniall Keokuk, the "princess" he named at Niagara Falls in 1911. He named her as the beneficiary on the second of his two life insurance policies, and she sometimes appeared with him at public events around the city of Cleveland. She married, divorced, eventually relocated to Eastlake, near Willoughby, and married again in 1950 at age thirty-nine.[2]

Thunderwater continued his humanitarian and political work on behalf of Indian people. In 1934 he worked with William Marsteller, the Cleveland attorney who represented him in his libel case in Louisville, to establish a rural refuge for himself and other Native people on a farm in Aurora, Ohio, about thirty miles southeast of Cleveland. Marsteller, who had a lifelong interest in Native people and cultures, owned the farm and persuaded Thunderwater to take over and manage it. Thunderwater stocked the farm with cows, horses, pigs, and chickens and for a time also rented adjacent land to raise corn and other crops. He operated the farm with the labor of Native men from Cleveland and elsewhere who were looking for a place to live or simply sought a haven from the hustle and bustle of city life. One of those men was Lee Miller, a Cherokee from Oklahoma, who came to the farm in 1937 after his wife died and he was left alone. Another was twenty-one-year-old Danny Tarbell of Akwesasne. By 1940 Tarbell was boarding in Thunderwater's Cleveland home and working in a local steel mill. In a May 1937 article the *Akron Beacon* wrote that Thunderwater described himself as an "Osaukee" and a "citizen chief" of the Six Nations Confederacy and that he visited the farm on weekends, "looking over the week's plowing and planting, the setting of hens, and the rest of the stock. . . . Peering from behind thick horn-rimmed glasses, the spry, white-haired chief spoke his mind about the present day form of government, about religions, and told of the presidents and generals he has known, and his own colorful life." The article quoted Thunderwater as saying, "The Indians had a communistic form of government. . . . [They] believed in the philosophy—no man has a right to anything he can't carry away and no man ever owned a thing." He continued with an interesting reference to the Six Nations Confederacy and the political symbolism of the longhouse: "That was the doctrine for which they formed their government and set up their wigwams and hodenosot" (see figure 12).[3]

One of the Cleveland residents to whom Thunderwater extended his assistance during these years was a white woman from Cleveland by the name of Elmina MacIntyre. MacIntyre was born in New York in 1870, and by 1910 she had moved to Cleveland, where she lived with an aunt. In 1920 Elmina and her aunt, both unmarried, purchased a home in Cleveland of which she became the sole owner when her aunt died in 1932. Around this time MacIntyre became associated with Thunderwater and in 1935, at about age sixty-five, she assigned him power of attorney to manage her financial affairs. Subsequently, MacIntyre became a regular visitor to the Thunderwater farm in Aurora, staying for several days a week on a regular basis for the next year and a half. Thunderwater supplied her with produce from the farm, including eggs, potatoes, vegetables, and meat; made repairs and provided upkeep to her home in Cleveland; and paid her gas, electric, water, and insurance bills. An accounting by Thunderwater in 1939 of the cost of his assistance to her over the course of several years put the total at more than $1,200. In payment for this debt, MacIntyre conveyed her Cleveland property to him, which he sold a year later. While the arrangement was an unusual one, there is no evidence that Thunderwater exploited legal control over MacIntyre's affairs for his own benefit, and after the transfer of the property he arranged for MacIntyre to remain in her former home until her death.[4]

Thunderwater also helped to care for Waunetta Griffin, "Princess Nita," the former Wild West performer who had testified on his behalf in his Louisville libel case. After she retired from the entertainment business, Griffin settled in Cleveland and by 1920 had been widowed, was living alone in a boarding house, and worked as a lithograph inspector. In 1935 she was hospitalized with mental illness, and for a time Thunderwater served as her court-appointed guardian, visiting her at a psychiatric facility in Euclid, Ohio, administering her small pension to pay her hospital bills, and arranging for the purchase of her clothing, shoes, and other necessary items. By 1938 Griffin was out of institutional care,

FIGURE 12. Chief Thunderwater in the early 1930s, soon after losing his libel case in Louisville, Kentucky.

Photograph courtesy of the Western Reserve Historical Society, Cleveland, Ohio.

indigent, and living on the streets in Cleveland. When Thunderwater learned of her circumstances, he again stepped in to arrange for her care and had her moved to a hospital, where she eventually died.[5]

Thunderwater was a regular presence at public events celebrating Cleveland history, which took place regularly in July of each year to mark the establishment of the city in 1796. In 1940 he appeared at a picnic in a local park organized by the Western Reserve Early Settlers Association. Accompanying him were two Senecas from New York, Iona Sky and Herman Jones. The event featured various games and competitions, one of which was won by Dan Tarbell, his boarder from Akwesasne. Thunderwater played an integral part in events celebrating the city's historic Erie Street Cemetery by officiating at a ceremony recognizing the city's mayor, Harold Burton. Ironically, Burton was made an honorary Indian chief at the event. In 1941 Thunderwater was part of a dramatization that marked the first meeting between the area's Native people and Moses Cleveland, the city's namesake, and in 1946 he and his granddaughter, Mahoniall, represented the area's historic Native population in a series of events and reenactments that marked the sesquicentennial anniversary of the city.[6]

Throughout these years Thunderwater continued to tend the grave of Joc-O-Sot, the Sauk warrior buried in Cleveland in 1844, as he had done since his move to the city nearly four decades earlier. In May 1938 the *Cleveland Plain Dealer* reported on his annual honoring of Joc-O-Sot and his dismay at the condition of the historic Erie Street Cemetery where his personal hero was buried. Setting the scene of the ceremony, the *Dealer* described the moment as Thunderwater, his "face as brown as a chestnut" and his "white hair tied behind with a rubber band," approached Joc-O-Sot's grave. "Almost 94 years ago this brave Indian was laid to rest with pomp and honor," he pronounced. "Then there were stately oaks and buckeyes here." With words that must have taken him back to his experience as a young man attending the reburial of Red Jacket in Buffalo in 1884 and his protests with others at the establishment of Seneca Indian Park in that same city in 1912, he continued. "Since then this sacred place has fallen into the hands of ruthless politicians who think only of their pocketbooks. . . . This place was given for the dead, but the politicians have already stolen part of it and tossed the bones away. How foolish people are to trust politicians who grin, pat your back until you vote and then don't want to see you again!" Recalling Joc-O-Sot's story and the lesson he found in the warrior's life, Thunderwater continued, "He was not like politicians, but brave and honest. After the Black Hawk War he volunteered to come east to gain help for his brothers. He came even though he was wounded in the lung, and found friends in Buffalo, Cincinnati and Cleveland, to help his people, until one day he died. He was a loyal Indian. . . . So I sprinkle corn on his grave. It's real Indian maize that I raise myself. It is sprinkled as a symbol that if he were alive I would raise corn for him, cook for him and feed it to him. It is the Indian symbol of eternal friendship." Asked by those in attendance if the ceremony would continue in the future, Thunderwater answered with a wearisome reply: "I don't know. There used to be so many Indians here. I'm the last one now. I don't know."[7]

Over the course of the next two years Thunderwater worked with Cleveland's Early Settlers Association, a local civic and historical organization, to protect the Erie Street Cemetery from development. A number of the city's earliest residents were buried in the graveyard as well, and he sought a fitting testimonial to honor Joc-O-Sot. Reporting on their successful efforts in July 1940, the *Plain Dealer* wrote, "Restored after 114 years, during which it has weathered various conditions and varying fortunes, the historical burial ground will be accepted for the city by Mayor Harold K. Burton—forever to remain in the municipality's care—undisturbed." Owing to Thunderwater's efforts, at the dedication of the newly renovated cemetery, his hero's grave was marked with a new monolith and dedicated with "tribal ceremonies."[8]

By 1948 Thunderwater was in deteriorating health. He had always been a conscientious letter-writer, but after this time correspondence from friends and inquiries from clients about his medicines often went unanswered. Perhaps as a sign of the decline in both his health and financial circumstances, in March 1948 he cashed in his two life insurance policies. In May 1949 Walter Rose, the son of his former business partner, wrote from Chicago with concern about a long lapse in their correspondence. "Long time no see, long time no hear," Rose noted in his letter. "I have been thinking about you for a long time. . . . I dropped a line about getting married, but I guess you did not get it." Another friend wrote from Towson, Maryland, in January 1950, "It seems like a long time passes and still not a word from you. . . . We looked for you around the holidays, thinking you might come down and see us. . . . I'm writing now to find out if everything is o.k. or not. . . . There's never a day goes by that we don't talk about you and wonder how you are. . . . Please write." A few months later Thunderwater became seriously ill, and in early June he was admitted to Mount Sinai Hospital in Cleveland. After a short hospitalization, he died on Saturday, June 10, 1950.[9]

The *Cleveland Plain Dealer* reported the news of Thunderwater's death the next day under the bold headline "Chief Thunderwater, Famous in Cleveland

50 Years, Dies." Reflecting the position and prestige he claimed for himself since he established the Council of the Tribes in 1914, the *Plain Dealer* identified "Oghema Niagara" as the "titular head of the Supreme Council of Indian tribes of the United States and Canada" and described his Cleveland residence as "the semiofficial capital of the North American Indian tribes." The *Plain Dealer* continued, "It was once the custom for the various tribes to send each year young men to visit the chief at his cottage tucked into the congested E. 67th Street-Central Avenue S.E. district." The caption of an accompanying photograph of an aged Thunderwater dressed in his Native regalia noted that "the 85-year-old peace chief of United States and Canadian tribes had lived in Cleveland half a century." The obituary went on to describe Thunderwater as a "dealer in Indian herbs and medicines" who "lectured vigorously in support of the American Indian" and recognized him for his regular presence at public and civic events around the city. Repeating a version of the story of his birth Thunderwater told many times over the course of his life, the tribute continued: "Chief Thunderwater, the best records indicate, was born in a covered wagon somewhere in New York State as his family was journeying from Niagara Falls to Iowa. . . . His mother was of the Sauk tribe and his father was of the Seneca-Iroquois." Perhaps with some confusion, but also clearly drawing on the story of Thunderwater's own claim regarding his political status, the *Plain Dealer* stated that "since his mother was the daughter of a chief in the Black Hawk War, Niagara became a chief by inheritance, or peace chief."[10]

Wire services picked up the news of Thunderwater's death, and over the next several days notices about his passing appeared in papers across the country. The *Democrat and Chronicle* of Rochester, New York, published an abbreviated version of the *Plain Dealer* obituary under the headline "Chief Thunderwater, Head of Indians." Similar and sometimes briefer reports appeared in newspapers in Ohio, Illinois, Michigan, Wisconsin, New York, Connecticut, Pennsylvania, Maryland, Florida, Louisiana, Missouri, Iowa, Montana, Wyoming, Arizona, and California. The *Gazette* of Montreal published an obituary, stating that "the aged chief's home, centre of Indian powwows in earlier years, was cluttered with arrow heads, stone axes, Indian war muskets and copies of the Congressional Record dealing with Indian affairs." The newspaper further noted, "His quarrels with the white man were legion."[11]

Chief Thunderwater—Oghema Niagara—was, and is, an enigma and an anomaly, a most unexpected Indian in the most unexpected places. He was written into history as a shadowy impostor who duped the unsuspecting people of

Kahnawake into a short but intense period of "hoax nativism" between 1915 and 1920, and who was driven back to Cleveland humiliated and without remorse once his deception was exposed. But his identity, character, life, and work have been badly misunderstood. Concerned about his rising influence and the expression he gave to increasingly intense Haudenosaunee political activism during the second decade of the twentieth century, Duncan Campbell Scott and Canada's Department of Indian Affairs orchestrated a campaign to discredit Thunderwater by using dubious information from suspect sources to cast him as a black man and child abuser who used a grifter's sense of showmanship and persuasion to lead his followers astray and cheat them out of their hard-earned money. In retrospect, it strains reason to believe that he could have bamboozled so many Haudenosaunee people in so many communities for such an extended period of time. Nevertheless, the image of Thunderwater as a fraud and con artist made its way into the anthropological literature, consigning him to a humorous, tragic, and ultimately inconsequential footnote in Haudenosaunee and Indigenous history. However, upon close examination, Thunderwater appears to have been what he always professed to be, and more.

Understanding Thunderwater's family history, childhood, and adult years has been a matter of piecing together his biography bit by bit from personal papers, Indian Department files, newspaper accounts, census and vital statistics records, and family oral histories. Some of the evidence is limited, and some of it derives from Thunderwater himself, but, taken together, the story it tells is coherent and consistent. His mother, "Au-Paw-Chee-Kaw-Paw-Qua," was Sauk and Algonquin and the daughter of one of Chief Keokuk's several wives. His father, "Jee-Wan-Ga," was Seneca. Both appear to have been part of the diaspora of Indigenous people unfolding in the United States during the mid-nineteenth century. Thunderwater was born in 1865 on or near the Tuscarora reservation in western New York State, after his parents crossed the international border at Niagara Falls while they were journeying between Quebec or Ontario and Iowa. He was named at those falls—"Oghema Niagara" or "Chief Thunderwater." Much of his early life was spent on the margins of Indian and Euro-American society. As he grew into adulthood, he followed his parents into entertainment work, performed in Buffalo Bill's Wild West Show, and settled for a time in Detroit, Michigan, where he had a relationship with a white woman who bore him a son, Louis Keokuk. Around 1900 Thunderwater and Louis settled in Cleveland, a city with a Native community he had come to know through his parents' travels and social connections. In Cleveland he continued his entertainment work and took up business as a maker and dealer of herbal medicines, a trade learned from his father. He became a political activist on behalf of Indian people, a commitment that began fifteen years earlier when he attended the reburial of Seneca chief Red Jacket in Buffalo, New York, in 1884.

Initially, Thunderwater's political activism focused on local issues in Cleveland, such as honoring the life of Joc-O-Sot and protesting unscrupulous saloonkeepers who sold liquor to Native people. His activism also had a humanitarian side. Following the example set by Native residents who offered hospitality to his family when they visited the city during his childhood, he opened his home and provided care to traveling and indigent Indians who visited the Cleveland area. It was a practice he maintained throughout his life. Drawing on his Seneca background and connections, Thunderwater gradually became involved in issues that concerned Haudenosaunee people in New York and Canada, including border crossing, liquor trafficking, and alcohol abuse, and abusive federal Indian policies and government officials. It appears likely that his Seneca and Sauk connections contributed to both his interest in these matters and his acceptance by members of the Haudenosaunee communities where he sought to give assistance. In 1909, members of one of those communities, the Tonawanda Band of Seneca Indians, appointed him as an official ambassador and "peace chief" to represent their interests. These experiences informed and intensified his political activism.

Thunderwater was an ambitious and effective self-promoter, as well as a committed political activist. He used his personal charisma, oratorical skills, and the showmanship learned in entertainment work to advance not only his political causes, but also himself. Throughout his adult life he made claims to political inheritance as a Sauk chief that were questionable and often exaggerated the scale of the political organizations he formed and the extent of his authority within them. While the Indian Department's estimates of the money raised by Thunderwater in Council of the Tribes membership dues—many tens of thousands of dollars—may be overblown, the funds were substantial, and his use of them remains unclear. No doubt, some of the funds supported council organizational activities, such as the conventions at Akwesasne, Tyendinaga, Kahnawake, and Grand River between 1915 and 1918. Also, it is likely that the money raised underwrote his frequent travel between Cleveland and Canada and between Haudenosaunee communities in Quebec and Ontario. There is limited evidence from the Louisville libel trial that local council members may have diverted membership dues for their personal use, but there is no evidence that Thunderwater did so. However, he never provided an accounting of his own use of those funds, so the possibility remains open that he also used them for his personal expenses. Thunderwater's involvement in the "Indians" newspaper subscription venture is even more challenging in this regard. The plan commodified Indians and "Indianness," and profit-making clearly was the intent of the enterprise. Though on paper the profits directed to Thunderwater were to support his political and advocacy work, the potential funds involved were significant, and it is not easy to dismiss a personal financial incentive. Nevertheless, Thunderwater's personal motivation seems to have been less economic than social and political. He did not live extravagantly, often aided others at his own expense, and died nearly penniless. Rather, he sought the limelight, envisioned himself a pan-Indian political leader, and yearned for public recognition and influence.

Thunderwater's combination of personal background, political commitment, political experience, self-interest, and the organization he established, the Council of the Tribes, proved to be critical in the revival of nationalism that had developed in Haudenosaunee communities in Canada in the late nineteenth century. There were several threads to that stalled current of nationalism, including opposition to the Indian Act, reestablishment of traditional government, reassertion of collective Haudenosaunee identity, political autonomy, and revival of the Six Nations Confederacy. Chief Thunderwater and the Council of the Tribes tapped into that dormant current of nationalism and provided an opportunity and a means for its resurgence. This political dynamic did not exist in the Haudenosaunee communities in the United States, an important factor that may explain why Thunderwater and the Council of the Tribes did not resonate in those communities. His first political successes were at Akwesasne, followed soon by success at Tyendinaga, Kanehsatake, Kahnawake, and Grand River. In response, he absorbed the influence and priorities of his Haudenosaunee supporters, and he adjusted and refined the goals of the Council of the Tribes. The Thunderwater movement became, in reality, a Haudenosaunee political movement. In effect, "Thunderwaterism" constituted the second phase in the rise of modern Haudenosaunee nationalism.

Duncan Campbell Scott and the Department of Indian Affairs determined the resurgence of Haudenosaunee nationalism in the form of the Thunderwater movement to be a retrograde development that challenged the assimilationist goals of federal Indian policy in Canada and threatened its wider implementation. They determined that a harsh and uncompromising response was required. In doing so they focused on the chief agitator and spokesperson of the movement, Thunderwater himself. Initially, they attempted to work with other government agencies to bar him from Canadian soil. Failing in that, they attempted to discredit him by portraying him as a black man, a child abuser, and a pedophile. It was a "dirty tricks" campaign that Scott would subsequently employ with success against other Native activists. Scott also worked behind the scenes to thwart one of the most important expressions of the Thunderwater movement, the attempt to incorporate the Council of the Tribes in Canada through an act of Parliament. By the early 1920s Thunderwater's influence had faded, and the Council of the Tribes ceased to be an effective political organization in Canada—the result of the Indian Department's campaign, the unrealized goals of Haudenosaunee nationalism, and the emergence of other individuals and organizations that took up those political goals. Though the Thunderwater movement had dissolved, "Thunderwaterism" lived on in traditionalist cultural and political developments that it helped to inspire in Haudenosaunee communities, in the Six Nations sovereignty movement for which it served as an important step, and in Indigenous political organizations in Canada for which it served as a building block.

Chief Thunderwater's funeral rites and burial were fitting to the life he had lived. Prior to his death he had ordered that his remains be cremated and his ashes interred in Erie Street Cemetery, the burial ground in Cleveland he had fought to preserve for so many years. For his grave he chose a plot next to Joc-O-Sot, his personal hero from the Black Hawk War. According to one newspaper report, Thunderwater's burial, five days after his death, was briefly delayed "pending the arrival of Indian envoys from reservations throughout the country." The "envoys" who were planning to attend the service were not identified, but presumably at least some were from the Haudenosaunee communities in Canada and the United States with which he had worked for so many years. His meager estate barely covered the expenses for the service and burial. Thunderwater's granddaughter, Mahoniall, attended the ceremony. Before his death she had promised him that she would continue his annual custom of honoring Joc-O-Sot's memory with flowers and Native tributes. She did so for both their graves for the next thirty-five years, until her own death in 1986.[12]

NOTES

Introduction

1. Susan Koessler Postal, "Hoax Nativism in Caughnawaga: A Control Case for the Theory of Revitalization," *Ethnology* 4, no. 3 (July 1965): 266–81; Robert F. Murphy, "Cultural Change," *Biennial Review of Anthropology*, 5 (1967): 42; Weston La Barre, "Materials for a History of Studies of Crisis Cults: A Bibliographic Essay," *Current Anthropology* 12, no. 1 (February 1971): 6; E. Brian Titley, *A Narrow Vision: Duncan Campbell Scott and the Administration of Indian Affairs in Canada* (Vancouver: UBC Press, 2004), 97–101.
2. Titley, *A Narrow Vision*, 97–101 (emphasis added).
3. This research was set forth in two publications. See Gerald F. Reid, *Kahnawà:ke: Factionalism, Traditionalism, and Nationalism in a Mohawk Community* (Lincoln: University of Nebraska Press, 2004); and Gerald F. Reid, "'To Renew Our Fire': Political Activism, Nationalism, and Identity in Three Rotinonhsionni Communities," in *Tribal Worlds: Critical Studies in American Indian Nation Building*, ed. Brian Hosmer and Larry Nesper (Albany: State University of New York Press, 2013), 37–64.
4. Rarihokwats, *How Democracy Came to St. Regis* (Rooseveltown, NY: Akwesasne Notes, 1971). In 2002 Rarihokwats updated his article with information about Thunderwater obtained from a website developed by Thunderwater descendants and reissued it under the title "The Thunderwater Movement: An Anthropological Study of an Indian Tribe." A copy of the reissued article can be found on *Academia* at http://www.academia.edu/20434959/The_Thunderwater_Movement_Anthropological_Study_of_the_Indian_Affairs_Tribe.
5. Philip J. Deloria, *Indians in Unexpected Places* (Lawrence: University of Kansas Press, 2004), 52–108.

Chapter 1

1. I first became aware of the "Oghema Niagara-Chief Thunderwater" family history document in 2004 when Dalene (McGroarty) Kelly contacted me about my Thunderwater research. Mrs. Kelly is a great-great-granddaughter of Chief Thunderwater, and she provided me with a photocopy of the document. Eventually, this connection led me to Mona Secoy, Mrs. Kelly's cousin and also a great-great-granddaughter of Thunderwater, who was in possession of the original document.

2. An image of the inscription on the flyleaf of the book is available on the website of Lighthouse Books, a rare book dealership in St. Petersburg, Florida. The image and other details of the book can be found at http://oldfloridabookstore.blogspot .com/2011/09/black-hawk-keokuk-and-legends.html. According to Michael Slicker, owner of Lighthouse Books, the book was sold several years ago to an unknown buyer. The owner of the flyleaf image is T. Allen Smith of St. Petersburg, Florida. I express my thanks to Mr. Smith for providing me with a copy of that image. Moses Keokuk remained the principal chief of the Sac and Fox Tribe until about 1884 or 1885, when he was succeeded by Chief Mahkosahtoe. Moses continued to serve the Sac and Fox as an assistant principal chief from that time until his death in 1903. An image and description of the photographic reprint on which the Thunderwater family history information is composed was provided to the author by Mona Secoy (personal communication, January 3, 2018). "C.H. Nielson, Manufacturer of All Kinds of Paper and Glass Views" is stamped on the reprint.

3. For translations of "oghema" and "niagara," see *The Ojibwe People's Dictionary*, https:// ojibwe.lib.umn.edu; and "Niagara Falls—Thunder Alley," http://www.niagarafrontier .com/. "Niagara" can also be translated as "the strait" or "a point of land cut in two." For translation of "okimawa," see Gordon Whittaker, *A Concise Dictionary of the Sauk Language* (Stroud, OK: Gordon Whittaker and the Sac and Fox of Oklahoma and the Missouri, 2005), 94, http://learn.bacone.edu/pluginfile.php/26452/mod_resource /content/1/sauk-concise-dictionary.pdf, accessed May 10, 2019. It is perplexing that the parents would use the equivalent of "chief" in the name of their child. In Sauk, Ojibwe, and Seneca cultures—the tribal backgrounds of Thunderwater's parents— the position of "chief" was an earned or hereditary title, a custom with which they would likely have been familiar. I address the matter of Thunderwater's political status later in this chapter.

4. William T. Hagan, "Keokuk," *American National Biography Online*, http://www.anb .org/, accessed July 10, 2017; WikiTree, "Har quo quar," www.wikitree.com, accessed July 10, 2017.

5. Thomas Burnell Colbert, "Keokuk," in *The Biographical Dictionary of Iowa* (Iowa City: University of Iowa Press, 2009), http://uipress.lib.uiowa.edu/, accessed August 17, 2018.

6. RootsWeb, "Chief Keokuk Family Tree," http://wc.rootsweb.ancestry.com/cgi-bin/igm .cgi?db=chief_keokuk&id=I1&op=GET, accessed November 22, 2017. Traditionally, Sauk culture permitted polygyny, but it was not the norm and was usually associated with a high level of male wealth, political influence, or social prestige. Green, in *Early Days in Kansas*, indicated that Chief Keokuk had as many as seven wives over the course of his lifetime. See Charles Ransley Green, *Early Days in Kansas: Along the Santa Fe and Lawrence Trails* (Olathe, KS: C. R. Green, 1913), 91, https://books.google .com/books?id=qVwvAAAAYAAJ, accessed December 30, 2017.

7. A handwritten four-page biographical document contained within Thunderwater's papers archived at the Western Reserve Historical Society in Cleveland, Ohio, states that Au-Paw-Chee-Kaw-Paw-Qua's "nation" was "Algonquin or Chippeway" in

addition to "Osaukee." The document also states that "Au-Paw-Chee-Kaw-Paw-Qua" translates as "Woman whose name shall never die." The document is unsigned and undated, but it may have been authored by Thunderwater sometime shortly before his death in 1950. See Western Reserve Historical Society (WRHS), MSS 3321, Oghema Niagara Papers, Folder 1, "Personal & Biographical Papers, 1913–1950," Thunderwater biographical note, n.d.

8. Michael Lee Weber, "Keokuk, Moses," in *Encyclopedia of Oklahoma History*, https://www.okhistory.org/publications/encyclopediaonline, accessed November 22, 2017.

9. WRHS, Folder 6, "Affidavits, 1915–1933," Affidavit of Chief Isaac Hill, June 16, 1930.

10. William A. Hunter, "Refugee Fox Settlements Among the Seneca," *Ethnohistory* 3, no. 1 (Winter 1956): 11–20.

11. WRHS, Folder 6, Affidavit of Mrs. Minnie Peck, June 9, 1927.

12. For discussions of Sauk political culture and Chief Keokuk, see Nancy Bonvillain, *The Sac and Fox* (Langhorne, PA: House, 1995); and William T. Hagan, *The Sac and Fox Indians* (Norman: University of Oklahoma Press, 1988). Other possibilities for Thunderwater's claim to chieftainship are to the Ojibwes through his mother and the Senecas through his father, but such claims would also be problematic. The Ojibwes, like the Sauks, were patrilineal and, thus, access to inherited political leadership could not have descended to him through his mother. The Senecas were matrilineal and, thus, access to inherited political leadership could not have descended to him through his father.

13. WRHS, Folder 1, "Personal & Biographical Papers, 1913–1950," Thunderwater biographical note, n.d. Thunderwater may have been the author of this unsigned biographical note. See also J. B. Patterson, *Life of Black Hawk, or Ma-ka-tai-me-she-kia-kiak: Dictated by Himself* (New York: Penguin Classics, 2008); Hagan, *Sac and Fox Indians*, 4; and *Louisville Times*, "Thunderwater's Case is Resumed," October 23, 1928.

14. James D. McCabe, *The Illustrated History of the Centennial Exhibition, Held in Commemoration of the One Hundredth Anniversary of American Independence* (Philadelphia: National Publishing Company, 1876), 331. A scanned image of the text is available at the Internet Archive at www.archive.org, accessed July 12, 2017. See also Tom Mensik, "How the Railroad and the Philadelphia Centennial Exposition Expanded the Hamill House," The Hamill House Museum, https://thehamillhouse.wordpress.com.

15. Paul Reddin, *Wild West Shows* (Urbana-Champaign: University of Illinois Press, 1999), 86–157. *Cleveland Press*, "He Treasures Letter from Buffalo Bill," May 12, 1951. The letter referred to and quoted was in the possession of a friend of Thunderwater's who acquired the chief's personal papers and collections after his death in 1950. A copy of the *Cleveland Press* article can be found in WRHS, Folder 7, "Newspaper Clippings." For an insightful and thought-provoking discussion of Native entertainers, artists, and professionals who defied convention and Indian stereotypes at the turn of the twentieth century, see Deloria, *Indians in Unexpected Places*, 52–108.

16. The photograph of Chief Thunderwater and the Oglala Lakotas in Buffalo was reproduced in the *Cleveland Press* in 1951, a year after Thunderwater's death. The

photograph was apparently part of Thunderwater's personal estate, which had been acquired by one of his friends. A copy of the reproduced photograph and an accompanying article can be found in WRHS, Folder 7, "Newspaper Clippings." The text accompanying the reproduced photograph states that it was taken at a "big pow-wow of Indian chiefs in Buffalo in 1910." This is almost certainly a reference to the "Indian Village and Congress" exhibition at the Pan-American Exposition in Buffalo, which was held in 1901, not 1910.

17. WRHS, Folder 6, "Affidavits, 1915–1933," Affidavit of Makes Mad, March 26, 1927, and Affidavit of Henry Eagle Head, May 14, 1927. "Mni wakan" can also be translated as "intoxicating liquor" or "whiskey." For information on Sherman Charging Hawk, see Ancestry.com, *1910 United States Federal Census* (database online), 2006, accessed November 29, 2017.

18. Ancestry.com, *1870 United States Federal Census* (database online), 2009, accessed November 29, 2017; Ancestry.com, *1880 United States Federal Census* (database online), 2009, accessed November 29, 2017; and Ancestry.com, *U.S. City Directories, 1822–1995* (database online), 2011, accessed November 29, 2017. According to a marriage application Louis Keokuk filed at age nineteen in Cleveland in 1908, he was born in Detroit, and his mother was Euphemia Blanchard. See Ancestry.com, *Ohio, County Marriage Records, 1774–1993* (database online), 2016, accessed November 29, 2017; and Ancestry.com, *Michigan, Death Records, 1867–1950* (database online), 2015, accessed November 29, 2017.

Chapter 2

1. David O'Neil, "Joc-O-Sot, or Walking Bear," in *Encyclopedia of Cleveland History*, www.case.edu/ech, accessed December 5, 2017; Paul Reddin, *Wild West Shows* (Urbana-Champaign: University of Illinois Press, 1999), 38.

2. *Cleveland Plain Dealer*, "Chief to Bury Chief," July 11, 1907, "Poor Lo's Not a Bit Uncivilized," July 15, 1907, "Selects Highland Park," July 19, 1908, "Memorial Day Observed," May 31, 1908, and "Would Protect Grave," August 31, 1908; Western Reserve Historical Society (WRHS), MSS 3321, Oghema Niagara Papers, Folder 2, "Correspondence, 1908–1950," Hawkins to Thunderwater, May 12, 1908.

3. Ancestry.com, *1910 United States Federal Census* (database online) 2006, accessed December 5, 2017. The 1910 U.S. Census population schedules list Thunderwater's son Louis and his daughter-in-law Blanche as "Louis Keokuk Palmer" and "Blanche Keokuk Palmer." The "Palmer" surname creates some confusion about Thunderwater's identity and family history, a detail that officials in Canada's Department of Indian Affairs later exploited to cast him as an impostor and undermine his credibility. The most likely explanation for the "Palmer" surname is one offered by Thunderwater himself when the issue arose during his libel case in Louisville in 1928. Testifying under oath, he stated that he was sometimes known as "Palmer" by some residents of Cleveland after having spent a number of his boyhood years living in the home of his godmother, "Mrs. Palmer."

4. WRHS, Folder 7, "Newspaper Clippings and Miscellaneous," asthma prescription, n.d., and Camp Niagara, May 22, 1908; WRHS, Folder 2, "Correspondence, 1908–1950," Business Men's Taft Club, October 30, 1908.

5. WRHS, Folder 7, "Newspaper Clippings and Miscellaneous, "Camp Niagara," May 22, 1908; and *Cleveland Plain Dealer*, "Big Schooners Entered," May 23, 1910, "Amateur Club Meetings," May 26, 1910, "Some Speed to New Cats," June 6, 1910, and "Keep Your Son's Weight 150 lbs. Court Warns Mother," September 17, 1910.

6. *Cleveland Plain Dealer*, "Cleveland Baby Is Made Princess," December 11, 1911. Louis and Blanche Keokuk had a second daughter, Marion Wanda, in 1914.

7. *New York Tribune*, "Chief Defends Pagan Faith; Indian Speaks at Christening of Granddaughter at Niagara," December 11, 1911; *Topeka Daily State Journal* "Defends His Faith," December 11, 1911; *Omaha Daily Bee*, "Indian Chief Raises Protest to Baptism," December 12, 1911; *Ocala Evening Star*, "A Sturdy Old Savage," December 16, 1911; and *Daily Gate City*, "An Indian Chief's Protest," December 14, 1911.

8. Rayna Green, "The Pocahontas Perplex: The Image of Indian Women in American Culture," *Massachusetts Review* 16, no. 4 (Autumn 1975): 698–714.

9. Gabriella Treglia, "Using Citizenship to Retain Identity: The Native American Dance Bans of the Later Assimilation Era, 1900–1933," *Journal of American Studies* 47, no. 3 (August 2013): 777–800; Gabriella Treglia, "The Consistency and Inconsistency of Cultural Oppression: American Indian Dance Bans, 1900–1933," *Western Historical Quarterly* 44, no. 2 (Summer 2013): 145–65; *Cleveland Plain Dealer*, "Calls Paleface Dance Immoral; Indian Chief Says White Man's is Worse Than His Ceremonies," December 8, 1907.

10. *Cleveland Plain Dealer*, "Indians on Warpath—Car Smashes Wagon Load and Custer Massacre Is All But Repeated," July 11, 1908.

11. *Cleveland Plain Dealer*, "White Man's Way, Indian's in Life, Cast Off When Great Spirit Calls," November 22, 1908, and "Chant Old Songs, Use Funeral Car—Indians' Burial of Brother is Almost Grotesque Blending of Past and Present," November 24, 1908.

12. *Cleveland Plain Dealer*, "Indian Will Be Actor—Son of Chief Rehearses for Part of Hiawatha with Y.M.C.A. Boys," July 19, 1909, and "Chippewa Braves Arrive for Show," October 7, 1910.

13. *Cleveland Plain Dealer*, "Objects to Fire Water—Indian Chief Asks That Law Protect His Fellow Aborigines," April 6, 1910.

14. Ancestry.com, *1910 United States Federal Census* (database online), 2006, accessed November 29, 2017. See also the 1900 U.S. Census for the Rosebud Indian Reservation in Meyer County, South Dakota, in Ancestry.com, *1900 United States Federal Census* (database online), 2004, accessed January 10, 2018; and the U.S. Indian census rolls for the Brule Sioux Indians in 1892 and 1895–96 in Ancestry.com, *U.S. Indian Census Rolls, 1885–1940* (database online), 2007, accessed December 7, 2017. Charging Hawk continued to work in the entertainment field for some time and had a good measure of success. In 1920 he was living in Chicago, where he worked as an actor for a motion picture company and by this time had appeared in silent films alongside

better-known actors such as James Young Deer and Lillian "Red Bird" St. Cyr. See Ancestry.com, *1920 United States Federal Census* (database online), 2010, accessed December 6, 2017.

15. WRHS, Folder 6, "Affidavits," Affidavits of Adrian A. Clark, Cephas Hill, and Gilbert Peterson, June 16, 1927, Isaac Hill, June 16, 1930, and Louis Blackman, June 17, 1927. Okmulgee, Oklahoma, where Boyd was born about 1883, was the capital of the Muscogee (Creek) Nation, and "Boyd" is a common surname on the nation's membership rolls from that time period. For information about Thunderwater's Native boarders, see Ancestry.com, *1930 United States Federal Census* (database online), 2002, accessed January 10, 2018; Ancestry.com, *Cuyahoga County, Ohio, Marriage Records and Indexes, 1810–1973* (database online), 2010, accessed January 10, 2018; and Ancestry.com, *1940 United States Federal Census* (database online), accessed January 10, 2018.

Chapter 3

1. Lauren Grewe, "'To Bid His People Rise': Political Renewal and Spiritual Contests at Red Jacket's Reburial," *Native American and Indigenous Studies* 1, no. 2 (Fall 2014): 44–68.

2. Western Reserve Historical Society, MSS 3321, Oghema Niagara Papers, Folder 2, "Correspondence, 1908–1950," Horthey to Niagara, November 5, 1908. For a discussion of the Kahnawake beadworkers petition to the U.S. Congress, see Gerald F. Reid, "Beadworkers and Border Lines: Kahnawà:ke Women Craftworkers and the Assertion of Rotinonhsiónni Border Crossing Rights in the Late Nineteenth Century." Paper delivered at the Annual Conference on Iroquois Research, Montreal, Quebec, October 4–6, 2019.

3. Dean R. Snow, *The Iroquois* (Cambridge, MA: Blackwell, 1994), 162–64. Despite the conclusion of the Everett Commission, the Cayuga land claim went unresolved and persists into the twenty-first century.

4. Laurence M. Hauptman and L. Gordon McLester III, eds., *The Oneida Indians in the Age of Allotment, 1860–1920* (Norman: University of Oklahoma Press, 2006), 260–77; and Laurence M. Hauptman, *In the Shadow of Kinzua: The Seneca Nation of Indians Since World War II* (Syracuse, NY: Syracuse University Press, 2013), 192.

5. United States, Office of Indian Affairs, *Annual Report of the Commissioner of Indian Affairs for the Year 1909* (Washington, DC: Government Printing Office, 1909), 36–37; and Vine Deloria Jr. and Raymond J. DeMallie, eds., *Documents of American Indian Diplomacy: Treaties, Agreements, and Conventions, 1775–1979*, vol. 1 (Norman: University of Oklahoma Press, 1999), 492–96.

6. WRHS, Folder 5, "Ambassadorial Credentials, 1909–1927 and General Legal Papers, 1893–1939," Oghema Niagara-Chief Thunderwater Ambassador Appointment by the Chiefs, Firekeepers Warriors of the Six Nations Tonawanda Band of Seneca Indians, 1909. For information about Freeman Johnson, see the biographical note in the description and inventory of the Freeman C. Johnson Collection at the Rochester

Museum and Science Center prepared by Sandra Gordon (1975). The description and inventory can be accessed at http://collections.rmsc.org/Library/JohnsonFreeman _findingAid.pdf.

7. For a discussion of the development of the hereditary council system at Tonawanda, see Deborah Doxtator, "What Happened to the Iroquois Clans? A Study of Three Nineteenth Century Rotinonhsyonni Communities," (PhD diss., University of Western Ontario, 1996), 277–311.

8. Snow, *The Iroquois*, 164–66 and 176–77; Anne Marie Shimony, *Conservatism among the Iroquois at the Six Nations Reserve* (Syracuse, NY: Syracuse University Press, 1994), 35; and Anthony F. C. Wallace, *Death and Rebirth of the Seneca* (New York: Vintage, 1969), 330–35.

9. *Buffalo Commercial*, "Habeas Corpus for Indian Girl," June 11, 1912; *Buffalo Enquirer*, "Charged by Chief Thunderwater that Detention of Eleven-Year-Old Miss Is Illegal," June 11, 1912; and *Buffalo Morning Express*, "Truant but Not Wayward," June 15, 1912.

10. *Buffalo Commercial*, "To Help Indians—Chief Thunderwater Works to Stamp Out Sale of Liquor," April 18, 1912.

11. *Buffalo Morning Express*, "No Whiskey for Braves," May 4, 1912; *Buffalo Courier*, "Thunderwater Swears Out Warrants on Allegations of Selling Indians Liquor," May 4, 1912; *Buffalo Morning Express*, "Chief Thunderwater Starts Crusade Against Those Who Sell His Braves Firewater," June 9, 1912; and *Buffalo Morning Express*, "Main Street Gamblers Routed by Thunderwater," August 20, 1912.

12. Bryan Printup and Neil Patterson Jr., *Tuscarora Nation* (Charleston, SC: Arcadia Publishing, 2007), 89; William E. Johnson, *The Federal Government and the Liquor Traffic* (Westerville, OH: American Issue Publishing Company, 1911), 184–85; William M. Beauchamp, *A History of the New York Iroquois* (Albany: New York State Education Department, 1905), 381–82; Thomas C. Moffett, *The American Indian on the New Trail: The Red Man of the United States and the Christian Gospel* (New York: Missionary Education Movement of the United States and Canada, 1914), 265; and Dorcas J. Spencer, "Indians and Prohibition," *American Indian Magazine* 4, no. 4 (October–December 1916): 311–14.

13. *Buffalo Sunday Morning News*, "Indians Protest at Tablet Unveiling," June 30, 1912; and *Buffalo Courier*, "Indians Protest But Offer No Violence When Ancient Cemetery Is Made City Park," June 30, 1912.

14. Joy Porter, *To Be Indian: The Life of Iroquois-Seneca Arthur Caswell Parker* (Norman: University of Oklahoma Press, 2001).

15. Porter, *To Be Indian*, 91–113.

16. Laurence M. Hauptman, "Designing Woman: Minnie Kellogg," in *Seven Generations of Iroquois Leadership: The Six Nations Since 1800* (Syracuse, NY: Syracuse University Press, 2008), 143–63; and Kristina Ackley and Cristina Stanciu, eds., *Laura Cornelius Kellogg: Our Democracy and the American Indian and Other Works* (Syracuse, NY: Syracuse University Press, 2015), xxiv and 1–30.

17. Hauptman, "Designing Woman," 149–52; Ackley and Stanciu, *Laura Cornelius Kellogg*, 8–10, and 26–30.

18. Postal, "Hoax Nativism," 279.

19. Snow, *The Iroquois*, 192; and Laurence M. Hauptman, *Formulating American Indian Policy in New York State, 1970–1986* (Albany: State University of New York Press, 1988), 4–6.

20. WRHS, Folder 3, "Council of the Tribes, 1914–1922 and undated," Address by George P. Decker Before Council of the Six Nations at Onondaga, November 10, 1914.

21. For example, see Library and Archives Canada (LAC), RG10, Vol. 3184, File 458,168 Pt. 1, Thunderwater to Roche, July 29, 1915; and WRHS, Folder 3, Council of the Tribes membership certificate, n.d.

22. Postal, "Hoax Nativism," 269–70; and Titley, *A Narrow Vision*, 97–101. While noting the similarity between the organizational structure of the Council of the Tribes and the Six Nations Confederacy, Postal suggested that this was a resemblance only, without depth or meaning.

23. Postal, "Hoax Nativism," 269; and Titley, *A Narrow Vision*, 97. My sincere thanks to Deborah Greene and her father, Clarence Green, grandson of Wellington Green, for providing me with a copy of Green's Council of the Tribes membership certificate.

24. Jon Parmenter, "The Meaning of *Kaswentha* and the Two Row Wampum Belt in Haudenosaunee (Iroquois) History: Can the Oral Tradition be Reconciled with the Documentary Record," *Journal of Early American History* 3, no. 1 (2013): 82–109.

25. The composition of the "Inner Council" of the Council of the Tribes in 1915 is identified on COTT letterhead from this time period. See LAC, RG10, Vol. 3184, File 458,168 Pt. 1, Thunderwater to Roche, July 29, 1915.

26. "Census Roll of Creek Indians," Creek Nation Collection, University of Oklahoma Libraries Western History Collections, https://digital.libraries.ou.edu/cdm/, accessed August 14, 2017. Interestingly, one other councillor in the Inner Council of the council was "Wanphia Spieche," who appears to be a relative of Boyd's, perhaps a brother. See Ancestry.com, *Cuyahoga County, Ohio, Marriage Records and Indexes, 1810–1973* (database online), 2010; and Ancestry.com, *1930 United States Federal Census* (database online), 2002.

Chapter 4

1. The following discussion of the rise of modern Haudenosaunee nationalism in the late nineteenth century is examined in detail in my chapter "'To Renew Our Fire': Political Activism, Nationalism, and Identity in Three Rotinonhsionni Communities," in *Tribal Worlds: Critical Studies in American Indian National Building*, ed. Brian Hosmer and Larry Nesper (Albany: State University of New York Press, 2013), 37–64. The discussion here is adapted from that chapter.

2. Wayne Daugherty and Dennis Madill, *Indian Government Under Indian Act Legislation, 1868–1951, Part I* (Ottawa: Department of Indian and Northern Affairs of Canada, 1980), 1–27; John L. Tobias, "Protection, Civilization, Assimilation: An Outline History of Canada's Indian Policy," in *Sweet Promises: A Reader on Indian-White*

Relations in Canada ed. J. R. Miller (Vancouver: University of British Columbia Press), 132–35.

3. Library and Archives Canada (LAC), RG10, Vol. 1862, File 241; Vol. 1876, File 933; Vol. 1991, File 6670; Vol. 2005, File 7784; Vol. 2015, File 8096; Vol. 2018, File 8246; Vol. 2084, File 12757; Vol. 2106, File 19383; Vol. 2184, File 37064; Vol. 2283, File 56785; Vol. 2320, File 63812–2; Vol. 2323, File 65108; and Vol. 2781, File 156468. See also Jack Aaron Frisch, *Revitalization among the St. Regis Mohawks* (PhD diss., Indiana University, 1971), 77–78; Reid, *Kahnawà:ke*, 50–92; William Sprague, "Report of the Indian Branch of the Department of the Secretary of State for the Provinces," in *Report of the Secretary of State for Canada for the Year Ending 30th June 1870.*

4. LAC, RG10, Vol. 1862, File 241; Vol. 1997, File 7073; Vol. 2015, File 8096; Vol. 2084, File 12757; Vol. 2016, File 19383; Vol. 2320, File 63812–2; and Vol. 2781, File 156468. See also Reid, *Kahnawà:ke*, 50–92.

5. Reid, *Kahnawà:ke*, 50–92.

6. Sally M. Weaver, "The Iroquois: The Grand River Reserve in the Late Nineteenth and Early Twentieth Centuries, 1875–1945," in *Aboriginal Ontario: Historical Perspectives on the First Nations*, edited by Donald B. Smith and Edward S. Rogers (Toronto: Dundurn Press, 1994), 213, 233–34, 239–41.

7. LAC, RG10, Vol. 2320, File 63812–2; and LAC, MG19, File 6.

8. LAC, RG10, Vol. 2320, File 63812–2.

9. LAC, RG10, Vol. 2320, File 63812–2, Hill to Superintendent General of Indian Affairs, July 30, 1888, and November 12, 1888, Maracle et al. to Governor General, October 29, 1888, Petition of 236 warriors, women, and people of the Six Nations Mohawks of the Bay of Quinte to the Governor General of Canada, October 29, 1888, "Results of the election of chiefs," November 7, 1888, Brant to Lord Stanley, December 13, 1888, Joseph I. Brant, n.d., Brant to Governor General, June 29, 1889, Brant to Deputy Superintendent General, August 17, 1889, Brant to Governor General, March 13, 1890, Brant to Dewdney, May 14, 1890, Maracle et al. to Stanley, November 20, 1890, and Chief Sachems to Governor General, November 1, 1891.

10. LAC, RG10, Vol. 2320, File 63812–2, Saro Tekaniaterekwen et al. to Governor General, December 4, 1890; LAC, RG10, Vol. 2320, File 63812–2, Petition of the Iroquois women residing at Caughnawaga village or reserve, December 8, 1890; LAC, RG10, Vol. 2320, File 63812–2, Onetotako et al. to the Governor General, March 1895; see also LAC, RG10, Vol. 2320, File 63812–2, Statement Addressed to the Honourable T. M. Daly, September 22, 1894, Reed to Daly, December 11, 1894, and Onetotako et al. to the Governor General, April 26, 1896.

11. LAC, RG10, Vol. 2320, File 63812–2 and Vol. 2781, File 156468. See also William N. Fenton, "Seth Newhouse's Traditional History and Constitution of the Iroquois Confederacy," *Proceedings of the American Philosophical Society* 93, no. 2 (May 1949): 141–58; and Sally M. Weaver, "Seth Newhouse and the Grand River Confederacy at Mid-Nineteenth Century," in *Extending the Rafters: Interdisciplinary Approaches to Iroquoian Studies*, edited by Michael K. Foster, Jack Campisi, and Marianne Mithun (Albany: State University of New York Press, 1984).

12. LAC, RG 10, Vol. 2781, File 156468–11 and Vol. 2930, File 192923. See also Darren Bonaparte, "Saiowisekeron: The Jake Ice Story," *Wampum Chronicles*, www.wampumchronicles.com/saiowisakeron.html. Accessed October 19, 2007.

13. Weaver, "The Iroquois," 233–41.

14. LAC, RG10, Vol. 2320, File 63812–2; Vol. 2781, File 156468–11; Vol. 7932, File 32–33 pt. 2; Vol. 7932, File 32–33 pt. 3. See also Weaver, "The Iroquois," 239–45; and Department of Indian Affairs, *Annual Report of the Department of Indian Affairs for the Year Ended 30th June 1898*, 495.

15. *Utica Observer*, "Indians Held a Monster Convention," November 21, 1914. A copy of the *Utica Observer* article is contained in the Thunderwater file maintained by the Department of Indian Affairs. See LAC, RG10, Volume 3184, File 458,168 Pt. 1. For the St. Regis reserve Indian agent's report, see LAC, RG10, Volume 3184, File 458,168 Pt. 1, Taillon to McLean, November 12, 1914.

16. Western Reserve Historical Society (WRHS), MSS 3321, Oghema Niagara Papers, Folder 3, "Council of the Tribes, 1914–1922," Louis Solomon et al., December 18, 1914. I would like to thank my colleague Roy Wright for his assistance in translating the name "Tehotiokwawakon."

17. LAC, RG10, Vol. 3184, File 458,168 Pt. 1, Oghema Niagara to Superintendent General of Indian Affairs, June 8, 1915 (emphasis in original).

18. WRHS, Folder 3, "Council of the Tribes, 1914–1922," "Programme—Thirtieth Annual Convention of the Council of the Tribes, 27 September to 1 October 1915." The program for the convention bills the event as the "thirtieth" annual meeting of the Council of the Tribes, implying that the Council of the Tribes was first organized in 1885. However, there is no evidence of the council prior to 1914. The date of 1885, though, did have some personal significance for Thunderwater. He claimed that the reburial of the remains of Red Jacket in Buffalo, New York, in October 1884 was a transformational moment his life and that he began his political activism on behalf of Native people the following year.

19. LAC, RG10, Vol. 3184, File 458,168 Pt. 1, Memorandum of J. D. McLean, June 14, 1916, and Williams to Scott, November 15, 1916.

20. The development of education and the schools in Kahnawake are discussed in greater detail in Reid, *Kahnawà:ke*, 107–18.

21. LAC, RG10, Vol. 6076, File 305–1B Pt. 1, Caughnawaga Agency—Caughnawaga Roman Catholic Boys School, Delisle to McLean, September 10, 1900. The development of education and the schools in Kahnawake are discussed in greater detail in Reid, *Kahnawà:ke*, 107–18.

22. Reid, *Kahnawà:ke*, 109–12.

23. Reid, *Kahnawà:ke*, 112–18.

24. WRHS, Folder 3, "Council of the Tribes, 1914–1922," "Official Programme, Thirty-First Annual Convention Council of the Tribes and Third of the Iroquois, September 10th to 15th, 1916, Caughnawaga, Quebec, Canada." Phillips (Sak Tehotionwasere), Mitchell Dailleboust (Wishe Tassennontie), and John Dailleboust (Sawatis Tawenrate) had served as elected band councillors during the late 1890s and early 1900s.

25. LAC, PA-181695, Chief Thunderwater Administering Indian Oath to Grand Councillor, September 14, 1916.
26. WRHS, Folder 3, "Council of the Tribes, 1914–1992," "Official Programme, Thirty-First Annual Convention Council of the Tribes and Third of the Iroquois, September 10th to 15th, 1916, Caughnawaga, Quebec, Canada." Chief Michael Montour is listed in the program as "Chief Mitchell Montour." "Chief Mitchell Montour" is almost certainly the person identified in early records as Michael Montour (Wishe Sakoientineta), hereditary chief of the Great Bear clan from 1881 to 1889. In these records, Montour/Sakoientineta is also sometimes referred to as "Mitchell." See Reid, *Kahnwá:ke*, 58–60. For the cap given to Thunderwater at the convention in Kahnawake in 1916, see WRHS, Permanent Collection 57.221.
27. LAC, RG10, Vol. 3178, File 449628–1, Gras to Scott, January 30, 1917, and *Eastern Door*, "Mohawk List of Chiefs (Band Councillors), 1889–1998," July 11, 1997.
28. WRHS, Folder 2, Correspondence, Chiefs and the Councillors of the Tribes to Chief Thunderwater, June 2, 1916. See also WRHS, Folder 2, Correspondence, Moses to Thunderwater, September 21, 1915, and Will Made by the Councillors of the Tribes, April 19, 1915.
29. WRHS, Folder 2, Correspondence, Mrs. Asa R. Hill to Martin, April 2, 1917. Mrs. Hill wrote to Thomas Walter Martin, Supreme Secretary of the Council of the Tribes in April 1917 with regard to the rights of members of the Six Nations band to hunt and trap on the Grand River reserve. Her letter was written on Council of the Tribes stationery, and in it she identified herself as the "official representative and secretary for the Council of the Tribes on the Grand River Reserve."
30. LAC, RG10, Vol. 3184, File 458168 pt. 1, Abraham to Scott; summary of Thunderwater's speech at Oshweken, October 2, 1916.
31. LAC, RG10, Vol. 3184, File 458168 pt. 1, Taillon to McLean, January 9, 1917, Great Counsel to the Council of the Tribes, January 18, 1917, and Thunderwater to SGIA, January 19, 1917.
32. LAC, RG10, Vol. 3184, File 458168 pt. 1, Memorandum for Mr. Meighen, October 29, 1917. *Ottawa Citizen*, "Indian Delegates Refused Audience by Govt. Official," October 26, 1917. A copy of the article is contained in LAC, RG10, Vol. 3184, File 458168 Pt. 1.
33. LAC, RG10, Vol. 3184, File 458168 pt. 1, "Bill 30—An Act to Incorporate the Council of the Tribes in Canada." The effort to incorporate the Council of the Tribes in Canada was preceded by the incorporation of the organization in Ohio in March 1917 under the name of "The Supreme Council of the Tribes." The stated purpose of the Supreme Council was to "promote the general welfare of the American Indians" and to "protect and preserve their rights and interests generally." See WRHS, Folder 3, "Council of the Tribes, 1914–1922" Article of Incorporation of the Supreme Council of the Tribes, March 10, 1917. For a copy of Chief Thunderwater's Six Nations membership certificate, see WRHS, Folder 1, "Personal and Biographical Papers, Undated and 1913–1950," Thunderwater Certification of Six Nations Membership, n.d. Thunderwater's membership certificate is undated but was most likely signed

around 1918. Levi General, who signed the certificate as the deputy speaker of the Six Nations Confederacy Council, was appointed to that position in 1918, after having been raised up as a hereditary chief with the title of Deskaheh the previous year; he was appointed speaker of the Confederacy Council in 1922. By 1920 Thunderwater's influence was ebbing, and the Thunderwater movement was in decline.

34. LAC, RG10, Vol. 7932, File 32–33 pt. 3, November 17, 1914, to July 15, 1915; and LAC, RG10, Vol. 7932, File 32–33 pt. 4, June 30, 1918, to September 18, 1918.

35. LAC, RG10, Vol. 3184, File 458168 Pt. 1, "Indians Want to Have Ambassador," *The Gazette*, October 2, 1918.

36. *Montreal Gazette*, "Indians Present at Trial of Chief," December 19, 1919, and "Chief Delisle was Acquitted," December 24, 1919; *Eastern Door*, Mohawk List of Chiefs (Band Councillors), 1889–1998, July 11, 1997.

37. LAC, RG10, Vol. 7933, File 32–34 Pt. 2, Barnhart to King George V, February 20, 1919, Minutes of Council Meeting, December 4, 1918, McLean to Campbell, December 10, 1918, and Correspondence, December 4, 1918, to March 7, 1919. Participation in the nomination meeting, which took place on December 20, 1918, may have involved as few as eleven people, the five nominees and the six individuals who nominated and seconded their nominations. See also "Installation of Life Chiefs on the Tyendinaga Reserve," Solomon J. Brant Papers, Kanhiote Library, Tyendinaga Mohawk Territory.

38. LAC, RG10, Vol. 7933, File 32–34 Pt. 2, Scott to Brant, March 13, 1919, Culbertson et al. to Superintendent General, October 6, 1919, and Sero et al. to His Majesty the King, n.d. The latter petition is undated, but an accompanying document signed by Chief Joseph J. Brant and others and dated April 9, 1919, suggests that the petition was prepared at about that same time. See LAC, RG10, Vol. 7933, File 32–34 Pt. 2, Brant et al. to His Most Gracious Majesty, April 9, 1919.

Chapter 5

1. Library and Archives Canada (LAC), RG10, Vol. 7932, File 32–33 Pt. 3, November 17, 1914, and M. C. Jacob et al., March 28, 1911; LAC, RG10, Vol. 2781, File 156468–11, Long to McLean, March 27, 1899; and LAC, RG10, Vol. 3184, File 458168 Pt. 1, Taillon to McLean, November 12, 1914, McLean to Chief Jocko et al., May 20, 1915, and Thunderwater to SGIA, March 19, 1915.

2. LAC, RG10, Vol. 3184, File 458168 Pt. 1, Thunderwater to SGIA, March 19, 1915, June 8, 1915, and July 29, 1915.

3. LAC, RG10, Vol. 3184, File 458168 Pt. 1, Parker to Scott, April 21, 1915, Scott to Parker, April 22, 1915, and Parker to Scott, April 26, 1915.

4. LAC, RG10, Vol. 7932, File 32–33 Pt. 3, White to Indian Department, June 28, 1915, Taillon to McLean, June 9, 1915, and Cook to Deputy SGIA, July 15, 1915.

5. LAC, RG 10, Vol. 3184, File 458168 Pt. 1, Brant to Scott, September 20, 1915.

6. LAC, RG 10, Vol. 3184, File 458168 Pt. 1, McLean to Brant, September 28, 1915.

7. LAC, RG 10, Vol. 3184, File 458168 Pt. 1, McLean to Loft, October 1, 1915.

8. LAC, RG 10, Vol. 3184, File 458168 Pt. 1, Parker to Scott, October 14, 1915.

9. LAC, RG 10, Vol. 3184, File 458168 Pt. 1, Leween et al. to Superintendent General of Indian Affairs, June 14, 1916, Claus to McLean, June 10, 1916, and Brant to McLean, July 31, 1916.

10. LAC, RG 10, Vol. 3184, File 458168 Pt. 1, Meritt to Hewitt, May 21, 1917. It is interesting to note that Hewitt wrote to the Office of Indian Affairs from Brantford, Ontario, near the Grand River reserve. By this point in time Thunderwater and the Council of the Tribes had been active in Haudenosaunee communities in Canada for over two years. He had been active at Grand River, where he had many council supporters and where a major convention of the council had been held just six months earlier. In addition, at this time Thunderwater and council members, many of whom were from Grand River, were preparing their case to incorporate the organization in Canada. However, Hewitt apparently mentioned none of this in his communication with the assistant commissioner and instead inquired about the "New York Indians." It is even more curious because Hewitt worked closely with Chief John Arthur Gibson and others at Grand River who were supporters of the hereditary chiefs system and, as discussed, there was a strong connection in Haudenosaunee communities between efforts to maintain and revive traditional government and the development of the Thunderwater movement.

11. LAC, RG 10, Vol. 3184, File 458168 Pt. 1, Brosseau, undated, and Brosseau to Secretary, August 21, 1916 (emphasis added). "Chief Beauvais" is a reference to Frank Beauvais, one of the elected band councillors. Noting the agent's concern that Chief Beauvais and the other elected councillors disregarded his directive and instead expressed support for Thunderwater, recall that Thunderwater supporters captured control of the Kahnawake band council in 1916 and dominated it until at least 1920.

12. LAC, RG 10, Vol. 3184, File 458168 Pt. 1, Taillon to McLean, September 1, 1916; and Clarke to Sherwood, September 11, 1916.

13. LAC, RG 10, Vol. 3184, File 458168 Pt. 1, Abraham to Scott, October 2, 1916.

14. LAC, RG 10, Vol. 3184, File 458168 Pt. 1, D. C. Scott to W. D. Scott, December 6, 1916, W. D. Scott to D. C. Scott, December 13, 1916, and Scott to Mulvey, January 12, 1917.

15. LAC, RG 10, Vol. 3184, File 458168 Pt. 1, Abraham to Scott, Summary of Thunderwater's speech at Oshweken, October 2, 1916; and P. Whitney Lackenbauer, *Battle Grounds: The Canadian Military and Aboriginal Lands* (Vancouver: UBC Press, 2007), 68–73.

16. LAC, RG10, Vol. 3184, File 458168 Pt. 1., Cooke Memorandum to Scott, October 31, 1917 (emphasis added).

17. LAC, RG10, Vol. 3184, File 458168 Pt. 1., Cooke Memorandum to Scott, October 31, 1917. For information on Cooke, see Brendan Edwards, "'A Most Industrious and Far-Seeing Mohawk Scholar': Charles A. Cooke (Thawennensere), Civil Servant, Amateur Anthropologist, Performer, and Writer," *Ontario History* 102, no. 1 (Spring 2010): 81–108; Katherine McGowan, "'In the Interest of the Indians': The Department of Indian Affairs, Charles Cooke and the Recruitment of Native Men in Southern Ontario for the Canadian Expeditionary Force, 1916," *Ontario History* 102, no. 1 (Spring 2010): 109–24; Timothy C. Winegard, "An Introduction to Charles A. Cooke within the Context of Aboriginal Identity," *Ontario History* 102, no. 1 (Spring 2010):

78–80; and Marius Barbeau, "Charles A. Cooke, Mohawk Scholar," *Proceedings of the American Philosophical Society* 96, no. 4 (August 1952): 424–26.

18. LAC, RG10, Vol. 3184, File 458168 Pt. 1, Scott to Meighen, November 6, 1917.

19. LAC, RG10, Vol. 3184, File 458168 Pt. 1, Mitchell Jack et al. to the Department of Indian Affairs, n.d., and Memorandum to Arthur Meighen, April 23, 1918; *Montreal Star*, "Indians Petition Government," April 13, 1918; Porter to Gogo, May 29, 1918.

20. LAC, RG10, Vol. 3184, File 458168 Pt. 1, Memorandum to Meighen, April 23, 1918 (emphasis added).

21. LAC, RG10, Vol. 3184, File 458168 Pt. 1, Porter to Gogo, May 29, 1918.

Chapter 6

1. Library and Archives Canada (LAC), RG10, Vol. 3184, File 458168 Pt. 1, Agreement for Adoption of Child by Mary Ann George and Oghema Niagara, September 27, 1916.

2. LAC, RG10, Vol. 3184, File 458168 Pt. 1, Indian Department correspondence, January 5 to February 4, 1919.

3. LAC, RG10, Vol. 3184, File 458168 Pt. 1, Thunderwater to George, January 8, 1919.

4. LAC, RG10, Vol. 3184, File 458168 Pt. 1, George to Indian Affairs, January 11, 1919.

5. LAC, RG10, Vol. 3184, File 458168 Pt. 1, Benedict to Indian Affairs, January 11, 1919.

6. LAC, RG10, Vol. 3184, File 458168 Pt. 1, Unsigned to Indian Affairs, January 11, 1919.

7. LAC, RG10, Vol. 3184, File 458168 Pt. 1, Scott to Smith, January 15, 1919.

8. LAC, RG10, Vol. 3184, File 458168 Pt. 1, Statutory Declaration of Mary Ann George in the Matter of Benedict and Thunderwater, January 22, 1919, Statutory Declaration of Mitchell Benedict in the Matter of Benedict and Thunderwater, January 22, 1919, Statutory Declaration of Mary Benedict in the Matter of Benedict and Thunderwater, January 22, 1919.

9. Western Reserve Historical Society, MSS 3321, Oghema Niagara Papers, Folder 6, "Affidavits, 1915–1933," Affidavit of Minnie Eaton, January 27, 1919, and Affidavit of George Stella, January 28, 1919.

10. LAC, RG10, Vol. 3184, File 458168 Pt. 1, Scott to Smith, January 15, 1919, and D. C. Scott to W. D. Scott, February 14, 1919.

11. LAC, RG10, Vol. 3184, File 458168 Pt. 1, W. D. Scott to D. C. Scott, February 27, 1919.

12. *Elyria Evening Telegram*, "The First Americans," June 30, 1918.

13. LAC, RG10, Vol. 3184, File 458168 Pt. 1, Cree to McLean, February 8, 1919, and Cree to McLean, February 21, 1919 (emphasis in original).

14. LAC, RG10, Vol. 3184, File 458168 Pt. 1, Orchard to McLean, May 5, 1919.

15. LAC, RG10, Vol. 3184, File 458168 Pt. 1, Edwards to McLean, May 6, 1919, and McLean to Edwards, May 8, 1919.

16. LAC, RG10, Vol. 3184, File 458168 Pt. 1, Edwards to McLean, May 15, 1919.

17. LAC, RG10, Vol. 3184, File 458168 Pt. 1, Edwards to McLean, November 19, 1919.

18. LAC, RG10, Vol. 3184, File 458168 Pt. 1, Brant to Meighen, November 6, 1919.

19. Postal, "Hoax Nativism," 271–72.

20. *Louisville Times*, "Thunderwater Held Not Chief," October 26, 1928.

21. WRHS, Folder 5, Ambassadorial credentials, Chief Solomon Brant, et al., July 27, 1920, and LAC, RG10, Vol. 7932, File 32–33 pt. 4, November 20, 1919, to March 2, 1928. I have discussed the development of the Longhouse in Kahnawake and the shift from the seven-clan to the three-clan system of hereditary chiefs in greater detail elsewhere. See Reid, *Kahnawà:ke*, 134–67.

22. Laurence M. Hauptman, "Designing Woman," 150–63; and Kristina Ackley and Cristina Stanciu, eds., *Laura Cornelius Kellogg: Our Democracy and The American Indian and Other Works* (Syracuse, NY: Syracuse University Press, 2015), 3–4, 47–52.

23. Titley, *A Narrow Vision*, 102–9.

24. Weaver, "The Iroquois," 213–57; Laurence M. Hauptman, *Seven Generations of Iroquois Leadership: The Six Nations Since 1800* (Syracuse, NY: Syracuse University Press, 2008), 117–42; and Titley, *A Narrow Vision*, 114–28.

Chapter 7

1. Western Reserve Historical Society (WRHS), MSS 3321, Oghema Niagara Papers, Folder 2, "Correspondence, 1908–1950," Correspondence, July 12 to September 8, 1920; Ancestry.com, *1930 United States Federal Census* (database online), 2002, accessed August 23, 2018; *Cleveland Press*, "Indian Chief Here Fashions Dream of Indian Empire," n.d.

2. Library and Archives Canada (LAC), RG10, Vol. 3184, File 458168 Pt. 1, Meritt to Paul, December 18, 1921, and Scott to Griffiths et al., January 3, 1922; WRHS, Folder 5, "Ambassadorial Credentials," Power of Attorney, May 14, 1927, and June 10, 1927; WRHS, Folder 1, "Personal and Biographical Papers, Writings, Printed Materials, Undated and 1913–1950," The Redman's Appeal for Justice, Rights of Indians, and Niagara to Dickinson, October 31, 1927. I discuss the Diabo case and the related grand council held in Kahnawake in 1927 in detail in "Illegal Alien? The Immigration Case of Mohawk Ironworker Paul K. Diabo," *Proceedings of the American Philosophical Society* 151, no. 1 (March 2007), 61–78; and Reid, *Kahnawà:ke*, 149–56.

3. *News-Journal*, "Tribes to Ask for Freedom," August 17, 1928; and the *Honolulu Advertiser*, "Indian Tribes Plan Fight to Seek Freedom," August 31, 1928.

4. The details of the "Indians" plan discussed here and in the following paragraphs are specified in an eight-page prospectus written by Burr, a copy of which is contained in the collection of Thunderwater's personal papers. The prospectus is undated but probably was prepared in late 1926. WRHS, Folder 4, "The Organization of Indians," Plan for the Organization of Indians, n.d.

5. WRHS, Folder 4, Agreement of Frank S. Burr and Michael A. Fanning, February 8, 1927.

6. Bureau of American Ethnology, *Circular of Information Regarding Indian Popular Names* (Washington, DC: Bureau of American Ethnology, 1915).

7. For several examples of the "Indians" honorary adoption and membership certificates, see WRHS, Folder 4, "The Organization of Indians."

8. WRHS, Folder 4, Honorary Memberships Endorsement of the Chiefs, Councillors, or both of the Thayendinaga Band of Mohawk Indians, n.d.
9. WRHS, Folder 4, *Indians* (1926).
10. WRHS, Folder 4, Agreement of Frank S. Burr and Michael Fanning, February 8, 1927, and Contract of Agreement between Michael Fanning and Herald Post Company, February 11, 1927.
11. *Louisville Herald-Post*, "Oghema Niagara," March 6, 1927; *Tennessean*, "Want to Become Indian—Paper Offers a Chance," February 27, 1927; and WRHS, Folder 4, "The Organization of Indians," Certificates of Adoption and Honorary Membership in the Mohawk Tribe of Frederick Lee Davis and 25 others. See the book's cover for the colorized photograph of Thunderwater that appeared in the *Herald-Post*, March 6, 1917.
12. *Louisville Times*, "Thousands of School Children Meet and Hear Chief Thunderwater in School Tour," March 10, 1927; Library and Archives Canada (LAC), RG10, Vol. 3184, File 458168-A Pt. 2, City Editor to Commissioner of Indian Affairs, March 11, 1927.
13. *Louisville Times*, Scott to City Editor, March 12, 1927, Managing Editor to Scott, March 12, 1927, and Scott to Managing Editor, March 14, 1927.
14. *Louisville Times*, "Thunderwater Takes Advantage of Board of Education," March 15, 1927.
15. *Courier-Journal*, "Thunderwater Denies He Is Fake, Declares That Charges Are False," March 16, 1927.
16. *Courier-Journal*, "Indian Called Trouble Source," "Not Registered in U.S. or Canada," and "'Chief' is Fake," March 16, 1927, "Chief's Denial Refuted by Teachers, Reporters," March 17, 1927, "$250,000 From Times Asked by Thunderwater," March 18, 1927, and "Thunderwater Asks $250,00 in C-J Suit," March 8, 1928.

Chapter 8

1. Western Reserve Historical Society, MSS 3321, Oghema Niagara Papers, Folder 4, "The Organization of Indians," Expenditures of Chief Thunderwater in his lawsuit against the *Louisville Times* and *Courier-Journal*, March 15, 1927, to December 2, 1929, and Agreement between Marsteller and Thunderwater, February 10, 1928.
2. LAC, RG10, Vol. 3184, File 458168-A Pt. 2, City editor to Scott, March 17, 1927, Statutory Declaration of Duncan Campbell Scott, April 2, 1927, Tabb to Williams, September 13, 1928, and Scott to Tabb, October 18, 1928.
3. For examples of the newspaper reports of legal battle threatened by Thunderwater, see *News-Journal*, "Tribes to Ask for Freedom," August 17, 1928; and the *Honolulu Advertiser*, "Indian Tribes Plan Fight to Seek Freedom," August 31, 1928.
4. The discussion of the first day in court of Thunderwater's libel case is based on the following sources: *Louisville Times*, "Thunderwater's Cases on Trial," October 22, 1928; *Louisville Times*, "Thunderwater Case is Resumed," October 23, 1928; and *Courier-Journal*, "$250,000 Suit Opened Here in U.S. Court," October 23, 1928.
5. As "Princess Nita," Griffin was especially known for her "William Tell" act, in which she and another marksman shot potatoes off each other's heads. "We used a pistol

and potato instead of a bow-and-arrow and apple," she said when interviewed by an Ohio newspaper reporter near the time of her death in 1938. "I stood up against a wall, too, while a man outlined me with daggers." See *Democrat and Chronicle*, "Wild West Star, 'Princess Nita,' in Hospital," August 16, 1938.

6. WRHS, Folder 6, "Affidavits, 1915–1933," Affidavit of Mrs. Minnie Peck, June 9, 1927, and Affidavit of Harry Eaton, n.d.

7. For reporting on the second day of the trial, see *Louisville Times*, "Thunderwater Case is Resumed," October 23, 1928, and *Courier-Journal*, "Dozen Indians Take Stand in $500,000 Suit," October 24, 1928. For the depositions of Cleveland residents in support of Thunderwater, see WRHS, Folder 6, "Affidavits, 1915–1933." Carl Mueller, one of the deponents, also testified that when orphaned at age twelve, he had been cared for by a Mohawk family and adopted into the Mohawk tribe and that for several years he assisted Thunderwater as the secretary of the Supreme Council of the Tribes.

8. *Louisville Times*, "Thunderwater Case is Resumed," October 24, 1928.

9. *Louisville Times*, "Thunderwater Case is Resumed," October 24, 1928.

10. WRHS, Folder 2, "Correspondence, 1908–1950," R. J. Barnhart et al., September 29, 1928.

11. WRHS, Folder 6, "Affidavits, 1915–1933," Depositions of Mike LaBorne, March 26, 1927, Adrian A. Clark, June 16, 1927, Cephas Hill, June 16, 1927, Gilbert Peterson, June 16, 1927, and Mike Kaine, June 21, 1927.

12. WRHS, Folder 6, Depositions of Makes Mad, March 26, 1927, Henry Eagle Head, May 14, 1927, Harry A. Coe, April 11, 1927, and Louis Blackman, June 17, 1927.

13. WRHS, Folder 6, Affidavits of Hooker Page, Ella White, October 9, 1928, and Affidavit of Nettie Edwards, October 11, 1928.

14. WRHS, Folder 5, "Ambassadorial Credentials, 1909–1927 and Undated," General Legal Papers, 1893–1939, Certificate and Record of Death of Wm. Peter Sands, April 13, 1927, and Copy of Death Certificate of Peter Sands, October 12, 1828.

15. WRHS, Folder 6, "Affidavits, 1915–1933," Affidavits of Gabriella Morrow, Elizabeth Morrow, and Blanche Willingham, March 19, 1927, and Affidavit of Mrs. Jesse Staples, June 3, 1927.

16. *Courier-Journal*, "Defense Side is Opened in $500,000 Suit," October 25, 1928.

17. *Courier-Journal*, "Defense Side is Opened in $500,000 Suit," October 25, 1928; and *Louisville Times*, "Tells Acts of Thunderwater," October 25, 1928.

18. *Courier-Journal*, "Defense Side is Opened in $500,000 Suit," October 25, 1928; and *Louisville Times*, "Tells Acts of Thunderwater," October 25, 1928.

19. WRHS, Folder 6, "Affidavits, 1915–1933," Affidavit of Mitchell Arquette, June 27, 1927, and Affidavit of Mitchell Arquette, June 10, 1929.

20. *Courier-Journal*, "Newspaper Men Heard in $500,000 Suit," October 26, 1928; and *Louisville Times*, "Thunderwater Held Not Chief," October 26, 1928.

21. *Courier-Journal*, "Newspaper Men Heard in $500,000 Suit," October 26, 1928; and *Louisville Times*, "Thunderwater Held Not Chief," October 26, 1928.

22. *Courier-Journal*, "Newspaper Men Heard in $500,000 Suit," October 26, 1928.

23. *Courier-Journal*, "$500,000 Suit Submitted to Federal Jury," October 27, 1928.

24. In the reporting on Jacobs's testimony, the *Louisville Times* erroneously connected him to the Tyendinaga reserve. See *Louisville Times*, "Thunderwater Held Not Chief," October 26, 1928; and *Courier-Journal*, "$500,000 Suit Submitted to Federal Jury," October 27, 1928. See also LAC, RG10, Vol. 3184, File 458168 Pt. 1, MacKenzie to Jacobs, September 19, 1928, and Jacobs to MacKenzie, September 20, 1928.

25. *Courier-Journal*, "$500,000 Suit Submitted to Federal Jury," October 27, 1928.

26. *Courier-Journal*, "$500,000 Suit Submitted to Federal Jury," October 27, 1928.

27. *Louisville Times*, "Thunderwater Case Weighed," October 27, 1928; and *Courier-Journal*, "$500,000 Suit Submitted to Federal Jury," October 27, 1928.

28. LAC, RG10, Vol. 3184, File 458168-A Pt. 2, Williams to Scott, October 27, 1928.

29. WRHS, Folder 6, "Affidavits, 1915–1933," Deposition of Louis Terrance, March 5, 1929, and "Depositions of Atonwa Akwirontonkwas et al.," August 18 to October 20, 1929. A total of fifteen signed statements are included in the collection of Thunderwater's personal papers. Each of the statements is numbered, with the highest being "93," suggesting that there may have been nearly one hundred such signed statements.

30. WRHS, Folder 6, Deposition of Chief Isaac Hill, June 16, 1930.

31. LAC, RG10, Vol. 3184, File 458168-A Pt. 2, McLean to McGibbon, November 20, 1928, McLean to Jacobs, November 20, 1928, Jacobs to McLean, November 28, 1928, and Jacobs to McLean, January 21, 1929. See also LAC, RG10, Vol. 3184, File 458168-A Pt. 2, Indian Department correspondence, March 2 to June 10, 1929.

32. *Courier-Journal*, "Thunderwater's Suits Ordered Dismissed," December 3, 1930.

Chapter 9

1. Western Reserve Historical Society (WRHS), MSS 3321, Oghema Niagara Papers, Folder 1, "Personal & Biographical Papers & Writings, 1913–1950 & Undated," Certificate of Title, November 25, 1840, and Certificate of Title, August 15, 1946; WRHS, Folder 2, "Correspondence, 1908–1950" and Folder 7, "Newspaper Clippings and Miscellaneous"; WRHS, Folder 8, "Financial Documents, 1914 & 1923–1950," Wilcox Drug Company price list, n.d., Cleveland Trust Company loan statements for Chief Thunderwater, September 15, 1928, to September 15, 1940, Irish Hospital Sweepstakes Ticket for Oghema Niagara, 1948, John Hancock Mutual Life Insurance Company Premium Receipt Book for Oghema Niagara; and *Cleveland Plain Dealer*, "Thunderwater Acquitted," May 8, 1942; *Cleveland Press*, "Ugh, Medicine Heap Bad, Lands 'Chief' in Court," March 4, 1942, and "Acquit Medicine Man," May 7, 1942.

2. Marion Wanda Palmer died in 1997 at age ninety-three. Blanche (Beckwith) Keokuk Palmer died in 1975 at age eighty-seven. Mahoniall (Keokuk) Cline died in 1986 in Ashtabula, Ohio, at age seventy-five. The history of Thunderwater's daughter-in-law Blanche and her daughters, Mahoniall and Marion, is based on U.S. Census and vital statistics records accessed through Ancestry.com and information provided by Mona Secoy and Dalene Kelly, both great-great-granddaughters of Chief Thunderwater. My thanks to Mrs. Secoy and Mrs. Kelly for their assistance in understanding this part of Thunderwater's family history.

3. *Akron Beacon*, "Chief Thunderwater Supervises Haven for Indians on Attorney William Marsteller's Farm at Aurora," May 25, 1937; WRHS, Folder 5, "Ambassadorial Credentials, 1909–1927 & Undated and General Legal Papers, 1893–1939," Contract Agreement between Chief Thunderwater and Albert Guth, April 27, 1937; and Ancestry.com, *1940 United States Federal Census* (database online), 2012, accessed January 10, 2018.

4. WRHS, Folder 5, "Ambassadorial Credentials, 1909–1927 & Undated and General Legal Papers, 1893–1939," Documents related to the affairs of Elmina MacIntyre, February 12, 1920, to December 2, 1939.

5. Ancestry.com, *1920 United States Federal Census* (database online), 2010; WRHS, Folder 5, "Ambassadorial Credentials, 1909–1927 & Undated and General Legal Papers, 1893–1939," Documents related to guardianship of Waunetta Griffin, April 1935 to February 1937; *Democrat and Chronicle*, "Wild West Star, 'Princess Nita,' in Hospital," August 16, 1938; and *Brooklyn Daily Eagle*, "Sic Transit Gloria," August 21, 1938.

6. *Cleveland Plain Dealer*, "Settlers Picnic in Lakewood's Park," June 23, 1940, "Mayor Burton Will Be Heap Big Indian Chief," July 18, 1940, "Rededicating the Erie Street Cemetery," July 20, 1940, "WCLE Will Broadcast Cleveland Day Program," July 14, 1941, "Cleveland Day," July 23, 1941, "Ceremony Welcomes Bride Across 150 Years," June 17, 1946, "Early Settlers Re-Enact Birth of City," June 30, 1946, and "150,000 Turn Out in Tribute to City's Sesquicentennial," July 23, 1946.

7. *Cleveland Plain Dealer*, "Indian Gets His Eulogy—in Maize," May 31, 1938.

8. *Cleveland Plain Dealer*, "Rededicating the Erie Street Cemetery," July 18, 1940.

9. WRHS, Folder 2, "Correspondence, 1908–1950," Connolly to Oghema Niagara, March 15, 1948, Rose to Chief, May 30, 1949, Breidenstein to Chief, January 30, 1950.

10. *Cleveland Plain Dealer*, "Chief Thunderwater, Famous in Cleveland 50 Years, Dies," June 11, 1950.

11. *Rochester Democrat and Chronicle*, "Chief Thunderwater, Head of Indians," June 11, 1950; *Dayton Daily News*, "Chief Thunderwater, Indian Chief, Dies," June 11, 1950; *Mansfield News-Journal*, "Top Indian Chief Dies," June 11, 1950; *Decatur Herald*, "Thunderwater, Indian Leader, Dies," June 12, 1950; *Detroit Free Press*, "Indians Big Chief Dies in Cleveland," June 11, 1950; *Minneapolis Star Tribune*, "Chief Thunderwater," June 11, 1950; *Green Bay Press-Gazette*, "Oghema Niagara," June 12, 1950; *Binghamton Press and Sun Bulletin*, "Indians' Chief Dies," June 11, 1950; *Hartford Courant*, "Oghema Niagara," June 11, 1950; *Philadelphia Enquirer*, "Oghema Niagara," June 13, 1950; *Cumberland Sunday Times*, "Chief Succumbs at 85," June 11, 1950; *Miami News*, "Oghema Niagara," June 11, 1950; *Palm Beach Post*, "Indian Chief Dies," June 11, 1950; *Tampa Times*, "Oghema Niagara," June 12, 1950; *Town Talk*, "Oghema Niagara," June 12, 1950; *St. Louis Post-Dispatch*, "Titular Head of Indians Dies," June 11, 1950; *Montana Standard*, "Chief of Indians Dies," June 11, 1950; *Casper Star-Tribune*, "Head of Indian Council of U.S. and Canada Dies," June 12, 1950; *Des Moines Register*, "Chief Thunderwater Dies, Head of Tribes," June 11, 1950; *Arizona Daily Star*, "Chief Thunderwater, Indian Tribal Leader, Is Dead at Cleveland," June 12, 1950; *Oakland Tribune*, "Death Takes Chief," June 12, 1950; *Los Angeles Times*, "Chief

Thunderwater, Indian Leader Dies," June 11, 1950; and *Montreal Gazette*, "Indian Tribes' Leader, 84, Dies in Cleveland," June 13, 1950.

12. *San Bernardino Daily Sun*, "Chief Thunderwater's Last Rites Conducted," June 15, 1950; *Cleveland Plain Dealer*, "Aid to Chief Thunderwater Earns Clevelander His Title," November 23, 1950; and "Indian Princess Honors Chief Each Year at Erie St. Cemetery," May 26, 1983.

BIBLIOGRAPHY

Archival and Primary Sources

Ancestry.com. Provo, Utah: Ancestry.com Operations, Inc.

    1870 United States Federal Census (2009).

    1880 United States Federal Census (2009).

    1900 United States Federal Census (2004)

    1910 United States Federal Census (2006).

    1920 United States Federal Census (2010).

    1930 United States Federal Census (2002).

    1940 United States Federal Census (2012).

    Cuyahoga County, Ohio, Marriage Records and Indexes, 1810–1973 (2010).

    Michigan, Death Records, 1867–1950 (2015).

    Ohio, County Marriage Records, 1774–1993 (2016).

    U.S. City Directories, 1822–1995 (2011).

    U.S. Indian Census Rolls, 1885–1940 (2007).

Bureau of American Ethnology. *Circular of Information Regarding Indian Popular Names.* Washington, DC: Bureau of American Ethnology: 1915.

Canada, Department of Indian Affairs. *Annual Report of the Department of Indian Affairs for the Year Ended 30th June 1898.*

"Census Roll of Creek Indians." Creek Nation Collection, University of Oklahoma Libraries Western History Collections. https://digital.libraries.ou.edu/cdm/. Accessed August 14, 2017.

Kanhiote Library (Tyendinaga Mohawk Territory). Solomon J. Brant Papers, "Installation of Life Chiefs on the Tyendinaga Reserve."

Library and Archives Canada (LAC)

    PA-181695. "Chief Thunderwater Administering Indian Oath to Grand Councillor, 14 September 1916."

    RG10, Vol. 1862, File 241, "Tyendinaga Reserve—Chiefs Express Their Affinity to the Six Nations and Question Their Timber and Women's Rights."

    RG10, Vol. 1876, File 933, "St. Regis Reserve—Survey of the Graveyard and Complaints Against Reverend Marcoux."

    RG10, Vol. 1991, File 6670, "St. Regis Reserve—Petition by Certain Band Members to Appoint Three New Chiefs."

    RG10, Vol. 1997, File 7073, "Tyendinaga Reserve—Election of Chief and Councillors."

RG10, Vol. 2005, File 7784, "St. Regis Reserve—Indians of Cornwall Island Requesting to be Allowed to Elect a Chief Under the Indian Act of 1876."

RG10, Vol. 2015, File 8096, "Tyendinaga Reserve—Complaints by the Chief Concerning the Disorderly Conduct at Council Meetings of Jacob Brant, William Green and David Powles."

RG10, Vol. 2018; File 8246, "St. Regis Reserve—Agent John Davidson Requesting Authority to Hold an Election for a Chief to Replace Loran Solomon."

RG10, Vol. 2084, File 12757, "Tyendinaga Reserve—Dispute Over the Proposed Trip of Chief Sampson Green to England to Collect Subscriptions for the Establishment of a School on the Reserve."

RG10, Vol. 2106, File 19,383, "Tyendinaga Reserve—Election of the Chief and Council."

RG10, Vol. 2184, File 37064, "St. Regis Agency—Correspondence Regarding the Election of Chiefs as Opposed to Life Appointments."

RG10, Vol. 2283, File 56784, "St. Regis Agency—Requisition Allowance for the Chiefs of the St. Regis Band."

RG10, Vol. 2320, File 63812–2, "Headquarters—Correspondence Regarding Hereditary Chiefs for the Iroquois in Ontario & Quebec."

RG10 Vol. 2323, File 65108, "St. Regis Agency—Correspondence Regarding Salaries & Pensions for the Chiefs of the Iroquois of St. Regis."

RG10, Vol. 2781, File 156468–11, "St. Regis Agency—Correspondence Regarding Elections of Chiefs and Councillors, Disputes Over Methods of Electing Chiefs, Charges Against Chiefs and Various Band Members (Poll Books)."

RG10, Vol. 2930, File 192923, "St. Regis Agency—Report on a Meeting of the St. Regis Council on 12 May Regarding the Permission to Choose Their Chiefs Rather Than Electing Them by Vote and Regarding the Extension of the Chiefs' Powers."

RG10, Vol. 3178, File 449628–1, "Caughnawaga Agency—Correspondence Regarding the Establishment of a Residence for the Sisters Who Are in Charge of the Caughnawaga Schools (Plans)."

RG10, Vol. 3184, File 458168 Pt. 1, "Correspondence Regarding an Organization Known as the Indian Rights Association or Council of the Tribes."

RG10, Vol. 3184, File 458168-A Pt. 2, "Correspondence Regarding an Organization Known as the Indian Rights Association or Council of the Tribes."

RG10, Vol. 6076, File 305–1B Pt. 1, "Caughnawaga Agency—Caughnawaga Roman Catholic Boys School."

RG10, Vol. 7931, File 32–33 Pt. 1, "St. Regis Agency—Elections of Chiefs and Councillors at St. Regis Reserve."

RG10, Vol. 7932, File 32–33 Pt. 2, "St. Regis Agency—Elections of Chiefs and Councillors at St. Regis Reserve."

RG10, Vol. 7932, File 32–33 Pt. 3, "St. Regis Agency—Elections of Chiefs and Councillors at St. Regis Reserve."

RG10, Vol. 7933, File 32–34 Pt. 2, "Tyendinaga Agency—Elections of Chiefs and Councillors on the Tyendinaga Reserve (Map)."

RG19, Vol. 5, File 6, "Joseph Brant and Family Fonds."

RootsWeb. "Chief Keokuk Family Tree." http://wc.rootsweb.ancestry.com/cgi-bin/igm
.cgi?db=chief_keokuk&id=I1&op=GET. Accessed November 22, 2017.
United States, Office of Indian Affairs. *Annual Report of the Commissioner of Indian
Affairs for the Year 1909*. Washington, DC: Government Printing Office, 1909.
Western Reserve Historical Society. MSS 3321. Oghema Niagara Papers.
Folder 1, "Personal & Biographical Papers, 1913–1950."
Folder 2, "Correspondence, 1908–1950."
Folder 3, "Council of the Tribes, 1914–1922 and undated."
Folder 4, "The Organization of Indians."
Folder 5, "Ambassadorial Credentials, 1909–1927 and General Legal Papers, 1893–1939."
Folder 6, "Affidavits, 1915–1933."
Folder 7, "Newspaper Clippings and Miscellaneous."
Folder 8, "Financial Documents, 1914 & 1923–1950."

Newspapers

Akron Beacon
Arizona Daily Star
Binghamton Press and Sun Bulletin
Buffalo Commercial
Buffalo Courier
Buffalo Enquirer
Buffalo Morning Express
Buffalo Sunday Morning News
Brooklyn Daily Eagle
Casper Star-Tribune
Cleveland Plain Dealer
Cleveland Press
Courier-Journal
Cumberland Sunday Times
Daily Gate City
Dayton Daily News
Decatur Herald
Democrat and Chronicle
Des Moines Register
Detroit Free Press
Eastern Door
Elyria Evening Telegram
Green Bay Press-Gazette
Hartford Courant
Honolulu Advertiser
Los Angeles Times
Louisville Herald-Post

Louisville Times
Mansfield News-Journal
Miami News
Minneapolis Star Tribune
Montana Standard
Montreal Gazette
Montreal Star
New York Tribune
News-Journal
Niagara Falls Thunder Alley
Oakland Tribune
Ocala Evening Star
Omaha Daily Bee
Palm Beach Post
Philadelphia Enquirer
Rochester Democrat and Chronicle
San Bernardino Daily Sun
St. Louis Post-Dispatch
Tampa Times
Tennessean
Topeka Daily State Journal
Town Talk
Utica Observer

Secondary Sources

Ackley, Kristina, and Cristina Stanciu, eds. *Laura Cornelius Kellogg: Our Democracy and the American Indian and Other Works*. Syracuse, NY: Syracuse University Press, 2015.

Barbeau, Marius. "Charles A. Cooke, Mohawk Scholar." *Proceedings of the American Philosophical Society* 96, no. 4 (August 1952): 424–26.

Beauchamp, William M. *A History of the New York Iroquois*. Albany: New York State Education Department, 1905.

Bonaparte, Darren. "Saiowisekeron: The Jake Ice Story." *Wampum Chronicles*, www.wampumchronicles.com/saiowisakeron.html. Accessed October 19, 2007.

Bonvillain, Nancy. *The Sac and Fox*. Langhorne, PA: Chelsea House, 1995.

Colbert, Thomas Burnell. "Keokuk." *The Biographical Dictionary of Iowa*. University of Iowa Press, 2009. http://uipress.lib.uiowa.edu/. Accessed August 17, 2018.

Daugherty, Wayne and Dennis Madill. *Indian Government Under Indian Act Legislation, 1868–1951, Part 1*. Ottawa: Department of Indian and Northern Affairs of Canada, 1980.

Deloria, Philip J. *Indians in Unexpected Places*. Lawrence: University of Kansas Press, 2004.

Deloria, Vine, Jr., and Raymond J. DeMallie, eds. *Documents of American Indian Diplomacy: Treaties, Agreements, and Conventions, 1775–1979.* Vol. 1. Norman: University of Oklahoma Press, 1999.

Doxtator, Deborah. "What Happened to the Iroquois Clans? A Study of Three Nineteenth Century Rotinonhsyonni Communities." PhD diss., University of Western Ontario, 1996.

Edwards, Brendan. "'A Most Industrious and Far-Seeing Mohawk Scholar': Charles A. Cooke (Thawennensere), Civil Servant, Amateur Anthropologist, Performer, and Writer." *Ontario History* 102, no. 1 (Spring 2010): 81–108.

Fenton, William N. "Seth Newhouse's Traditional History and Constitution of the Iroquois Confederacy." *Proceedings of the American Philosophical Society* 93, no. 2 (May 1949): 141–58.

Frisch, Jack Aaron. *Revitalization, Nativism, and Tribalism among the St. Regis Mohawks.* PhD diss., Indiana University, 1971.

Gordon, Sandra. "Freeman C. Johnson Collection." Rochester, NY: Rochester Museum and Science Center, 1975. http://collections.rmsc.org/Library/JohnsonFreeman _findingAid.pdf.

Green, Charles Ransley. *Early Days in Kansas: Along the Santa Fe and Lawrence Trails.* Old Ridgeway, 1912. https://books.google.com/books?id=qVwvAAAAYAAJ. Accessed December 30, 2017.

Green, Rayna. "The Pocahontas Perplex: The Image of Indian Women in American Culture." *Massachusetts Review* 16, no. 4 (Autumn 1975): 698–714.

Grewe, Lauren. "'To Bid His People Rise': Political Renewal and Spiritual Contests at Red Jacket's Reburial." *Native American and Indigenous Studies* 1, no. 2 (Fall 2014): 44–68.

Hagan, William T. "Keokuk," *American National Biography Online.* http://www.anb .org/. Accessed July 10, 2017.

———. *The Sac and Fox Indians.* Norman: University of Oklahoma Press, 1958.

"Har quo quar." www.wikitree.com. Accessed July 10, 2017.

Hauptman, Laurence M. *Formulating American Indian Policy in New York State, 1970–1986.* Albany: State University of New York Press, 1988.

———. *Seven Generations of Iroquois Leadership: The Six Nations Since 1800.* Syracuse, NY: Syracuse University Press, 2008.

———. *In the Shadow of Kinzua: The Seneca Nation of Indians Since World War II.* Syracuse, NY: Syracuse University Press, 2013.

Hauptman, Laurence M., and L. Gordon McLester III, eds. *The Oneida Indians in the Age of Allotment, 1860–1920.* Norman: University of Oklahoma Press, 2006.

Hunter, William A. "Refugee Settlements Among the Seneca." *Ethnohistory* 3, no. 1 (Winter 1956): 11–20.

Johnson, William E. *The Federal Government and the Liquor Traffic.* Westerville, OH: American Issue Publishing Company, 1911.

La Barre, Weston. "Materials for a History of Studies of Crisis Cults: A Bibliographic Essay." *Current Anthropology* 12, no. 1 (February 1971): 3–44.

Lackenbauer, P. Whitney. *Battle Grounds: The Canadian Military and Aboriginal Lands.* Vancouver: UBC Press, 2007.

McCabe, James D. *The Illustrated History of the Centennial Exhibition, Held in Commemoration of the One Hundredth Anniversary of American Independence.* Philadelphia: National Publishing Company, 1876.

McGowan, Katherine. "'In the Interest of the Indians': The Department of Indian Affairs, Charles Cooke and the Recruitment of Native Men in Southern Ontario for the Canadian Expeditionary Force, 1916." *Ontario History* 102, no. 1 (Spring 2010): 109–24.

Mellatti, Julio Cezar. "Áreas Etnográficas da América Indígena, 2016." http://www.juliomelatti.pro.br/areas/00areas.pdf. Accessed September 3, 2017.

Mensik, Tom. "How the Railroad and the Philadelphia Centennial Exposition Expanded the Hamill House." The Hamill House Museum. https://thehamillhouse.wordpress.com.

Moffett, Thomas C. *The American Indian on the New Trail: The Red Man of the United States and the Christian Gospel.* New York: Missionary Education Movement of the United States and Canada, 1914.

Murphy, Robert F. "Cultural Change." *Biennial Review of Anthropology* 5 (1967): 1–45.

Ojibwe People's Dictionary. https://ojibwe.lib.umn.edu. Accessed July 11, 2017.

O'Neil, David. "Joc-O-Sot, or Walking Bear." *Encyclopedia of Cleveland History.* www.case.edu/ech. Accessed December 5, 2017.

Parmenter, Jon. "The Meaning of *Kaswentha* and the Two Row Wampum Belt in Haudenosaunee (Iroquois) History: Can the Oral Tradition be Reconciled with the Documentary Record." *Journal of Early American History* 3, no. 1 (2013): 82–109.

Patterson, J. B. *Life of Black Hawk, or Ma-ka-tai-me-she-kia-kiak: Dictated by Himself.* New York: Penguin Classics, 2008.

Porter, Joy. *To Be Indian: The Life of Iroquois-Seneca Arthur Caswell Parker.* Norman: University of Oklahoma Press, 2001.

Postal, Susan Koessler. "Hoax Nativism at Caughnawaga: A Control Case for the Theory of Revitalization." *Ethnology* 4, no. 3 (July 1965): 266–81.

Printup, Bryan, and Neil Patterson Jr. *Tuscarora Nation.* Charleston, SC: Arcadia Publishing, 2007.

Rarihokwats. *How Democracy Came to St. Regis.* Rooseveltown, NY: Akwesasne Notes, 1971.

Reddin, Paul. *Wild West Shows.* Urbana-Champaign: University of Illinois Press, 1999.

Reid, Gerald F. "Beadworkers and Border Lines: Kahnawà:ke Women Craftworkers and the Assertion of Rotinonhsionni Border Crossing Rights in the Late Nineteenth Century." Paper delivered at the Annual Conference on Iroquois Research, Montreal, Quebec, October 4–6, 2019.

———. "Illegal Alien? The Immigration Case of Mohawk Ironworker Paul K. Diabo." *Proceedings of the American Philosophical Society* 151, no. 1 (March 2007): 61–78.

———. *Kahnawà:ke: Factionalism, Traditionalism, and Nationalism in a Mohawk Community.* Lincoln: University of Nebraska Press, 2004.

———. "'To Renew Our Fire': Political Activism, Nationalism, and Identity in Three Rotinonhsionni Communities." In *Tribal Worlds: Critical Studies in American Indian*

Nation Building, edited by Brian Hosmer and Larry Nesper, 37–64. Albany: State University of New York Press, 2013.

Shimony, Anne Marie. *Conservatism among the Iroquois at the Six Nations Reserve.* Syracuse, NY: Syracuse University Press, 1994.

Slicker, Michael. *Lighthouse Books.* http://oldfloridabookstore.blogspot.com/2011/09 /black-hawk-keokuk-and-legends.html.

Snow, Dean R. *The Iroquois.* Cambridge, MA: Blackwell, 1994.

Spencer, Dorcas J. "Indians and Prohibition," *American Indian Magazine* 4, no. 4 (October–December 1916): 311–14.

Sprague, William. "Report of the Indian Branch of the Department of the Secretary of State for the Provinces." *Report of the Secretary of State for Canada for the Year Ending 30th June 1870.* Ottawa: Canada Department of the Secretary of State, 1871.

St. Regis Mohawk Tribe. "Tribal History." http://www.srmt-nsn.gov/. Accessed January 9, 2008.

Titley, E. Brian. *A Narrow Vision: Duncan Campbell Scott and the Administration of Indian Affairs in Canada.* Vancouver: UBC Press, 2004.

Tobias, John L. "Protection, Civilization, Assimilation: An Outline History of Canada's Indian Policy." In *Sweet Promises: A Reader on Indian-White Relations in Canada,* edited by J. R. Miller, 127–44. Vancouver: University of British Columbia Press, 1991.

Treglia, Gabriella. "The Consistency and Inconsistency of Cultural Oppression: American Indian Dance Bans, 1900–1933." *Western Historical Quarterly* 44, no. 2 (Summer 2013): 145–65.

———. "Using Citizenship to Retain Identity: The Native American Dance Bans of the Later Assimilation Era, 1900–1933." *Journal of American Studies* 47, no. 3 (August 2013): 777–800.

Wallace, Anthony F. C. *Death and Rebirth of the Seneca.* New York: Vintage, 1969.

Weaver, Sally M. "The Iroquois: The Grand River Reserve in the Late Nineteenth and Early Twentieth Centuries, 1875–1945." In *Aboriginal Ontario: Historical Perspectives on the First Nations,* edited by Donald B. Smith and Edward S. Rogers, 213–51. Toronto: Dundurn Press, 1994.

———. "Seth Newhouse and the Grand River Confederacy at Mid-Nineteenth Century." In *Extending the Rafters: Interdisciplinary Approaches to Iroquoian Studies,* edited by Michael K. Foster, Jack Campisi, and Marianne Mithun. Albany: State University of New York Press, 1984.

Weber, Michael Lee. "Keokuk, Moses." *Encyclopedia of Oklahoma History.* www.okhistory .org. Accessed November 22, 2017.

Weeks, Philip, and Lynn R. Metzger. "American Indians." *Encyclopedia of Cleveland History.* https://case.edu/ech/articles/a/american-indians. Accessed February 7, 2020.

Whittaker, Gordon. *A Concise Dictionary of the Sauk Language.* Stroud, OK: Gordon Whittaker and the Sac and Fox of Oklahoma and the Missouri, 2005. http://learn .bacone.edu/pluginfile.php/26452/mod_resource/content/1/sauk-concise-dictionary .pdf. Accessed May 10, 2019.

Winegard, Timothy C. "An Introduction to Charles A. Cooke within the context of Aboriginal Identity." *Ontario History* 102, no. 1 (Spring 2010): 78–80.

INDEX

Page numbers in *italic* typeface indicate illustrations.

Made in the USA
Monee, IL
13 October 2023

44565293R00116